PSYCHOLOGY, HUMANISM, AND SCIENTIFIC INQUIRY

PSYCHOLOGY, HUMANISM, AND SCIENTIFIC INQUIRY
The Selected Essays of Hadley Cantril

Edited by

ALBERT H. CANTRIL

Transaction Books
New Brunswick (U.S.A.) and Oxford (U.K.)

BF
204
.C36
1988

Library of Congress Catalog Number: 87-16189
ISBN 0-88738-176-6
Printed in the United States of America

Library of Congress Cataloging in Publication Data

Cantril, Hadley, 1906-1969.
  Psychology, humanism, and scientific inquiry.

  Bibliography: p.
  Includes index.
  1. Humanistic psychology.   2. Psychology,
Physiological.   3. Psychology—Philosophy.
I. Cantril, Albert Hadley, 1940-   . II. Title.
BF204.C36   1987   150.19   87-16189
ISBN 0-88738-176-6

Contents

Acknowledgments

This collection of essays has benefited from the counsel of friends and colleagues: W. Phillips Davison, Albert H. Hastorf, William H. Ittelson, Kenneth E. Livingston, Nelson W. Polsby, Henry W. Riecken, M. Brewster Smith, and Hans Toch. Alfred Imhoff lent a sharp pencil in bringing editorial consistency to articles published over a twenty-year period. The Institute of Politics at Harvard University has provided sanctuary for completion of this project. I also gratefully acknowledge the support of my father's colleague over the years, Lloyd A. Free and my sister, Mavis Cantril Jansky. My wife, Susan Davis Cantril has assisted in all phases of bringing together this collection of essays of a man she was never lucky enough to have known and who, himself, would have so cherished her.

Introduction

The concept for this collection of essays grew out of many long discussions I had with my father, Hadley Cantril, in his later years. The recurring theme in these discussions was his quest for a science of human nature that was faithful to data from the phenomenal world yet held out hope for a systematic accounting of the full range of experience we call "human."

As becomes clear somewhat sequentially in the essays in this volume, he became ever more frustrated with the orthodoxies of various schools of thought in psychology. Increasingly, his terms of reference reached out to the wider community of students of the human condition, whether they be psychologists, neuroscientists, semanticists, psychiatrists, philosophers, theologians or poets. He was impatient with formulations whose precision was sustained by the narrowness of their scope of inquiry, just as he was uneasy with appealing general theories that were at variance with empirically demonstrable insights into the qualities of the experience of humankind.

An unintended consequence for him was growing isolation from his peers in the discipline of psychology. His energies did not flag, however, as he let his unfettered inquiry lead him on. The irony is that this feeling of isolation can now be juxtaposed against his legacy in many areas: the nature of social attitudes, the psychology of radio, the psychology of social movements, the method of public opinion research, the implications for the War effort of polls he conducted for Franklin D. Roosevelt in the early 1940s, experimental work with the Ames demonstrations in visual perception, the paradoxes in the attitudes of the American people toward "government" and the development of cross-cultural survey techniques in pursuit of a general theory of human aspirations.

As a teenager I recall answering the phone one evening and responding "yes" to the query of whether Professor Cantril was in. The caller, it turned out, was Helen Dukas, secretary to Albert Einstein, a neighbor who lived but four doors away on Mercer Street in Princeton. Einstein had heard of the work with Adelbert Ames, Jr. and was interested in learning more about it, in particular, about the trapezoid window demonstration, central to the "transactional" approach being developed.

My father spent the next evening with Einstein. He later reported that immediately upon viewing the illusion of oscillation in the rotating window, Einstein exclaimed, "Ah hah, what you have there is not a rectangle!" Einstein also quickly grasped the larger point of the individual's creative role in shaping what is perceived as "real" and the implied need to free psychology from the shackles of the mechanistic approach that was then dominating the field. When my father spoke of the resistance of mainstream psychology to what he saw as the liberating implications of the transactional point of view, Einstein was amused and commented: "Well, I learned a long time ago, don't waste time trying to convince your colleagues."

The spirit of that injunction is what sustained my father in his later years. Ever affirmative in outlook, he did nonetheless come to know the solitude that comes with independence of spirit.

At the time of his death in 1969, he was working on a book that was to bring together in a systematic formulation his understanding of what made human experience what it is. He was not far enough along, however, for the manuscript to be published posthumously.

The "Why" of Man's Experience, published in 1950, spells out the transactional approach, insofar as it had been developed to that point. But there has been no integrated volume since then that pulls together his systematic thinking. That is the purpose of this collection. In the 1950s and 1960s, his writings of a theoretical nature appeared in widely dispersed professional journals, not readily accessible to the general audience.

This collection is, therefore, a crude proxy for the systematic book he might have written. It is redundant in parts. Yet, it attempts to select from dozens of his essays those that portray his evolving understanding of how a science of human nature can be both true to the complexity of its subject and still be "scientific."

The central theme of the essays in this volume is that the task of psychology is to develop an understanding of human nature that has a naturalistic foundation yet encompasses the full range of human experience. That is, psychological theory must be fully consistent with scientifically established propositions about the nature of human experience. At the same time, subject matter of psychology must include those aspects of experience usually considered more the province of the philosopher, the artist, or the theologian.

Much of Hadley Cantril's writing, particularly in his later years, dealt with the tensions inherent in this view of psychology's task. On the one hand, my father was critical of formulations that, in an attempt to be scientific, focused on "partial problems in precise ways." On the other, he objected strongly to the positing of some explanatory concept from which extrapolations are made with little regard to "the possibility of any naturalistic bases for speculation." In his words:

> We see ... a wide gulf between behavioristically inclined psychologists, on the one hand, and those psychologists concerned with the full gamut of human behavior including the apparent self-generation of motives, on the other hand. The former often convey the impression that man is a robot, made up of various neurological centers, glandular activities, and moving parts, but without any overall motive power. The latter are impatient with any traditional mechanistic stimulus-response formulations, seem rather unaware of the revolution in neurophysiology, and continue to use a variety of abstractions as 'explanations' without much concern as to what their naturalistic bases might be, getting around the problem with speculative qualities or attributes assigned to the intangible 'mind' or 'person' and creating systems, subsystems, and taxonomies of all sorts, fitting human experience and behavior into them.

By insisting on an approach that is both naturalistic in its foundation and holistic in its scope, the problem of developing a system of psychology is greatly complicated. To devise theoretical constructs, abstractions must be derived about human experience in such a way that they do not compromise the nature of that experience.

> The task of starting with naive experience and formulating systematic constructs on the basis of naive experience is a particularly difficult undertaking. For the very essence of living is its unity and flow. Yet in order to get any grasp of this most complicated subject matter and to communicate this understanding to others, the psychologist is forced to break up into distinguishable parts what really constitutes an indivisible, functional aggregate; he is forced to consider separately the various aspects of living which are all interrelated and interdependent and none of which would function as they do except for all the others. ... If the psychologist, then, is to be faithful to his subject matter, he must always bear in mind that living is an orchestration of ongoing processes and that any process he may choose to differentiate out of this aggregate of ongoing processes of living can be understood only if it is recognized as referring to a phase of man's orchestrated functioning.

It was the transactional point of view that my father felt presented the most adequate accounting of human experience. This orientation represented for him an overarching set of abstractions consistent with empirical work, both in and out of the laboratory, and a useful takeoff point for consideration of the larger philosophical questions toward which he felt psychology should be able to contribute some insight. It is to be distinguished from "transactional analysis" that has been recently popularized.

The contemporaneity of the articles in this collection is apparent in the current difficulties of "humanistic psychology" in establishing itself as a subdiscipline within psychology. Evolving out of frustration with the constraints of the mechanistic character of behaviorism, on the one hand, and the determinism of psychoanalysis, on the other, humanistic psychology has searched for postulates that affirm the inner- and self-directed aspects of behavior. Unfortunately, much of humanistic psychology was sidetracked by the counterculture of the 1960s and is still uncertain how to be integrated with the mainstream of psychology.

M. Brewster Smith, the influential American psychologist, sees an important lesson for all of psychology: abandon the aspiration of creating one unified science of psychology. While he is alert to the limits of "hardnosed" behaviorism, and the positivistic tradition in general, he is also reluctant to subscribe to the "irrationalist and anti-scientific affinities of the humanistic psychology movement." In his view, the tension is simply too great for productive efforts to build a unified discipline.

The essays in this volume underscore my father's affirmative view of psychology's potential in this regard. Indeed, a major theme of the collection is that a unified psychology is what we must strive for. While Cantril lived to see his contributions in public opinion research and visual perception gain wide acceptance, he felt equally significant was his work at the intersection of the domains of psychology and humanism in search of the bridging concepts that would advance a unified psychology.

Such a bridging concept for Cantril was "value satisfaction" which derives from the uniquely human capacity to attribute value significance to experience. A Bach partita can inspire, just as we can get satisfaction from doing something we know to be "good," or "right," or "true." Hence, it is appropriate for psychology to presume to wrestle with the question of what role ethical and moral systems play in human functioning. While mindful of the ultimate need for a naturalistic grounding for any explanatory system, he felt the presumption of psychology's legitimate role in this domain was justified if a longer-term view of "science" is taken. With regard to the concept of "value satisfaction," he noted:

> While such concepts, like others in the history of science, may have no explanation today, they are neither mystical nor by any means outside the bounds of scientific explanation tomorrow. Progress in scientific inquiry can only come about if a notion is postulated that seems to be intrinsically reasonable, whose existence may not be verifiable today but which nevertheless holds out the possibility of yielding to scientific verification in the future.

This book of articles is divided into four sections. The first, "Psychology and Scientific Inquiry," contains three articles written with Adelbert Ames,

Jr., Albert H. Hastorf, and William H. Ittelson and published in 1949 in *Science*. The basic statement of the transactional approach therein reflects the concern that psychology not be constrained by a mechanistic view of humankind in the attempt to be "scientific." The essays concern the epistemology of a science of human nature.

The second section, "Toward a Humanistic Psychology," includes four articles that present a recurring theme in Cantril's writing—the need for conceptual clarity regarding those qualities that make experience uniquely "human." The first article, published in 1950, poses the problem: how to develop a system of psychology that accounts for the "full-bodied experiences of everyday life." It touches for the first time on the "value attribute" of experience—a theme that was to recur: "An outstanding characteristic of man is his capacity to sense the value quality of his experience." "The Qualities of Being Human," which appeared in 1954, develops the value attributes theme and includes a discussion of the search for assumptions, including ethical and moral certainties that will be functional in a fast-moving world. The third article is from a paper, presented to the Second International Congress of Classical Studies in Copenhagen in 1954, which outlines the dilemma of the psychologist in describing and abstracting human experience without compromising its very nature. The concluding article, "The Human Design," is the 1964 reexamination of the problem, drawing upon his seven-year cross-cultural study with Lloyd A. Free of human aspirations in thirteen countries.

"Psychology in the Humanistic Realm" includes four articles in which my father attempted to take psychology into those domains of experience that engage the humanist. The first is his address as president of the Society for the Psychological Study of Social Issues in 1948. It deals with factors that must be weighed in judging what psychology can contribute for the "good" of humankind. Next is a paper prepared for delivery at the American Philosophical Association in 1955. It draws implications from research in transactional psychology for an understanding of the evolution and operation of ethical and moral systems. The section concludes with two essays applying general propositions of transactional psychology to "the nature of faith" and leadership in a democratic political system.

In the early 1960s, my father was introduced to the revolutionary developments in neurophysiology, and in particular to the work of William K. Livingston, who had been working independently at the University of Oregon Medical School on what he called "transactional neurology." The collaboration of the two was to have been exciting and productive except for Livingston's death just days after they had outlined a systematic book spelling out the psychological and neurological underpinnings of the transactional point of view.

The fourth section of the book deals with this phase of work. It commences with "A Transactional Inquiry Concerning Mind," written just before he met Livingston, and evidencing his continuing search for a naturalistic approach that would free psychology from the lingering influence of Descartes' mechanistic mind-body dualism. "The Concept of Transaction in Psychology and Neurology" and "Brain, Mind, and Self," taken together, indicate the scope and import of the book he and Livingston intended. A further elaboration is found in "Sentio Ergo Sum: 'Motivation' Reconsidered." Neither man lived to see the publication of "Brain, Mind, and Self" which appears here for the first time.

The book concludes with F.P. Kilpatrick's interpretive essay, "Hadley Cantril (1906-1969): The Transactional Point of View."

Albert H. Cantril
Cambridge, Massachusetts
June, 1987

Editor's note   The articles appear in the form in which they were first published (except, as noted, "Brain, Mind, and Self"). However, spelling, punctuation, capitalization and references have been made consistent throughout. Hadley Cantril's use of "man," "he," and so forth, is in a gender-free sense, and reflects the era in which he wrote rather than implying sexual bias.

I
Psychology and scientific research

1

The nature of scientific inquiry

with Adelbert Ames, Jr., Albert H. Hastorf,
and William H. Ittelson

> *The traditional code of science—that is, the objec-*
> *tives sought and the methods of investigation—*
> *cannot satisfy the requirements of our critical times,*
> *and this is why science has failed to measure up to*
> *the opportunities and obligations before it. The gen-*
> *erally accepted ideas of what natural science is and*
> *what it is for are out of date and need radical*
> *revision.*
>
> —C. J. Herrick (1949: v)

A feeling of urgency for a more adequate understanding of man and his social relations can be sensed in today's intellectual atmosphere. People are becoming more and more anxious about the ability of psychologists and social scientists to help solve the problems arising from our technological advances and from the swift social transitions they leave in their wake. But unfortunately what Herrick has said about the natural sciences applies especially to those sciences which deal with man—psychology and the social sciences in general. Moreover, in these sciences, in contrast to the physical sciences, there seems to be less agreement as to what constitutes significant research.

Obviously, an increase in our understanding of man can come about only as we extend our empirical knowledge and improve our formulations through research of demonstrated significance. And before that is possible, we must increase our understanding of the scientific process through which

Originally published as "Psychology and scientific research. I. The nature of scientific inquiry." Reprinted by permission from *Science* 110, no. 2862 (Nov. 4, 1949): 461-4.

3

discoveries are made. But sometimes the scientist's interest in building up the content of his discipline sidetracks him from a consideration of the scientific process itself and creates a lag in the understanding and improvement of scientific tools. What follows is an attempt to clarify our thinking about the nature of scientific research in those fields which take upon themselves the primary responsibility of accounting for man's thoughts and behavior. Only then will such research accomplish what we have a right to expect of it.

We shall first consider the nature of scientific inquiry, trying to find out why man pursues scientific inquiry, anyway—what function it serves him, and what steps seem to be involved. We shall then distinguish between scientific inquiry and scientific method—a distinction which seems necessary to avoid certain pitfalls and to assure scientific progress. Then we shall try to point out some of the specific implications to be derived for psychology from a better understanding of the nature of scientific inquiry and the role of scientific method and we shall indicate to what degree science can be "objective." Finally, some suggestions will be made which might accelerate the kind of scientific research that will increase our understanding of man.

The apparent reason for scientific inquiry is essentially the reason for any inquiry—to solve a problem. Scientific inquiry can never be understood if it is somehow put on a pedestal and viewed as something remote and apart from man's everyday activities. "Science," says Conant, "emerges from the other progressive activities of man to the extent that new concepts arise from experiments and observations." (1947: 24)

These activities of life are carried through in an environment which includes people, artifacts, the phenomena of nature. Man's only contact with this environment is through his senses. And the impressions man's senses give him are cryptograms in the sense that they have no meaning unless and until they become functionally related to man's purposive activities. The world man creates for himself through what Einstein has called the "rabble of the senses" is one that takes on a degree of order, system, and meaning as man builds up through tested experience a pattern of assumptions and expectancies on which he can base action.

Man builds up his assumptive or form world largely in an unconscious and nonintellectual way, in the process of adjustment and development as he goes about the business of life, that is, as he tries to act effectively to achieve his purposes. Man often uses many of his assumptions without being at all aware of them, such as those involved in reflex activity, habits, stereotypes, and a whole host of perceptual activities. Man is aware of other assumptions from time to time as they become relevant to the situation at hand, such as loyalties, expectancies, ideals. Still others, such as intellectual abstractions, can be brought to voluntary recall. Man's actions cannot be effective unless and until he builds up an assumptive or form world that has some degree of constancy and verifiability.[1]

What man brings to any concrete event is, then, an accumulation of assumptions, of awarenesses, and of knowledge concerning the relatively determined aspects of his environment as derived from his past experiences. But since the environment through which man carries out his life transactions is constantly changing, any person is constantly running into hitches and trying to do away with them. The assumptive world a person brings to the "now" of a concrete situation cannot disclose to him the undetermined significances continually emerging. And so we run into hitches in everyday life because of our inadequate understanding of the conditions giving rise to a phenomenon, and our ability to act effectively for a purpose becomes inadequate.

When we try to grasp this inadequacy intellectually and get at the why of the ineffectiveness of our purposeful action, we are adopting the attitude of scientific inquiry. Man as scientist tries to understand what aspect of his environment is responsibile for a hitch and then calls upon what knowledge he has that is relevant to an understanding of the determined, predictable nature of the particular phenomenon in question. Modern man uses the scientific method as a tool because he has found empirically that he can increase his understanding and act more effectively if his pursuits are guided by some knowledge concerning the determined aspects of the phenomenal world. G.H. Mead pointed out (1939: 41) that

> every discovery as such begins with experiences which have to be stated in terms of the biography of the discoverer. The man can note exceptions and implications which other people do not see and can only record them in terms of his own experience. He puts them in that form in order that other persons may get a like experience, and then he undertakes to find out what the explanation of these strange facts is.

Since the scientist's acquired purpose is to increase his understanding of a certain range of phenomena, when he experiences a hitch in his understanding of such phenomena he tries to bring to conscious awareness the reason for the hitch, that is, he tries to formulate intellectual concepts that will explain away the hitch. He does this by examining the probable conditional relationships except for which he, as an experiencing individual in a concrete situation, would not be faced with the hitch. He abstracts out of the hitch-situation those aspects he believes are probably necessary to his understanding of the original hitch. In his inquiry, the scientist arbitrarily treats these abstracted aspects of a phenomenon as if they existed in their own right. He does not do this simply because he wants to but because he has to, in order to recall and manipulate the phenomenon intellectually. The abstractions man is able to form have on him what Dewey and Bentley (1945: 225) characterize as a tremendous "liberative effect," making possible the voluntary, controlled conceptual thinking necessary for scientific inquiry and for the use of scientific method.

From this point of view, we might say in general that science is an activity designed by man to increase the reliability and verifiability of his assumptive world. For it would appear that in the last analysis any scientific pursuit—no matter how abstruse it seems—is carried on because it is somehow of concern to man. Science is the human effort to understand more about nature and human nature in verifiable, determined terms. The word *determined* is used here in the scientific sense as meaning high in prognostic reliability. From this it is clear that real progress in any science involves an awareness of our assumptive worlds, a consciousness of their inadequacy, and a constant, self-conscious attempt to change them so that the intellectual abstractions they contain will achieve increasing breadth and usefulness. Real progress in science means much more than merely adding to existing knowledge.

The processes involved in scientific inquiry would seem to be somewhat as follows: (1) sensing the inadequacy of the conceptual aspects of our assumptive world, thereby being faced with a problem for which we must seek an answer; (2) deciding on all those aspects of a phenomenon that might have a significant bearing on the problem: deciding on those aspects except for which the functional activities in question would not exist; (3) picking out from the various aspects assumed to be involved those that seem most important in terms of the original hitch we faced and that will serve as bases for standards we can think about and manipulate; (4) working out some method of changing those aspects we have chosen as variables or bases for standards and conducting our empirical investigations accordingly; (5) modifying our assumptive world on the basis of the empirical evidence concerning the validity of formulations that have resolved an immediate problem.

The solving of the immediate problem will automatically give rise to new hitches, and the above process constantly repeats itself.[2]

Specifically, it seems that scientific inquiry has two major functions for man. First, it provides man with a bundle of what are called "scientific facts." This bundle is composed of his up-to-the-now understandings of the determined, predictable aspects of nature and is used by him for purposes of prediction and control. There are essentially two varieties of these scientific facts: first, general statements of relationships of determined aspects of nature which we refer to as "scientific laws" and which, in the physical sciences, tend to be expressed in mathematical formulas; second, applications of these general laws to concrete situations for purposes of verification, specific prediction, or control. The characteristic of all these generalized scientific laws is that they disclose predictable aspects of types of phenomena no matter where or when they occur, irrespective of actual concrete situations.

A second function of science is that it provides a conceptual reorganization of the knowledge man has already acquired of the determined aspects of nature. Here we are trying to increase our range of understanding, or, as Dewey and Bentley phrase it, to improve our "specification," that is, our accuracy in naming (1945, 1946). Here, for example, the specifications involved in relativity are more accurate namings of phenomena than are Newton's concepts, and in this sense, Newton's concepts are not to be regarded as "wrong." This function of science includes that of increasing the range of man's conceptual knowledge through the discovery of more and more predictable aspects of nature that up to the present time remain undetermined.

Understanding and prediction

The aim of science is often defined as the attempt to increase the accuracy of our predictions. While the accuracy of predictions is clearly a most important criterion of progress in scientific formulation, emphasis on prediction alone can easily obscure the more fundamental aim of science covered by the word *understanding*. When we use the word understanding we are giving emphasis to the importance of increasing the range of our conceptual knowledge. Increased accuracy of prediction will be an inevitable coproduct of increased understanding in this sense. Any increase in understanding is also inevitably accompanied, sooner or later, by an increased ability to control variables and to apply our knowledge. Understanding also avoids the implication of a rigid determinism which seems, among other things, to be inconsistent with the fundamental indeterminism of modern physics.

Every scientific investigator must bear in mind that it is impossible for scientific research to disclose the unique specificity involved in any one actual occasion—for example, the student of modern physics knows that there is no law governing the behavior of an individual atom. And the investigator must also remember that it is impossible to predict with any complete accuracy the specific nature of growth and emergence, which are themselves undetermined. While it is impossible to determine the undetermined nature of emergence, it is still possible to increase our scientific knowledge about emergence through understanding more about the relatively determined phenomena immediately related to these undetermined emergent aspects. For example, we may hope to understand more about the extent of the undetermined field; to understand more about the conditions which make it possible for the undetermined aspects to emerge. In other words, our understanding of emergence can imporve only insofar as we become more and more aware of the boundaries of our determined world.

It is here that many of those who equate science with prediction or who use a narrow working definition of operationism are also those who will say they want nothing to do with the speculations of philosophy. And yet it is only by taking the philosopher's point of view, by bringing in freely all factors that might conceivably be involved in a single situation, that we can become aware of the boundaries of our up-to-the-now, determined scientific world. In discussing the role of philosophy, Conant writes that "there must be constant critical appraisal of the progress of science and in particular of scientific concepts and operation" (1947: 13f.). In their book *The Evolution of Physics*, Einstein and Infeld repeatedly emphasize the new philosophic views which have both helped to evolve and have evolved from physical research. Any scientific investigator who pushes his field of inquiry beyond the realm of the determinable and the repeatable out into the no man's land of emergence will inevitably become entangled with metaphysical problems. In so doing, he can hope that what is metaphysical for him today can tomorrow be part of the understood, physically determined, repeatable, and verifiable.

Transactional observation

Our own philosophical basis for our thinking concerning the nature and function of scientific inquiry and scientific method should be made explicit. We are using as our takeoff point what Dewey and Bentley have referred to in a series of articles as a "trans-actional approach."[3] What they mean by the term *transactional* can best be gathered by their own words. "Observation of this general (transactional) type sees man-in-action not as something radically set over against an environing world, nor yet as merely action 'in' a world, but as action *of* and *by* the world in which the man belongs as an integral constituent" (1945: 228). Under this procedure all of man's behavings "including his most advanced knowings," are treated as "activities not of himself alone, nor even as primarily his, but as processes of the full situation of organism-environment" (1946: 506). "From birth to death every human being is a *Party,* so that neither he nor anything done or suffered can possibly be understood when it is separated from the fact of participation in an extensive body of transactions—to which a given human being may contribute and which he modifies, but only in virtue of being a partaker in them" (Dewey 1948: 198).

Dewey and Bentley distinguish this transactional procedure from two other procedures which they feel have largely dominated the history of science up till now. First is what they call the antique view of "self-action; where things are viewed as acting under their own powers." Second is the interaction view of classical mechanics, "where thing is balanced against thing in causal interconnection." In transactional observation, "systems of description and naming are employed to deal with aspects and phases of action, without final attribution to 'elements' or other presumptively detachable or independent 'entities,' 'essences,' or 'realities,' and without isolation of presumptively detachable 'relations' from such detachable 'elements'" (1946: 509).[4]

While it is easy enough to understand this point of view intellectually, it is not nearly so easy to put it into operation in pursuing actual scientific inquiry. It tends to go against the grain of the psychologist's working procedures to regard any formulation merely as a certain "connection of conditions" (Dewey 1946: 217). And it is perhaps particularly difficult for psychologists to understand the full implications of the transactional point of view, because, as Dewey and Bentley have pointed out, "The interactional treatment, as everyone is aware, entered psychological inquiry just about the time it was being removed from basic position by the physical sciences from which it was copied" (1946: 546). But we must remember that psychology, by comparison, is still in its infancy, that the transactional approach, which Dewey and Bentley trace to the preface of Clerk Maxwell's *Matter and Motion,* dated 1877, antedated the first psychological laboratory.

Notes

1. The nature and function of man's assumptive or form world is much too large a subject to treat in any detail here and must be reserved for later consideration.
2. There seems to be a striking similarity between the processes used in scientific inquiry and the processes man makes use of in building up the assumptive world. Both science and common sense can be regarded as functional activities man uses in carrying out his life transactions. And the method of scientific inquiry seems in many ways to be an unconscious imitation of those age-old processes man has employed in his common-sense solutions of problems. In common-sense activity, the assumptions and awarenesses on which man depends for effective action are the hypotheses he has built up from his many experiences: weighted averages he unconsciously uses to give him a high prognosis for effective action.

   There are, however, certain important differences between the steps involved in pursuing scientific inquiry and the apparent processes that constitute common sense. A most important difference is the fact that in using scientific inquiry, man is the operator who decides what he is going to operate on and how. In an everyday life situation, however, man is not only the operator but he is also being operated on and must carry out his activities in the midst of the situation itself. When we meet hitches in everday life and try to overcome them with hunches for effective action, we test these hunches by the action itself in a more or less insightful, more or less conscious way. In scientific inquiry, on the other hand, hunches are tested by controlled experiments and a deliberate attempt is made to intellectualize the processes involved (cf. Dewey 1948: 197).

3. Since this article was written, Dewey and Bentley have brought together in a single volume, *Knowing and the Known* (Boston: Beacon Press, 1949), the references to Dewey and to Dewey and Bentley cited here together with other articles previously published by them.

4. In citing these distinctions made by Dewey and Bentley we are not implying (and they may not be) that in our own view either self-action or interaction can by any means be completely ruled out in any adequate explanation. Self-action is seen in the behavior of the simplest bodily cell, in the uniqueness of individual behavior, in the behavior of "nations," etc., while interactional assumptions appear to be essential first steps in providing an intellectual grasp of the form for the flow of transactional processes. The role of self-action and interaction in an inclusive transactional view must be left open as a problem and cannot be considered here in detail.

References

Conant, J.B. 1947. *On understanding science.* New Haven: Yale University Press.
Dewey, J. 1946. *Problems of men.* New York: Philosophical Library.
Dewey, J., and Bentley, A.F. 1945. "Terminology for knowings and knowns." *J. Phil.* 42:225.
———. 1946. "Interaction and transaction." *J. Phil.* 43: 505.
———. 1946. "Transactions as known and named." *J. Phil.* 43: 533.
———.1946. "Specification." *J. Phil.* 43: 645.
Herrick, C.J. 1949. *George Ellett Coghill.* Chicago: University of Chicago Press.
Mead, G.H. 1939. *Mind, self and society.* Chicago: University of Chicago Press.
Dewey, J. 1948. "Common sense and science: their respective frames of reference." *J. Phil. 45: 197.*

2

Scientific inquiry and scientific method

with Adelbert Ames, Jr., Albert H. Hastorf,
and William H. Ittelson

[In chapter 1] We have had to discuss the nature of and the apparent reason for scientific inquiry because "scientific research" has so often been thought of merely as a technique or method of investigation. What we know as the scientific method is a means for pursuing scientific inquiry. If we do not bear this in mind, real progress in scientific research is apt to be thwarted. For the implicit equating of scientific inquiry and scientific method to a technique of investigation leaves out an all-important consideration: the problem of formulating a problem for scientific investigation. For the formulation of the problem for investigation must contain within itself the possibility of going beyond what is now scientifically established if it is to satisfy the definition of scientific research. If the formulation of the problem does not do this, then succeeding steps in investigation are futile.

Although there is likely to be little argument here, some "research" in psychology seems to reflect only a lip service to this fundamental tenet. It may be appropriate to underscore the point here in the words of modern scientists. Whitehead has pointed out that "no systematic thought has made progress apart from some adequately general working hypothesis, adapted to its special topic. Such an hypothesis directs observation, and decides upon the mutual relevance of various types of evidence. In short, it prescribes method" (1933: 286). Einstein and Infeld have written that "the formulation of a problem is often more essential than its solution, which may be merely a matter of mathematical or experimental skill. To raise

Originally published as "Psychology and scientific research. II. Scientific inquiry and scientific method." Reprinted by permission from *Science* 110, no. 2863 (Nov. 11, 1949): 491- 7.

new questions, new possibilities, to regard old problems from a new angle, requires creative imagination and makes a real advance in science" (1942: 95). Oppenheimer indicates that the experimental techniques of science enable us to define and detect our "errors of conception" (1947: 22).

It should be emphasized that if an hypothesis is to be regarded as adequate it must be more than a statement or description of current data and more than a prediction that data will reproduce themselves. An hypothesis must be tested both in terms of its ability to predict immediate events and its promise of leading to further, more adequate hypotheses. For in scientific procedure there is a never-ending process of hypothesizing, a constant flow of one hypothesis from another, with each hypothesis trying to go beyond established formulations in its inclusiveness.[1]

It is the way in which the investigator poses his problem that determines where he will come out—what functional activities he will feel have a bearing on the problem, which of these he will use as the bases for standards in empirical investigation, and what methodological procedures he will follow or try to devise. In this connection it is relevant to note that the popular conception of what makes a scientist "great" is that he has solved problems that have long baffled others. While this may be true enough, a review of the history of science will show that in general the solution of a problem is relatively easy once the problem has been posed and that the real scientific contribution of those scientists we now regard as outstanding is due to the way in which they have formulated problems which they or others have solved. The tremendous advances in the physical sciences since the seventeenth century, for example, are due more to improved formulations than to changes in methodology. In the seventeenth century and continuing into the twentieth, science sought all-inclusive "laws" and felt that reality was firmly in hand. But today both all-inclusive laws and reality seem more elusive than ever. Contemporary physics is seeing its ultimate particle disappear, physiology is realizing that it is not dealing with the classical closed-energy system. The need for a basic conceptual reformulation to bring about newer and greater understanding is apparent on all sides. In his history of science, Dampier-Whetham has noted that "insight, imagination, and perhaps genius, are required firstly to pick out the best fundamental concepts" (1929: 457).

Search versus research

Much that now passes for scientific research, not only in psychology but in many fields, has precious little to do with what may be honestly called scientific pursuit. But the surface similarity between much current work and real scientific investigation may be sufficient to deceive the investigator himself. If investigators are not to hoodwink themselves and each other and pervert scientific inquiry for some end that has little if anything to do with increasing our understanding of man, it is clearly imperative that they be concerned as consciously as possible with research that will bring about major reformulations. Otherwise they are forced to close their eyes to important problems that face them or to devote themselves only to methodological problems, rationalizing these activities as research.

One variety of this perversion is represented in the shotgun approach, in which the idea seems to be that if one only gathers enough data, possibly with the use of new gadgets or apparatus, one must sooner or later come out with some sort of scientific result. A precedent for this type of activity was set by Francis Bacon, who held that "by recording and tabulating all possible observations and experiments, the relations would emerge almost automatically" (Dampier-Whetham 1944: 58). And in the three hundred years since Bacon's time, many investigators have proceeded either without any clear hypothesis or with what they call "limited hypotheses," often so limited that they cannot possibly provide a springboard for further emergence. Much of such data today is concerned with correlational relationships. The situation is such that to an outside observer reviewing the history of modern thought, psychology seems to be merely "trying correlation after correlation in the hope of stumbling on something significant" (Randall 1926: 495).

Another perversion of scientific method is found in the tendency in some areas of psychology to work out elaborate classifications, with the implication that if the behavior of an individual can only be properly pigeonholed in some static system, then further analysis of a functional nature is relatively unimportant for understanding. Karl Pearson's emphasis on classification as a major pursuit of science undoubtedly did a great deal to establish this misconception. One needs only to review the literature in the field of personality or to watch many clinicians diagnose psychiatric patients to see how some men in these areas are struggling to free themselves from older classificatory systems.

Scientific inquiry and scientific method are also not to be confused with investigations limited solely to a so-called "quantitative approach." An overconcentration on problems of measurement as such can easily sidetrack the investigator from the more important concentration on what data are significant to gather and can blind him completely to the problem of problemization, with its concurrent problem of selecting the standards worth measuring. Furthermore, those who are wedded solely to a quantitative approach are all too frequently unwilling to tackle problems for which there are no available quantitative techniques, thus limiting themselves to research impressive only in the elaborate quantitative treatment of data. Current attempts to refine sampling techniques in the field of public opinion research, for example, while indispensable, run the danger of making investigators myopic to certain areas of inquiry that would seem much more important for an understanding or prediction of public be-havior—for example, the problem of asking the right questions, of deter-mining the surety of opinion under different circumstances, or the effect of different interviewing situations on response. The current vogue of factor analysis in the study of personality, while most significant as a means of testing a theory, as Eysenck's report shows (1947), frequently reflects insuffi-cient consideration of the relevance or adequacy of the variables thrown into the hopper for analysis.

The function of experimentation and measurement

In saying that what now passes for research (scientific inquiry instru-mented by scientific method) is often only scientific pretension, we do not mean to imply at all that reasonable problems for scientific research can be formulated or operated on without including empirical investigation. Ex-perimentation is clearly indispensable as a test of formulation. An hypoth-esis can be tested only if one is able to do something with it. But it is often forgotten that the value of an experiment is directly proportional to the degree to which it aids the investigator in formulating better problems. And while a single experiment may solve a problem, it can never give us complete understanding. If an investigator believes that by solving a prob-lem he has achieved complete understanding it only shows that his prob-lem has been defined inadequately and is not a step in the constant, never-ending scientific search for more and more comprehensive formulations.

The importance of any scientific experiment in which relevant variables are manipulated must be in terms of the breadth of the formulation it has a bearing on. It should be borne in mind that the first and most significant step in experimentation is to determine *if* the variation of one abstracted phenomenon affects other abstracted phenomena at all. The next most disclosing step is to determine *how* the variation of one abstracted phe-nomenon affects other abstracted phenomena. We confirm or deny the validity of an hypothesis by determining if and how the manipulation of one variable affects another variable or the total group of phenomena in which we are interested. In the process of using the scientific method of relevant variables, the investigator can discover if and how variables are affected only with reference to some inclusive, higher-order formulation. Otherwise relevant variables could be manipulated forever without making any scientific advance at all. It is also imperative to bear in mind that how much a change in one variable affects another variable does not give us new insight on the "if" and "how" relationship. We determine how much one variable affects another in order to increase our prediction and control, not to increase our range of understanding.

In the process of experimentation, the investigator must be ready to use whatever procedures appear most relevant to an understanding of the problem at hand. These procedures will be both quantitative and nonquantitative. Obviously if we select some phenomenon or characteristic as a variable for experimentation we can do so only because it exists in some degree, some amount, some quantity in relation to the abstracted standard upon which it is based. In scientific research quantitative and nonquantitative procedures are interdependent, and highly refined quantitative investigation may be necessary before one can establish a nonquantitative formulation as, for example, the relationship between the Michelson-Morley experiment and Einstein's formulation. Thus the establishment of any dichotomy between quantitative and nonquantitative procedure is an artificial barrier to scientific progress, separating and taking apart what really belong together in scientific method. Scientific inquiry will be strapped if the investigator feels that he cannot be scientific without being one hundred percent quantitative.

Because scientific methodology is now so often equated solely with quantitative procedures, it may be useful here to distinguish what seems to us to be the function of quantitative procedures in scientific method.

First is the design of controlled experiments or other systematic investigations which involve measurement for the specific purpose of checking a hunch, validating an hypothesis, or testing a general law in a specific concrete situation. As we have already emphasized, the verification of this hypothesis is itself to be regarded only as a stepping stone to further, more inclusive hypotheses. In the fields of psychology and the social sciences, this general function usually translates itself into the purpose of checking some experienced relationships and causalities in an effort to intellectualize and systematize hunches that seem significant.

A second role played by quantitative measurement is the systematic recording of data. But it must be emphasized again in this connection that the accumulation of quantitative results is profitable only to the extent that some previous intellectual excursions have led to an hypothesis which is subjectively held with some degree of surety. Recording without an hypothesis in mind, if it is indeed possible at all, has no place in scientific method.[2]

A third function of quantitative research is to establish norms for the purpose of studying single cases—in psychology, for example, individual or group variations. As any experimental, clinical, or social psychologist knows, quantitative standards are of the utmost importance in predicting how specific individuals or groups of individuals will react in specific situations. But again it must be borne in mind that one undertakes measurement for such purposes only after the formulation of some hunch which may itself be based on nonquantitative evidence. And we must furthermore remember that we can only measure something relative to an arbitrarily established norm.

Whereas most investigators would undoubtedly give a nod of approval to the thesis that quantitative and nonquantitative procedures are interdependent in scientific method, much current work in psychology and the social sciences indicates that in practice this kind of thinking and research-planning is not followed, and that, on the contrary, there is often a conscious or unconscious attempt to imitate physical scientists, in the false belief that their success has been due chiefly to the quantitative techniques they have designed. It may therefore be worth a brief historical glance at Isaac Newton's procedure to gain some perspective on the role of quantitative experimentation in verifying and extending nonquantitative observations.

Although Newtonian concepts have been superseded, the Newtonian method remains essentially unchanged and still provides the framework for most of modern science. While Newton's aim was to find absolute, mathematical "laws of nature," his method clearly consisted of (1) simplification and isolation of fundamental concepts, (2) formulation of relevant hypotheses on the basis of these essentially nonquantitative concepts, and (3) intensive quantitative verification and amplification of these hypotheses. Although the concepts of mass and the mutual attraction of gravitation are inherent in a falling apple, it is doubtful if they would ever emerge from a statistical study of *all* falling objects on the face of the globe. As Newton expressed it, "Our purpose is only . . . to apply what we discover in some simple cases, as principles, by which . . . we may estimate the effects thereof in more involved cases." The inverse of this, the attempt to find the "principles" in the welter of "involved cases," would have seemed senseless to Newton.

In developing his methodology, which he nowhere explicitly defines, Newton was in effect systematizing what had become over the centuries the de facto method of the "natural philosophers." Nineteen hundred years before Newton, there was sufficient evidence for Aristarchus to advance his heliocentric concept of the universe. This significant concept was, of course, lost until Copernicus, reading the ancients, discovered that some philosophers had "thought the earth was moved." "When for this reason, therefore, I had conceived its possibility, I myself also began to meditate upon the mobility of the earth." The immediate result of this fruitful hypothesis was, of course, a systematic theory which, however, still depended for its acceptance on the principle of mathematical simplicity. Galileo, sensing the importance of experimental verification, provided the last historic step by means of his telescope.

The Newtonian era probably represents one of the most significant and fruitful epochs in human thought. Relevant to our discussion here, the birth of scientific inquiry was accompanied by a formulation of concepts which have determined and dominated thinking up to the present day. Copernicus meditated "upon the mobility of the earth." Newton, age 23, "began to think of gravity extending to ye orb of the Moon." Kepler gave support to the Copernican system because "I have attested it as true in my deepest soul," and "I contemplate its beauty with incredible and ravishing delight." Harvey "began to think whether there might not be a motion [of the blood], as it were, in a circle." Huygens and others formulated the principle of the conservation of what later was termed kinetic energy. The list is virtually endless. In every area of human thought starting and productive contributions were made. Since there is no reason to suppose that the seventeenth century was especially propitious for the birth of genius, one wonders if the productivity of this period may not be attributed to a fortunate blending of unfettered speculation coupled with a new awareness of the need for empirical verification at every step. Remove the speculation and only barren measurement remains.

Operationism

In the past quarter-century the basic tenets of operationism have so interested all science and have become so ingrained in the thinking of most scientific investigators that no discussion of the role of experimentation in scientific inquiry can be complete without a consideration of the place of operationism which is, historically, a "recent formulation of some of the essential features of the experimental method and of empiricism generally"(Feigl 1945: 250).

The impetus for operationism came from Bridgman in physics with the recognition that concepts such as distance have different meanings when used in different contexts. The concept is, therefore, a construct of the observer and not "a thing in itself." It follows that if the variables with which an experimenter deals are products of the experimenter's ingenuity and cannot be specified by pointing to them, then they must be specified by pointing to the procedures employed by the experimenter in creating his constructs. It is only by pointing out the procedures employed in experimentation that the investigator can convey to others the constructs he is dealing with.

Unfortunately, however, the generality of Bridgman's approach has sometimes been lost sight of. There is nothing in the general statement of operationism which delimits or in any way prescribes the defining operation to be used. Bridgman himself has asserted that "any method of describing the conditions is permissible which leads to a characterization precise enough for the purpose in hand, making possible the recovery of the conditions to the necessary degree of approximation" (1945: 246). Those writers who assert that defining operations must necessarily be "physicalistic" are gratuitously adding a restriction not inherent in the operational approach. This insistence probably traces back to the feeling that physicalistic constructs are somehow more "real" than others and has led to a fundamental misconception and perversion of the operational approach as originally stated.

The inhibiting effect of this artifical restriction has probably not been severe in those sciences more closely concerned with the physicalistic. In psychology, however, this has tended to exclude the use of psychological constructs and, as Pratt has stated, "to place a stamp of approval on certain limited fields of research in which hypotheses can be neatly formulated in the language of the older sciences" (1945: 268). We have indicated that a study of relationships alone does not constitute scientific research. Real research must always involve constantly higher-order abstractions. In the field of psychology many of these abstractions cannot possibly be "pointed to" in any narrow operational sense and many of them are not easy to manipulate experimentally. While a scientific investigator must rely upon operational concepts, he must remember at the same time, as Feigl has said, that "operationism is not a system of philosophy. It is not a technique for the formation of concepts or theories. It will not by itself produce scientific results. These are brought about by the labor and ingenuity of the researchers (1945: 258).

Selection of standards

A major problem confronting any investigator is the selection or discovery of the standards to use in his investigation. The dictionary defines as a standard "that which is set up and established by authority as a rule for the measures of quantity, weight, extent, value, or quality."

The problem of selecting standards is much more complicated than is often realized, for the reason that the conditional relationships we abstract out of a total situation and except for which the situation would not exist do not themselves exist in their own right. Nor is there any adequate intellectual explanation of their existence. These conditional relationships or aspects of a total phenomenon that the scientist calls "variables" are not God-given and are not limited. Einstein and Infeld point out that "physical concepts are free creations of the human mind, and are not, however it may seem, uniquely determined by the external world" (1942: 33). Any adjective or any adverb can serve as a potential basis for a variable. Variables that provide the bases for standards are purely the creations of man, enabling him to formulate an abstract, common, determined phenomenal world. The variables employed in any scientific research are based on intuitive judgments and in any concrete investigation depend upon the way in which the investigator has formulated his problem. Since problems are formulated differently in different fields of inquiry, the aspect of a phenomenon that we choose in one field to serve as the basis for a standard in that field will not necessarily be applicable in another field of inquiry. Furthermore, the aspect of a phenomenon that may serve as a basis for standards within any one field will vary according to the nature of the hitch in a concrete situation.

Here words play their familiar tricks even with the thinking of the scientist, who may tend to forget that in his necessary use of word symbols for his thinking and communication (*space, time, IQ, attitude, etc.*) he is employing abstractions which he cannot, as a scientist, implicitly or unconsciously assume as real in investigation. And it is only to the extent that the investigator is aware of his own transformation of adjectival or adverbial relationships into noun qualities that he maintains the possibility of discovering new conditional relationships except for which a phenomenon would not exist. If abstracted characteristics of the situation are unconsciously reified, complacency or a defensive attitude results.

When we decide on a standard, we take some aspect of a phenomenon, some variable, as a basis for measurement. Since the phenomena with which science deals are so enormously varied, the quantitative units employed in any investigation will depend on the nature of the problem at hand—for example, distance will be measured in angstrom units or in light years. Also, obviously, we cannot necessarily quantify one standard in the same way we do other standards. While precise units of measurement may be applicable in the physical sciences, in psychology, if we are using some aspect of experience as the basis for a standard, we may have to be satisfied with crude introspective measures such as "more than" or "less than." Whitehead has pointed out that "we must entirely separate psychological time, space, external perception, and bodily feeling from the scientific world of molecular interaction. This strange world of science dwells apart like the gods of Epicurus, except that it has the peculiar property of inducing our minds to play upon us the familiar antics of the senses:" (1922: 62).

Since every standard is based on a man-made assumption, and since it is possible for man to use an infinite number of abstracted subphenomena as bases for standards, the criterion for the selection of what shall be used as the basis for a standard is essentially its usefulness in determining whether or not the abstracted subphenomenon with which we are dealing is constant, verifiable, and potentially helpful in solving our original problem. Also, of course, the basis to be used for our standard must be subject to voluntary recall and to intellectual manipulation.

How do we proceed to select the standards we will use in actual empirical investigation? Since we must start with the nature of the particular hitch we have experienced, abstract generalizations or rules cannot be given. The best that can be done is to describe the apparent functional process that goes on.

It seems to be something like this: In the course of following an acquired interest in understanding why certain phenomena occur (in physics, biology, psychology, and other sciences) we encounter a difficulty which no previous investigator has resolved to our intellectual satisfaction or perhaps has faced as we face it now. The assumptive world we have built up from experience (which includes the abstracted scientific concepts that have a bearing on the problem) proves inadequate as we try to intellectualize the hitch we have run into. There is no empirical evidence we can find that describes all the conditions except for which the phenomenon that puzzles us would not exist.

In trying to intellectualize the inadequacy of our assumptive world, we discover that a certain condition or set of conditions have not been taken into account. We abstract out of the hitch-situation those aspects we believe are probably necessary to our understanding of the original hitch. We use these aspects of a phenomenon as the bases for our standards, and we vary their "amount." We may have an understanding of why such conditions are important at the time we think of them or we may only have a vague hunch that they are important and may intellectualize them much later. If we have an immediate understanding, we can design our investigation rather precisely. If we have only a hunch, a certain amount of trial and error in experimentation is necessary. But this trial and error takes place within boundaries we set and is not to be mistaken for a shotgun approach. In either case, we design the empirical test of our new basis for a standard with reference to other phenomena that have already been established as bases for standards. We do this in an attempt to determine whether or not the variation in the new basis we have selected for a standard affects old standards and is affected by them according to our formulation.

Our formulation may be validated in some circumstances if the new aspect of the phenomenon we have introduced is affected by other functional aspects. Or, under other circumstances, our formulation may be confirmed if the new aspect we have introduced is not affected by other standards. If our empirical test confirms our formulation and we find that we have abstracted out an aspect of the phenomenon that is the necessary condition for the existence of the total phenomenon, then we can say that we have the basis for a new standard and can proceed to think of it quantitatively.

Once an investigator has discovered new aspects of a phenomenon that can serve as the bases for standards, it is only too easy for him to slip into the misconception that the particular operation on which he has settled as suitable to the problem at hand exhausts the subject and says all there is to be said about it. This leads to the reification of the very construct which operationism, for example, was devised to avoid. Any science becomes stagnant if it does not regard the discovery of new variables as its primary concern.

We cannot agree with those investigators who believe that the basic variables of all sciences are the same if we can only find them. As we have already pointed out, in psychology this leads to an artificial restriction of the problems dealt with, sometimes to the extent of eliminating from consideration the most pertinent variables. For example, in the attempt to study certain perceptual phenomena, emphasis has been placed on such easily defined variables as "farther than" and "bigger than," where the more psychologically meaningful variable in many cases is probably the subjective feeling of "surer than." If our awareness of a change in an external event is to be considered at all functional in nature, then the subjective sense of surety accompanying the perception must be of primary psychological significance. In the case of those perceptions we label attitudes, investigation of the surety with which attitudes are held under different conditions has lagged far behind our interest in measuring the "direction" of the attitude or opinion.

A note on analysis

The use of the term *analysis* is a poor and misleading way by which to describe the processes involved in determining the variables we will use in our scientific thinking. For analysis assumes the existence of entities existing in their own right which together make up a total phenomenon, and suggests that all we have to do is somehow isolate them, by analysis, for manipulation. Analysis becomes synonymous with the classification of variables in terms of abstracted, fixed, and reified standards.

As we have already indicated, there is an infinity of variables that provide the bases for an infinity of standards. We have said that all adjectives and adverbs furnish a potential basis for standards. And from a study of the history of our language we know that emerging situations bring their own new bases for standards—for example, the "snafu" of the GI. When we analyze by using existing standards we make nouns out of adjectival or adverbial relationships often without knowing. For analysis is possible only by using existing standards. Analysis thus does not add anything to our understanding of the functional activities involved in transactional relationships. Hence analysis is not at all similar to what must be regarded as the scientist's constant obligation to discover those aspects of a phenomenon except for which it would not exist. Likewise synthesis—the putting together of that which we have taken apart—is a process by means of which we cannot get any more into the synthesis than is included in the standards made use of in analysis.

The functional activities we pick out for attempted intellectual understanding are those related to the immediate hitch we face. This means, then, that although an infinite number of conditional relationships exist, in any concrete scientific pursuit the range of conditional relationships an investigator might pick out as important will be limited, and will be bounded by the nature of the hitch he has encountered. Scientific progress results from the ability to pick out the most relevant conditional relationships for empirical investigation, not by further analysis of established variables alone.

Notes

1. In a memorandum concerning the conceptualization of novel problems, Horace Fries has called attention to the necessity of making a distinction between an increase in our understanding and the solution of an immediate problem. He points out that "the degree of success in the resolution of the difficulty is always relative, i.e., better or worse relative to the interests or desires affected. But the *solution* of a problem brings about an adequate *resolution* of the difficulty in proportion to the adequacy in which the difficulty is organized into a problem, i.e., the adequacy of the problemization of the difficulty" (unpub.).
2. Occasionally Charles Darwin's work has been used as an illustration of the way in which an hypothesis suddenly appears if one can only accumulate sufficient data. But in the famous first paragraph of his introduction to the *Origin of Species* (1859), Darwin clearly belies any such contention:

   When on board H.M.S. "Beagle" as naturalist, I was much struck with certain facts in the distribution of the organic beings inhabiting South America, and in the geological relations of the present to the past inhabitants of that continent. These facts, as will be seen in the latter chapters of this volume, seemed to throw some light on the origin of species—that mystery of mysteries, as it has been called by one of our greatest philosophers. On my return home, it occurred to me, in 1837, that something might perhaps be made out of this question by patiently accumulating and reflecting on all sorts of facts which could possibly have any bearing on it. After five years' work I allowed myself to speculate on the subject, and drew up some short notes; these I enlarged in 1844 into a sketch of the conclusions, which then seemed to me probable: from that period to the present day I have steadily pursued the same object. I hope that I may be excused for entering on these personal details, as I give them to show that I have not been hasty in coming to a decision.

And we find in Darwin's letter this further statement (1888: 183):

In October 1838, that is, fifteen months after I had begun my systematic enquiry, I happened to read for amusement Malthus on population, and, being well prepared to appreciate the struggle for existence which everywhere goes on from long-continued observation of the habits of animals and plants, it at once struck me that under these circumstances favorable variations would tend to be preserved, and unfavorable ones to be destroyed. The result of this would be the formation of new species. Here then I had at last got a theory by which to work.

References

Bridgman, P.W. 1945. "Some general principals of operational analysis." *Psychol. Rev.* 52: 246.

Dampier-Whetham, W.C.D. 1929. *History of science.* New York: Macmillan.

_____. 1944. *Shorter history of science.* Cambridge: Cambridge University Press.

Darwin,C. 1859. *Origin of species.*

Darwin, F. (ed.) 1888. *Life and letters of Charles Darwin.* New York: Appleton.

Einstein, A., and Infeld, L. 1942. *Evolution of physics.* New York: Simon and Schuster.

Eysenck, H.J. 1947. *Dimensions of personality.* London: Routeledge.

Feigl, H. 1945. "Operationism and Scientific Method." *Psychol. Rev.* 52: 250.

Fries, H.H. (n.d.) Cultural function of art relative to the conceptualization of novel problems. Unpublished paper, University of Wisconsin.

Oppenheimer, J.R. 1947. *Physics in the contemporary world.* Cambridge, Mass.: Massachusetts Institute of Technology (Little Memorial Lecture).

Pratt, C.C. 1945. "Operationism in Psychology." *Psychol. Rev.* 52: 262.

Randall, J.H., Jr. 1926. *Making of the modern mind.* Boston: Houghton Mifflin.

Whitehead, A.N. 1922. *Principle of relativity.* Cambridge: Cambridge University Press.

_____. 1933. *Adventures of ideas.* New York: Macmillan.

3

The transactional view in psychological research

with Adelbert Ames, Jr., Albert Hastorf,
and William Ittelson

When psychology emancipates itself from dependence on interactionism alone by taking a transactional view of the phenomena which come within its province, we should expect that the division of psychologists into schools would rapidly disappear. Schools (Gestalt, behaviorism, psychoanalysis, etc.) would disappear not because they are "wrong" or "have been overthrown" but because the formulations of each school that meet empirical tests would be encompassed within wider formulations of problems. What are some ways to speed this development?

First of all, the psychologist must not only realize intellectually, but must make a part of his functional assumptive world, the idea that man's thought and behavior can be understood only as processes of a "full situation of organism-environment." The point has been made by H.A. Murray and collaborators in their contention that "the main body of psychology started its career by putting the wrong foot forward and it has been out of step with the march of science much of the time. Instead of beginning with studies of the whole person adjusting to a natural environment, it began with studies of a segment of a person responding to a physical stimulus in an unnatural laboratory environment" (1948: 466). Brunswik, in his "ecological analysis," has pointed out the need to understand the complete "representativeness of circumstances" operative in any situation under ob-

Originally published as "Psychology and scientific research. III. The transactional view in psychological research." Reprinted by permission from *Science* 110, no. 2864 (Nov. 18, 1949): 517- 22.

servation (1949). But while an increasing number of psychologists are calling for a revision in traditional psychological procedure, their voices are still those of men crying in the wilderness of the universe which constitutes so much of psychological inquiry today. The psychological investigator, of all people, cannot separate the observer from what is being observed, the process of knowing from what is known, what is "out there" from whatever goes on in the experiencing organism. Psychology must disavow completely any "field theory" which implies that an environmental field acts *on* a person rather than *through* a person.

Because man inevitably builds up for himself an assumptive world in carrying out his purposive activities, the world he is related to, the world he sees, the world he is operating on, and the world that is operating on him is the result of a transactional process in which man himself plays an active role. Man carries out his activities in the midst of concrete events which themselves delimit the significances he must deal with.

In the process man is himself changed in greater or lesser degree by having his own assumptive world changed through confirmation or denial as a result of action. In his immediate activity man abstracts from the immediate situation certain determined aspects according to his assumptive world. And this, as we indicated, includes far more than the immediate occasion: it is a continuum which includes the past and the future, a storehouse of both past experience and ideals. As Bentley has pointed out, "Behaviors are present events converging pasts into futures. They cannot be reduced to successions of instants nor to successions of locations. They themselves span extension and duration. The pasts and the futures are rather phases of behavior than its control" (1941: 485). Psychologists must be constantly aware of the effects man's own actions have both on his assumptive world—confirming or denying certain aspects of it—and concurrently on the "environment out there" as it is perceived and experienced.

Another implication of the transactional mode of observation is that the psychologist, like any other scientific investigator, must be sensitive to the pitfalls involved in reifying anything as an entity that has been given a proper name—a pitfall that philosophers since Plato have inveighed against. Psychologists, like other scientists, must become increasingly self-conscious of the dangers to their scientific progress inherent in catchwords, whose use, as Dewey and Bentley point out, "shatters the subject matter into fragments in advance of inquiry and thus destroys instead of furthering comprehensive observation for it" (1945: 243). Any uncritical use of traditional abstractions makes it difficult or impossible to see together what has already been taken apart.

While academic psychologists have long since given up the entity of the *soul,* and while most of them, at least in their professional writing, refuse to talk of the *mind,*[1] many other entities have slipped into the professional jargon of psychology to make transactional observation difficult. We have, for example, *need, IQ, schizophrenic, trait, attitude, Oedipus complex,* and *mesomorph.* The uncritical use of such words as specifications can easily lead to redundancy and double talk.

Psychology runs the risk of retarding its discovery of new bases for psychological standards through the use of bases for standards employed successfully in the past by the physical sciences. For example, psychologists refer to "the size of the retinal image," "visual angles," "intensity of opinion," "field forces," "gradients," "positive or negative valences," "vectors," "depth psychology," and some even search for the physical dimensions of consciousness, limiting physical dimensions to a handful of constructs. Psychology has by no means emancipated itself yet from the standards of the physical sciences and is not rapidly enough discovering standards appropriate for the phenomena with which it deals.[2] By refusing to place firm reliance on standards whose bases are necessarily subjective, psychology sometimes complacently throws out some of the most important problems with which it should be concerned. Nouns such as *surety, anxiety, ego-involvement, expectancy, happiness,* imply adjectival or adverbial relationships that are purely subjective. There are plenty of bases available for standards if the psychologist dares use them as he becomes sensitive to the importance of the problem of selecting bases for standards appropriate for the inquiry at hand.

It has become increasingly clear in recent years in the fields of chemistry and biology, for example, that standards appropriate to the subject matter of investigation must be sought and that reliance on the standards of classical or modern physics alone will hamper investigation. For example, J.G. Hoffman, a professor of biophysics, has recently noted that "the word biophysics . . . is a ridiculous combination of incongruous extremes. Disciplined scientific thought has never taken more diverse forms than it has in the fundamental modes of thinking in biology and in physics" (1949: 7). In pointing out the limitations of a physical mode of observation for the study of living systems, Hoffman quotes Delbrück's statement that "instead of aiming at the whole of the phenomena exhibited by the living cell we now expect to find natural limits and, thereby, implicitly, new virgin territories, on which laws may hold which are independent of those of physics, by virtue of the fact that they relate to phenomena whose appearance is conditioned on *not* making observations of the type needed for applying atomic physics" (p. 14).

There is also a tendency in psychology to use catchwords in labeling the fields of social, clinical, educational, or industrial as "applied" fields of psychology and to separate them from the more traditional "experimental" psychology. Any such division is absurd unless the person who uses it consciously reserves it for rough descriptive purposes. Investigators in these fields must, of course, also rely on experiments. But beyond that, any such distinction acts as a deterrent in the search for more adequate formulations which will better account for human behavior, whether in the laboratory, the clinic, the factory or in everyday social life. It is especially in fields such as these that one encounters hitches in interpretation because of the huge number of variables involved in the concrete situations that constitute each of the areas of inquiry. When such hitches are encountered, the investigator does not merely "apply" to their resolution some theory he has read in a book or learned from laboratory experiments. To be sure, he brings such knowledge and experience into the process of hypothesis formation. But the chances are very high indeed that any theory which is not itself based in large part upon the understanding of similar full-bodied concrete situations will turn out to be extremely inadequate.

We can illustrate the way in which psychological inquiry has been restricted by the use of terms with reference to the field of perception, which has so often been a weathervane in psychology. In working on perception, psychologists early found that certain variations in objective or physiological factors produced marked subjective variations. This naturally led to the idea of correspondence between subjective factors on the one hand and objective and physiological factors on the other hand. Since an alteration of objective and physiological factors could so easily be shown to cause subjective effects and since the converse could not so easily be demonstrated, the assumption was built up that the subjective aspects of perception had their origin largely in the corresponding objective factors and the accompanying physiological disturbances they caused. Studies of perception have thus concentrated largely on the analysis of objective and physiological factors. And since these objective or physiological factors could be varied quantitatively, scientific methodology in psychology tended to become identified with measurement alone.

This led to a long neglect of those factors not amenable to precise measurement. These neglected factors were, of course, subjective factors described by such symbols as past experience, loyalties, expectancy, and purpose, whether these were operating consciously or unconsciously. This methodological dam has recently been cracked, largely through research in social and clinical psychology, where the effects of subjective factors on perception are especially obvious. More recently, in an attempt to liberate investigators somewhat from correspondence between subjective and objective or physiological factors, the Hanover Institute has designed demonstrations of perceptual phenomena which deliberately make use of illusions. By using illusions, the investigator gains more freedom to understand the nature of the functional activities that are involved in the scientific inquiry of perception and thereby gets a better toehold on the function of perception in man's purposive behavior. For example, it can be demonstrated that the perception of *where* a thing is depends upon the perception of *what* a thing is and on *when* it is perceived. Carr has pointed out that "illusions contrasted with correct perceptions are the experimental variants that reveal the common principle involved in both" (1935: 326).

On the basis of an interactional view alone, an investigator could study the interdependence of various aspects of a perception forever and never get at the reason for such relationships until he asked himself what function such an interrelationship of phenomena served in the transaction of living. When he asks himself this question it appears that variables such as size and distance are experientially related because it is only through their relationship in past experiences that high prognostic reliability is built up. Prognostic reliability becomes itself, then, a new dimension of experience, a new basis for a standard the psychologist can use for experimentation. And if the investigator continues, as he must, to ask the next question concerning the function of prognostic reliability in a life transaction, the apparent answer is that prognostic reliability of a perception increases effective action. So the effectiveness of action becomes another variable that can be used as a basis for a standard in experimentation. And there must follow, of course, the question: Effective action for what? We then see that we cannot understand even the simplest perception without bringing in the variable of purpose.

The transactional mode of observation seems, then, to be peculiarly appropriate for psychologists if they are going to seek what Collingwood has called more abstract, more universal "logical grounds" for the understanding of subordinate abstractions or phenomena (1940). Obviously, if we do not understand the logical ground that causes relevant variables to be relevant, then our scientific methods will be sterile indeed. Hence progress in psychology is to be measured largely in terms of the discovery of logical grounds which increase our understanding because of their intrinsic reasonableness and the possibility they hold out of verification by experimental methods. Many of the abstractions Freud created are a case in point.

The transactional view has a third implication for psychology which concerns the method of experimentation that must be involved in real research. Different subjects for scientific inquiry pose different kinds of problems that can only be solved by adapting or creating methods appropriate to them. In saying that any one scientific discipline has special circumstances of its own which determine the techniques to be used, we are not in any way denying the indispensability of the universal characteristic of scientific method: the controlled experiment. All we are saying is that we must increase our self-consciousness and our ingenuity concerning the use and meaning of *controlled* and not claim that we are undertaking controlled scientific investigation when our assumptive world artificially limits the number of potential controls we are aware of.

One difficulty in the use of experimental techniques in psychology and the social sciences is that of approximating in a controlled experiment any concrete situation in which thought and behavior normally occur. Although this has been pointed out many times, and although the difficulty is easily recognizable, psychologists must be particularly on their guard to see that, in the experimental situations they devise, they have not left out so many of the subjective variables involved in normal experience that their experimental results will have little subsumptive power.

A second and much less frequently realized difficulty is that in dealing with the human organism we are dealing with a particular variety of "world stuff" which perceives complicated significances. Unless we make a special effort to understand the particular significance a particular organism at a particular time and place attaches to all the stimuli involved in our investigations, we shall again have abstracted out of the situation perhaps the most important variables for study. In psychology it is imperative that the investigator be as aware as possible of the unconscious assumptions brought by his subject to any experimental situation. Otherwise he will not have the slightest idea of what aspects of the phenomenon under investigation are most important. This awareness of assumption is as important for the psychologist to have in mind in understanding the perception of a chair as it is in understanding social perceptions.

Still another difficulty facing the psychologist is the comparative lack of any agreed-upon bases for standards by means of which experimental situations can be described and repeated and results can be interpreted. The search for appropriate bases for standards is obviously one which requires great caution and wisdom in an area such as psychology because of the number of unknown variables apt to be involved in any standards set. Much careful research is still needed to discover what variables should be used as the bases for standards to provide the most useful analysis of man's experience.

Value judgments and "objectivity"

A great deal of discussion has taken place in recent years concerning the possibility or the desirability of complete "objectivity" in science. The publication of Karl Pearson's *Grammar of Science* in 1892 (1911 [3d ed]), with its contention that an understanding of scientific method can train "the mind to an exact and impartial analysis of facts" and can free the individual from bias in the formation of judgments, gave a great boost to the myth that real scientific inquiry somehow goes on in a world devoid of personal judgments. The contrasting point of view has been expressed by Whitehead (1929a: 228ff.):

> Judgments of worth are no part of the texture of physical science, but they are part of the motive of its production. Mankind have raised the edifice of science, because they have judged it worth while. In other words, the motives involve innumerable judgments of value. Again, there has been conscious selection of the parts of the scientific fields to be cultivated, and this conscious selection involves judgments of value. These values may be aesthetic, or moral, or utilitarian, namely, judgments as to the beauty of the structure, or as to the duty of exploring the truth, or as to utility in the satisfaction of physical wants. But whatever the motive, without judgments of value there would have been no science.

It is becoming increasingly clear that the process of mentation invo ved in scientific inquiry is not a simple one of bringing "impartial analysis" to bear on a set of conditions. The scientist's own value judgments are involved in (1) sensing the inadequacy of his conceptual structure—posing a problem for himself; (2) sensing the functional activities or subphenomena which may be involved in the phenomenon that has caused the original hitch; (3) deciding on which aspects of a phenomenon (variables) can fruitfully be used as bases for standards in experimentation; and (4) designing an experimental procedure to test the validity of these bases for standards. Scientific research thus involves an elaborate process of weighing and integrating which may take place largely on an unconscious level.

In this process, all of the unconscious assumptions, all of the awarenesses, and all of the conceptual abstractions of the individual investigator's assumptive world are operative. Whether any scientist likes to admit it or not, any interpretation he makes must be regarded as a value judgment. To be sure, rational thought and the conscious intellectual manipulation of abstracted variables can, often do, and obviously should play a most important role in the process of scientific inquiry. But to assume that rational thought and conscious manipulation alone are the determinants of the judgments involved in scientific research is to go against the overwhelming evidence already obtained from scientific research itself. The dictionary definition of the word *objective*, in the sense it is used in discussions concerning the objectivity of science, is: "Emphasizing or expressing the nature of reality as it is apart from self-consciousness; treating events or phenomena as external rather than as affected by one's reflections or feelings." For example, our knowledge of perception, showing that "the nature of reality" as we experience it would not exist *except for* the assumptive world we being to a concrete situation, flatly contradicts the contention that the scientist can be objective in any such sense.

The objectivity of science can therefore only refer to the use of accepted rules of empirical research *after* the problem, the variables, and the experimental design have been decided upon. Here the scientific investigator takes every precaution he can to see that he does not misinterpret what he observes by allowing any subjective bias to enter into the actual conduct of the experiment itself.

Not only is objectivity illusory in the sense of eliminating personal bias: it is also undesirable. We cannot improve on the conclusion reached by Herrick (1949: 180f.) after a lifetime of productive research in neurology:

> The bias which arises from unrecognized personal attitudes, interests, and preconceptions is the most treacherous of all the subversive enemies of sound scientific progress; yet these attitudes and interests are the key factors in all really original scientific investigation. This issue must be faced frankly and courageously. The easy way out is to ignore the troublesome personal ingredients of the problem and say that science has no concern with them. This is now generally regarded as the standard or normal scientific method. But actually this cannot be done, and we cannot afford to try to do it; for the interests and the attitudes of the inquirer shape the whole course of the investigation, without which it is meaningless and fruitless. To neglect these components of scientific work and the satisfactions of a successful outcome is to sterilize not only the process but also the results of the inquiry. The vital germ of untrammeled imaginative thinking is thrown into the discard, and too often we seem quite content with the dead husk which is so easily weighed, measured, classified, and then stowed away in the warehouse.

In the social sciences, Robert Lynd has made the same point in his plea for "outrageous hypotheses" (1939).

The myth that "science is objective" may tend to be fostered in most cultures today in an attempt to preserve whatever status quo exists by giving it scientific blessing. But any scientist will resent boundaries placed on his thinking by social, economic, political, religious, or any other ideological barriers and taboos. This danger is especially prevalent in the field of inquiry labeled "social psychology" and in the social sciences, where the data gathered have been largely determined and preconditioned by the purposes and conditions within which the investigator has worked.

Psychologists and social scientists who honestly try to bring their most mature value judgments to bear on concrete social problems are all too frequently labeled as biased, crackpot reformers if they even implicitly criticize existing social relationships. Yet it is because scientific inquiry is shot through with value judgments that no scientist can avoid some responsibility for the judgments he makes. And because value judgments play so important a role in scientific thinking, ways and means must be discovered of making value judgments themselves the subject matter for scientific inquiry (Cantril 1949). Value judgments concern the significance of the constant emergents which are not subject to explanation in determined and verifiable terms. Here the scientist has a freedom of choice; here conscience, the "sense of oughtness," must be recognized as the highest standard for effective action. When the subject matter with which the scientist deals consists of human beings trying to act effectively to carry out their purposes, then the social responsibility of anyone who pretends to be an expert obviously becomes very great indeed.

Accelerating research in psychology

Our recurring theme has been that any truly scientific investigation involves much more than the use of an accepted methodology of experimentation. We have tried to show why the progress men hope for in their understanding of themselves can come about only to the extent that those who are professionally concerned with such an understanding become increasingly sensitive to the problem of problemization.

But readers already sympathetic with our emphasis may be reminded of the drama critic who, after pointing out the second-rate quality of then-current productions, ended his comments with the statement that what we need are better plays. Are there any concrete suggestions which might speed up the search for more and more adequate formulations psychologists would seek to verify experimentally? A few have occurred to us.

We have pointed out that scientific inquiry, like any inquiry, begins when we meet a hitch, when we sense the limitations of or doubt the adequacy and reliability of our assumptive worlds as we try to act effectively. From this it follows that every attempt must be made to increase an investigator's consciousness of the range of hitches that must be faced and that are inherent in attempts to resolve problems. We must get across the notion that hitches are not obstacles to be avoided but, on the other hand, challenges which alone make productive research possible. No one can be "trained" to do research merely by having a set of rules spelled out for him. A good investigator, like a good clinician, a good avertising man, or a good labor leader, will be produced only when there is a real desire and ability to use ingenuity in meeting the hitches that occur in carrying out purposive action.

It has long been apparent that no one person today can be thoroughly competent, knowledgeable, and experienced in the diversified areas of inquiry that impinge on and are necessary for a proper understanding of man. More than mere cross-fertilization or broadened specialization is needed. Can ways and means be found to make it possible to bring together investigators who agree on the probable common significance of the hitches they face and on the probable order of importance of the hitches that must be resolved for improved understanding? Perhaps informal organizations are required which will make it possible for men of diverse experience to work and commune together as the occasion demands, on common problems and on the same level without reliance on one another's authority and unrestricted by limitations of time or any goal other than the search for more adequate concepts. Psychologists and social scientists will have to work out organizational and communicating techniques so their search for the more adequate conceptualizations people expect of them will not be hampered by formalities or administrative duties.

All investigators are caught in and influenced by a traditional mode of thinking and teaching cluttered up with catchwords, with an emphasis on the interaction of variables, with an overconcentration on methodology for its own sake. In academic circles the tendency all too often is to feel that the student—and the professor—have essentially "covered" the problem of formulation if various systems and theories of psychology have been reviewed. The psychologist's relative lack of concern with the problem of more adequately formulating emerging problems is often reflected in what seems to be his extreme self-consciousness in respect to the short history of his discipline.

We are not in the least denying, of course, that rigorous methodological standards must be insisted upon or that the history of the subject should be reviewed. But we do feel that progress in psychology can be brought about more rapidly only if methodological procedures are considered in relation to concrete problems and if the history of psychological investigations can be viewed from the perspective of problems that now seem significant, rather than vice versa. Whitehead has nicely stated both points in his dicta that "the main evidence a methodology is worn out comes when progress within it no longer deals with main issues" (1929: 13) and that "a science which hesitates to forget its own history is lost" (1929a: 162).

Notes

1. A good example of a scientist who used the transactional method of observation was G.E. Coghill, who taught himself to see every organism in terms of a manifold of three inseparable constituents—structure, function, and mentation. The word *mentation* Coghill used as a substitute for *mind*, to connote the constant organism–environment transaction (1949: 198).
2. It is significant that psychological terms describing capacities of human beings

are occasionally used by natural scientists as rough specifications of certain phenomena they encounter. For example, mathematical physicists, in describing the behavior of some of their electronic computing machines when they become overloaded, call then "neurotic;" while biologists occasionally speak of the phenomenal "memory" which the cells of the body exhibit for certain stimuli.

References

Bentley, A.F. 1941. "Factual space and time of behavior." *J. Phil.* 38: 477.

Brunswik, E. 1949. In *Proc. Berkeley symp. math. statistics and probability*, pp. 143-202. Berkeley: University of California Press.

Cantril, H. 1949. "Toward a scientific morality." *J. Psychol.* 27: 363.

Carr, H.A. 1935. *Introduction to space perception.* New York: Longmans, Green.

Collingwood, R.G. 1940. *An essay on metaphysics.* Oxford: Clarendon.

Dewey, J., and Bentley, A.F. 1945. "Terminology for knowings and known." *J. Phil.* 42: 225.

Herrick, C.J. 1949. *George Ellett Coghill.* Chicago: University of Chicago Press.

Hoffman, J.G. 1949. *Physics Today* 2, no. 7: 6.

Lynd, R. 1939. *Knowledge for what?* Princeton: Princeton University Press.

Murray, H.A., et al. 1948. *Assessment of men.* New York; Rinehart.

Pearson, K. 1911. *Grammar of science.* 3d ed. London: Black.

Whitehead, A.N. 1929a. *Aims of education.* New York: Macmillan.

———. 1929b. *Function of reason.* Princeton: Princeton University Press.

II
Toward a humanistic psychology

4

An inquiry concerning the characteristics of man

People everywhere seem to be searching for a more adequate understanding of man, for some positive directives, some guidance to help them create a world with more order and predictable development amid the social consequences of rapid technological advances.[1]

The great spread of scientific knowledge has made people less sure that man is on a high pedestal as a special creation of a God who endowed man with certain purposes and who is somehow particularly interested in him. Men are beginning to see themselves as natural phenomena that must be understood. One result is that people become increasingly frustrated if they have to integrate a scientific attitude toward some phases of life with a prescientific attitude toward others.

The social scientist, the philosopher and the puzzled layman, naturally wonder what the psychologist has to offer in the way of scientific evidence concerning the character of the thing we call "human nature." In 1894, G. Stanley Hall wrote: "In the opinion of many of its more sanguine devotees, [experimental psychology] is showing itself not only to be the long hoped for, long delayed science of man, to which all other sciences are bringing their ripest and best thoughts, but is introducing a period that will be known hereafter as the psychological era of scientific thought, even more than a few recent decades have been marked by evolution. . . . It is asking the old question, what is man, in many new ways, and giving, bit by bit, new and deeper answers in a way that I deem it not too much to say makes every prospect of our own national future and of the republican type of government generally, brighter; and promises to be a realization of all that

Originally given as the presidential address to the Eastern Psychological Association, April 21, 1950. Reprinted from *The Journal of Abnormal and Social Psychology* 45, no. 3 (July 1950): 490- 503.

the old professors of logic, ethics, and religion, in their best days, dimly strove for—and more" (1894: 160–1).

But so far psychology does not seem to have provided the understanding of man which Hall hoped for and which people have a right to expect it should have provided.

The usual procedure in trying to understand and write about man's behavior is to proceed from one logical step to another, treating each aspect of man's behavior in a separate and isolated fashion. But if we view man's behavior as a process of living, as we must to be realistic, we cannot be satisfied with a description of isolated aspects of experience which neglects other aspects in the process and which merely relates the interaction of one variable on another. For each aspect depends upon the others for its very existence and function, and the interdependence of all the aspects which constitute behavior and experience in any one occasion of life is complicated indeed.

When man tries to understand himself, he is in a peculiarly difficult position. The traditional mode of thinking about man's problems has involved setting up a "person" on one side and an "environment" on the other side and then studying the effects of the interaction of one on the other. But such a procedure greatly oversimplifies and distorts the existing situation. For man's life is a continual process of transactions, a series of processes of participation in a natural and social setting. This setting is something *through* which we act and which takes on significance only through our own action in it. The "environment" involved in the total environment–person situation is an environment which the individual himself has helped to create. Dewey and Bentley state the situation this way: "From birth to death every human being is a *Party*, so that neither he nor anything done or suffered can possibly be understood when it is separated from the fact of participation in an extensive body of transactions— to which a given human being may contribute and which he modifies, but only in virtue of being a partaker in them" (1949: 271).

It is difficult to get used to this way of thinking. Most people have been brought up with the idea that the physical and social environment is something "out there," outside of themselves, something they act on or that acts on them. Even if the idea is grasped intellectually that man and his environment are inseparable, there may be difficulty making the idea part and parcel of daily thinking and behavior. Furthermore, those scientists who have taken upon themselves the responsibility for the understanding of man—psychologists and social scientists—are just beginning to emancipate themselves from the more traditional point of view which was discarded by the more sophisticated natural scientists about seventy years ago when their older concepts of "matter" began to disappear.

The way in which a scientist poses his problem determines where he will come out. For the way in which the problem is posed will determine what particular aspect of a dilemma is to be studied and the techniques that will be used or devised for carrying out the investigation. A scientist is called "great" not so much because he has solved a problem as because he has posed a problem the solution of which, either by himself or his successors, will make for real progress. Einstein and Infeld have noted that "the formulation of a problem is often more essential than its solution, which may be merely a matter of mathematical or experimental skill. To raise new questions, new possibilities, to regard old problems from a new angle, requires creative imagination and marks real advance in sci nce" (1942: 95).

The selection or discovery of the particular variables to use in an investigation is a major problem confronting any scientific investigator. The problem of selecting proper and sufficient variables is much more complicated than often is realized. For the variables scientists use do not exist in their own right. They are only aspects abstracted out of a total situation by scientists as inquiring human beings endowed with the capacity to manipulate ideas. These aspects that scientists call "variables" are not God-given and are not limited. This holds for the physical sciences as well as for psychology. Any adjective or any adverb can serve as a potential basis for scientific variables. The nature of the variables selected will vary with the particular kind of situation with which the scientist is confronted.

The history of science shows that any science becomes stagnant when those who work within it become complacent about the particular way they have compartmentalized the subject matter of their discipline. When this complacency occurs, problems are artificially restricted, important variables that might upset the nice scientific structure so created are consciously or unconsciously eliminated. In this sense, real scientific pursuit involves the breaking down and revamping of our up-to-the-now formulations. Scientific progress thus required much more than merely "adding to" existing knowledge.

The problem

It is apparent to nearly anyone familiar with attempts to understand man's behavior, whether he is a professional psychologist or not, that the full-bodied experiences of everyday life have in them much more than any "explanatory system" so far seems to take into account. For many of us, no one of them rings quite true. There does not seem to be yet an explanatory system that is intrinsically reasonable in its account of why man's experience is what it is.

The reasons for the apparent inadequacy of the contemporary understanding of experience may be seen by referring back to almost any area of psychological inquiry and seeing how problems have been posed and how research has been conducted. From this some useful lessons should be drawn for the future.

We can use as an illustration the area of psychological inquiry concerned with man's awarenesses: the field technically known as the study of perception. This is a reasonable field to choose since the directions of attack on the ancient problem of how and why man is aware of anything often have been a weathervane in psychology as well as in philosophy.

In studying the way man perceives anything, psychologists concentrated first on the effects on perception when the stimulus was altered or when there were changes in the physiological processes involved. This naturally led to the idea that there was a certain correspondence between the subjective factors in experience on the one hand and the objective and physiological factors on the other hand. And since it was so easy to show how an alteration of "objective" or physiological factors could cause "subjective" effects, the idea was built up that experience could be largely accounted for by corresponding stimulus events and the accompanying physiological disturbances. It was not nearly so easy to demonstrate the reverse effect: the role played by such "subjective" factors as past experience, loyalties, expectancies, and purpose in determining the nature of perception. Furthermore, it was relatively easy to measure and to put in quantitative terms changes in the objective stimulus situation or the physiological factors. But precise measures of past experience and loyalties obviously could be made only in a very crude form.

Of course, normally there is no awareness unless something exists of which to be aware and unless the intricate mechanisms of the body are functioning properly. But this is by no means all of the story. The relations between perception and the physiological processes could be studied forever and still never get at the reason why such relationships seem to exist. The reason why such relationships exist would not be uncovered until the question of what function such relationships serve in the process of living is asked.

Many of us now share the feeling that psychology has not gone farther in getting at the reasons for man's awarenesses because it has dealt so often with isolated human experience in which isolated physical stimuli are related to isolated sensory processes in an isolated individual usually studied in a situation where his isolation in time and space is not realized. This would mean, too, that while the emphasis of Gestalt psychologists on the interdependence of various parts of a stimulus situation is obviously in the right direction, it still provides no underlying account of *why* "relational determination" functions as it does. No amount of study of the immediate relationship involved in a situation seems to account for the fact that the awareness of *where* a thing is depends on *what* the thing is assumed to be. The why of such relationships can be understood only when the functions such relationships apparently serve are examined in actual transactions of living. Any experience in the "now" cannot be explained without realizing that the "now" is only a transition point carrying the past into the future.

Psychology will meet the challenge it has imposed on itself and which men everywhere expect it to meet only when it becomes fully emancipated from a point of view which permits or encourages the study of isolated individuals, isolated experiences, isolated relationships. Man's thought and behavior can be understood only as *processes* which take place in full-bodied situations. And the cross-relationship of factors which must be taken into account becomes complicated indeed as the psychologist tries to account for the experiences of man in his social life, for his family ties, his friendships, his frustrations, ambitions, responsibilities, desire for affection, his strikes and his wars. As Bridgman has recently pointed out, "The world of daily life . . . is obviously enormously more complex than the world of the physicist" (1950: 2).

The job is not a simple one of selecting and choosing what appear to be the most significant parts of different explanatory systems and simply adding them together without attempting to understand the cross-relationships involved, as psychologists labeled "eclectic" would suggest. For this would be failing to make a distinction between taking apart what really belongs together and putting together processes that are inseparable in any actual occasion of life and without which there would be no experience at all. It is because of their failure to make such a distinction that eclectics label anyone a "radical" who adopts a synthesizing explanatory system. Eclecticism by its very nature discourages imagination and leads to sterility.

If the nature of man's everyday life experience is to be fathomed, it is necessary first of all to try to describe man's experience in appropriate terms. Those processes that play significant roles in man's living and their cross relationships must be sought and understood. An account of man's experience will become intrinsically reasonable only insofar as all of those factors are taken into account without which man's experience would not be what it is.

This emphasis may appear to be self-evident. But it is apparently true that the reason why the scientist's understanding of the nature of man's experience and behavior is not greater than it is today is because he has either neglected to search for and discover the characteristics of man's experiences or has deliberately limited those characteristics to a few easy ones psychologists have favored for one reason or another and that still leave much unexplained. Sometimes a psychologist can boast of being scientific only because he is closing his eyes to pressing problems. Obviously such a procedure is not consistent with the spirit of scientific inquiry.

An authority on evolution, G.G. Simpson, has pointed out that "it is important to realize that man is an animal, but it is even more important to realize that the essence of his unique nature lies precisely in those characteristics that are not shared with any other animal" (1949: 284). Whitehead has stated as a "general principle" that "low-grade characteristics are better studied first in connection with correspondingly low-grade organisms, in which those characteristics are not obscured by more developed types of functioning. Conversely, high-grade characteristics should be studied first in connection with those organisms in which they first come to full perfection" (1927: 5).

All organisms, including man, are ongoing, living processes. And all higher organisms, including man, have biological needs or physiological tension systems that must be satisfied periodically if life and growth are to continue. But there is something about man that is unique. The biologist sees his enormous adaptive and creative abilities; the poet sees his "divine discontent"; the religious prophet sees him searching for the Kingdom of God. Each observer in his own way sees that something has been added in the latest chapter of the long evolutionary story.

It seems hopeless to try to account for man's behavior solely in terms of variables as crude as reflexes, instincts, or physiological tensions. For example, attempts to account for man's motivation in terms of the reduction of physiological tensions seem inadequate to "explain" the many situations in which man's satisfactions and happinesses are actually related to an increase, rather than a decrease, in the state of "tensions" experienced. When a person deliberately undertakes a new task, when he deliberately strives to meet new levels of aspiration, he often knows well enough that he will experience new and perhaps more disturbing inner tensions. Man's psychological tensions seem to be more the coproducts of his strivings than basic explanations of them. When the characteristics of individual experiences are observed, their variety and subtlety are apparent. They are by no means all described appropriately by words that may be suitable for lower organisms.

The quality of experience

An outstanding characteristic of man is his capacity to sense the value in the quality of his experience. This experienced value attribute is a pervasive and inseparable aspect of every experience. All human wants, urges, desires, and aspirations are permeated with some value attribute.

You can see best what is meant by the value attribute in experience by referring to your own experience. A value attribute of a relatively low order is experienced in situations where physical needs are satisfied in a crude and elemental way: that is, the sense of well-being and taste in the satisfaction of hunger by any kind of food you can get hold of. The satisfying quality of these sensations is apparently the result of some evolutionary process insuring our survival. Man experiences a "higher," subtler, richer, more satisfying value attribute with the satisfaction of his needs in other situations which have become desiderata of civilized men: for example, satisfaction of hunger with food that is prepared tastefully, served nicely, eaten in attractive surroundings and in the company of congenial people.

You sense the satisfying value of experience from a job well done, from helping to accomplish a community, national, or humanitarian task, from having met or exceeded your own expectations or the expectations others have of you. You sense a value attribute in the exhilaration, the sense of well-being you may get from climbing a mountain, from a swim in a lake or the sea, from a good game of tennis or golf. You feel a richness of experience as you watch your children grow and develop. You sense a high quality from the experience of helping a friend or doing a deed which you know is good. You sense a value attribute in creativity whether that creativity involves baking a tasty loaf of bread, making your garden grow, raising hogs, cattle, or grain, putting together a homemade radio, repairing a broken machine, painting a picture, or writing a poem or a sonata. You sense a value attribute in experience when you learn something useful for your purposes, when you make sense out of something; and you share the value attributes of a child's experience when you see his sense of satisfation in learning to tell time, in learning to read, in learning his first simple additions. You sense value attributes in the humble, ordinary activities of life: in saying "hello" to a neighbor, in cleaning your house, in taking a bath after a hard day's work. You sense the value attributes of disappointment, disturbance, or sorrow when things go wrong.

Man's unusual capacity to sense the value of experience in so many diverse ways provides the possibility of working out a plausible explanation for the many divergent types of activity men seek to repeat. Man tries to recapture qualities he has experienced on previous occasions: in his social gatherings, his ways of satisfying physical needs, his aesthetic experiences, his work or his play. He wants to recapture these experiences simply because he enjoys experiencing the value attribute related to them. However, it should be pointed out that in everyday life, situations never repeat themselves identically and, if they tend to, man will often try to create variation, for with the repetition of very similar situations there can be a decreased sense of satisfaction. Habitual activity may become monotonous and boring; or we may become aware of it only subconsciously.

The value attribute that pervades every experience is a crucially important fact. It is the catalyzer needed to produce nearly all of our actions. The sensed value of any experience differs in some subtle way from that of any other experience. To describe the full quality of an experience it is generally necessary to resort to a whole string of adjectives as in describing a person or a landscape. Sometimes analogies are used. Sometimes we think of bits of poetry or passages from a novel where those who are expert in putting our feelings into words have managed somehow to capture, or remind us of, a feeling approximating our own. The value attributes of experience characteristic of man seem to occur largely in what Korzybski has aptly described as "non-verbal," "silent" levels (1949: 4).

We remember the values experienced in life and we store them up, building out of them a standard or system of values which we inevitably, though generally unconsciusly, use for later reference. Against this system of values derived from past experiences, we sense the quality of our present experience. It is the only value standard we know. On the basis of our acquired pattern of values we characterize our present experiences variously as "worthwhile," "satisfying," "pleasant," "fruitless," "disappointing," and the like.

It is in terms of the values of experience that the "worthwhileness" of an action is tested. The value of the quality in experience comes into being only in concrete situations. In general it is not subject to recall, as are conceptual abstractions.

A sense of quality in experience is achieved only by participating actively in life transactions. And conversely, if no value attribute in action is experienced, there is no participation in the ongoing process of living and growing. This is the situation with certain psychiatric patients and with those who live entirely in the past, dreaming of the good old days and wishing they would come again.

The richness and variety of the quality we are able to get out of experience depends on the scope and variety of the life situations in which we can participate, especially with the opportunity we have to share experience with others. The richness of the quality of our experience will depend, too, on the extent to which we can create some order, some meaning, some direction in life situations through our own participation in them.

There is considerable evidence both from the laboratory and from everyday observation that the behavior of animals reflects an increasing sense of value attributes as one moves up the phylogenetic scale. The lowly laboratory rat displays "hierarchies" of path preferences in moving through a maze to a goal. The number and variety of activities shown by a dog in an effort to regain his master's favor suggests a considerable ability to sense value attributes. The descriptions Köhler and Yerkes give of the excited behavior of primates when they reach an insightful solution to a difficult problem leaves no doubt that a fairly high order of value attribute is being experienced. But while the capacity to sense a value attribute of some sort is not peculiar to man's experience alone, the capacity has been developed to such a degree in man that it may be considered sufficiently unique to distinguish man from all other animals. Sensed value attributes characterize all of man's experience.

The enhancement of the value attribute of experience

While the concept of the sensed value attribute of experience seems to me indispensable in providing a toehold to account for some of the characteristics of man, still it is not enough by itself. On this basis alone it would be impossible to account for man's curiosity and inquiry, for all the new fears and anxieties that beset him, for his self-conscious search to increase the range of the setting in which he can act effectively, for his constant lack of perfect "adjustment," for his will-o'-the-wisp search for peace of mind, or for his feeling of personal development and growth.

This points to the conclusion that the ultimate, the most generalized goal of man is what can be called the enhancement of the value attributes of experience. This can be regarded as the top standard of human experience, a standard in its own right. It is the capacity man has to sense *added* value in his experience that accounts for his ceaseless striving, his search for a direction to his activities, for his characteristic unwillingness to have things remain as they are.

In supposing that the enrichment of the value attributes of experience is the outstanding characteristic of man, there are no teleological implications whatever. There is no implication that the course man's life is pursuing inevitably follows some overall intrinsic design. Neither is there any acceptance of a hedonistic doctrine with its contention that the aim of life is to seek pleasure, nor any thought that the achievement of increments of value attribute means "improvement" or "progress" in any Western sense.

The concept of the "enhancement of the value attributes of experience" has been adopted because it seems intrinsically reasonable in itself and because it provides the possibility of explaining plausibly the other characteristics of man's experience. Some such concept must be used and its scientific explanation sought if we are to avoid the inadequacy of any account of man's experience solely in terms of influences that are operating in the "now." For the behavior of the "now" is not something that can be neatly isolated from the past *and* the future.

All observations of man indicate that most people who are attuned to anything approximating normal life will not be satisfied with their role unless it offers some potentiality for one experience to lead to another, for change to occur in some apparent direction. Steinbeck expressed the situation in one of his novels: "For it is said that humans are never satisfied, that you give them one thing and they want something more. And this is said in disparagement, whereas it is one of the greatest talents the species has and one that has made it superior to animals that are satisfied with what they have" (1947: 37). It is this characteristic to which the naturalist Coghill referred when he said that his philosophy of life was "not of *being*, but of *becoming*; not of *life*, but of *living*" (Herrick 1949: 230). It is what lies behind the remark I heard a woman make in a crowded railway station: "Most things excite me only once." It lies behind the colloquialisms "It gave me a lift," "I got a kick out of it."

The ongoing process described here is distinguished from and should not be confused with the normal "stages of growth" which an individual goes through from conception through birth, adolescence and old age as determined by his chromosome activity and glandular processes. Nor is the process described here to be confused with growth and development in the evolutionary sense.

What is meant by a desired increment in the value attribute of experience can again be seen best by observing one's own life and the lives of others. The skilled worker who gets the job he wants will soon become relatively dissatisfied if it offers no "future"—if there is no chance for increased responsibility, for increased creative effort, or for greater usefulness in his social group. A young woman may have her whole heart set on marriage. But after marriage she will use this new situation as the springboard for obtaining new, emergent qualities of experience through her children, her new social intercourse, her new community responsibilities. Or a farmer's first goal may be to own his own farm. Once he achieves this goal, he will want to "develop" and "improve" his farm. A young man who has acquired the ambition to go to college will rapidly acquire other ambitions as soon as he enters college. He will want to make a certain team or club, or he may strive for a certain academic record. Once he gets into a club or makes a team, the chances are that he will strive within his social groups to raise his status, to become an important member. And once he makes the grades he desires, he will probably raise his sights. Gangsters will strive within the gang of their hearts' desire to "be" somebody.

It should be particularly emphasized that the satisfaction sought in experience is a satisfaction within the particular culture or group of which the individual is a participating member. In Western society there is a tendency to think of increased satisfaction in terms of hustling and bustling activities that spell "progress," "wealth," "fame," or "advancement" in terms of our particular norms. It may at first appear, then, that persons in "primitive," "backward," "easygoing," or "static" cultures or groups show no behavior that could properly be described as attempts to experience increments of satisfaction. Yet intimate participation in the social life of any cultural group and an understanding of the significance of individual behavior reveals that the people who compose that group do seek increased satisfactions according to standards and expectancies of their own. While it may appear that the life of a Chinese coolie, a Russian peasant, a South African native, a Navajo Indian in New Mexico, or an Arapesh of New Guinea may go around only in a constant circle, they in turn might wonder what modern Americans could possibly get out of a life that might seem to them a hectic rat-race. Wherever we look in any culture, man has aspirations of some kind and never seems completely satisfied with his lot.

An increment of the value of experience is possible only if there is some standard, some form to use as a springboard for emergence. We cannot sense an enhancement of quality in experience if we have no standard as a takeoff. It is for this reason that the concept of the value attributes of experience was introduced earlier. Otherwise the concept of an enhanced quality of experience would make no sense. Both are required for an adequate, intrinsically reasonable explanatory system.

The supposition of the enhancement of the value attributes in experience accounts for the aspect of growth. It is dependent on the capacity of man to look into the future as he takes part in and becomes part of emerging situations. What is experienced as an increment of value today becomes part of the value standard tomorrow if experiences can be repeated in similar future occasions. The process of development in the individual is a constant pyramiding of the set of value standards necessarily used as the test of the next experiences. Participation in any occasion of living alters for good or evil the standard of value built up which provides the only stepping stone for the next participation.

We experience increments of value attributes when we overcome the obstacles facing us constantly in new situations. By the very nature of things, when we overcome one difficulty we are faced with new difficulties which in turn demand resolution and in turn necessitate continued emergence. When our difficulties are of major proportions and when we sense that we are on the way to a better resolution of them, then an increment of value in our experience may have considerable duration. In such cases, we are not bothered by temporary frustrations because we realize we are going on to a richer experience.

Man more than any other animal is faced with the problem of choice.

His choice often is between the security he feels fairly certain he can obtain if he does one thing and, on the other hand, the experience of new, emergent quality if he does another thing. For this reason man's judgments are frequently and inevitably tinged with both hope and fear.

Usually man will not choose the path leading to a possible increase in the value attribute of his experience unless a certain minimum feeling of security is guaranteed. Yet it is the nature of man to strive for an increment in the value attribute of his experience even though he may know full well it will involve sacrifice and pain. On the basis of the many cases he has treated, Rogers concludes that "the urge for a greater degree of independence, the desire for a self-determined integration, the tendency to strive, even through much pain, toward a socialized maturity, is as strong as—no, is stronger than—the desire for comfortable dependence, the need to rely upon external authority for assurance. . . . I have yet to find the individual who, when he examines his situation deeply, and feels that he perceives it clearly, deliberately chooses dependence, deliberately chooses to have the integrated direction of himself undertaken by another. When all the elements are clearly perceived, the balance seems invariably in the direction of the painful but ultimately rewarding path of self-actualization or growth" (1948: 218).

The whole process of life is dialectical in the sense that the "normal" individual keeps going on to new experiences insofar as his security framework allows. From his observations of children, William Stern concluded that "self-preservation and self-development unite and blend in the process of growth. . . . The activities which first develop are exactly those which are of the most primary importance for self-preservation; and whilst self-development hastens on the ever-new triumphs in the growth of powers and the spiritual conquest of the material, the motive-power and capacity of self-preservation works away in the subconscious with unerring surety of purpose. . . . Each single goal, aimed at by struggling self-development, is no sooner reached than it immediately exists solely to be replaced by others, and not only so, but it becomes a permanent acquirement of the personality. . . . For there is indeed nothing in development of only momentary value, everything keeps on working, even if only as a tool for other efforts, everything heaps up powers, makes reserves, opens roads, that determine future life" (1930: 52ff).

Value attributes and increments of value in experience are always relative. They are unique to the experiencing individual. There are, and can be, no absolute units of the standard of value upon which increments of value are based for *all* individuals. The standard of value for each person is determined by his particular unique biological and life history. There are enormous individual differences in both the quality and the degree of value increment sought. People in lowly stations of life may experience much greater value than persons who are "successful," or "famous." A humble cobbler may "get more out of life," for example, by watching the success of his children as a result of the education he has struggled to furnish them than a millionaire who sees no upward trend in his development as life goes on.

Nor can an increment of value attributes for any single individual be judged in terms of any accepted social standards no matter how these may affect the general direction of a person's activities. Conformity may be only a matter of expediency, not of gratification. There are again huge individual differences. Some people, through circumstance or learning, will place enormous reliance on security, others will more readily take a chance on the satisfaction to be derived from exploring unfamiliar roads. Even within the same culture what one person regards as success, another will regard as failure; what one calls a virtue another will call a vice.

In trying to increase our valueful experiences, we also try, of course, to decrease the number of situations which we know from past experience will either provide no such satisfactions or will keep us from participating in situations that we believe would be satisfying. Similarly, many of us spend a great deal of our lives avoiding situations of various kinds as we attempt to minimize the occasions of life which we predict will give us no increments of value in the immediate or distant future.

The direction any individual's development takes depends largely on the particular situations in which he participates. In the process of development and socialization, specific possibilities providing increments of value to experience are learned. The particular environment through which growth takes place gives a particular individual a particular sense of the direction in which he may look for a richer, more satisfying way of life. Stated somewhat differently, a person's unique environment provides a particular way of instrumenting his pattern of growth with its intrinsic desire for an increment of the value of experience.

Furthermore, it is known from studies of genetics and individual differences that an individual will develop in *his* particular way depending on *his* particular abilities and temperamental traits, *within* the directional framework provided by his participation in a particular social context. Thus, if you are a farmer, your particular abilities and temperamental traits will help determine how good a farmer you will be; if you are a labor leader your abilities and capacities and temperamental traits operating through an environment will largely determine your effectiveness within the situation you face. The same holds true for the talent of a musician or novelist, the creativity of a scientist, the genius of some comedians. The characteristics unique to every person are rooted in his chromosome activity.

A naturalistic basis

Why is it that concepts associated with man's capacity to sense a value attribute in experience have not been previously introduced in psychology? It may be due in part to the fact that if such concepts are thought of, they appear to be metaphysical and without any scientific underpinning. But while such concepts, like others in the history of science, may have no explanation today, they are not mystical and by no means outside the bounds of scientific explanation tomorrow. Progress in scientific inquiry can only come about if a notion is postulated that seems to be intrinsically reasonable, whose existence may not be verifiable today but which nevertheless holds out the possibility of yielding to scientific verification in the future. It has been necessary to postulate man's capacity to sense value attributes and an increment of value in experience in order to take into account all of those aspects that characterize man's experience. For if any explanatory system leaves out any characteristic of man's experience then it must itself be ruled out as an adequate account of man.

These concepts have not been pulled out of thin air. What they name are experiences that can be operationally defined as standards that provide man with his most reliable guides for purposeful action. They are the compass which gives man his direction both as to how he should act and what this action is for.

The neurologist Herrick has pointed out that no mechanical model of nervous structure and action has been devised which successfully bridges the gap between the order of objective nature as we know it empirically and the subjective experience of knowing. He says, "Our bodies think as naturally as they breathe and if we do not yet understand how we understand, the thing to do is to try to find out. . . . It is not unreasonable to hope that a scientific formulation of the mind-body problem may be found in terms of principles different from those of both Newtonian and quantum mechanics and still within the domain of nature—of human nature—as we experience it" (1946: 40ff.).

More and more it is becoming apparent in studies of the life process at all levels that because of the particular organization of the mechanisms of an organism, they are themselves instrumental in determining the course of their own development. The physicist Schrödinger writes that the chromosomes "are law-code and executive power—or, to use another simile, they are architect's plan and builder's craft—in one" (1946: 21). In trying to answer the question, "What is life?" Schrödinger concludes, "What I wish to make clear in this last chapter is, in short, that from all we have learnt about the structure of living matter, we must be prepared to find it working in a manner that cannot be reduced to the ordinary laws of physics. And that not on the ground that there is any 'new force' or what not, directing the behaviour of the single atoms within a living organism, but that because the construction is different from anything we have yet tested in the physical laboratory" (p. 76). . . . "We must therefore not be discouraged by the difficulty of interpreting life by the ordinary laws of physics. For that is just what is to be expected from the knowledge we have gained of the structure of living matter. We must be prepared to find a new type of physical law prevailing in it" (pp. 80f.).

An imposing amount of research in physiology, neurology, genetics, and physics already is beginning to clarify the problem sufficiently so that something approximating a naturalistic explanation of experience seems eventually possible. As Herrick has stated, the apparent order science finds in both the organic and the inorganic world is due to mechanisms which are "intrinsic to the natural system in operation" and "is not imposed upon it from without" (1947: 258). In this conception of any underlying mechanism, the mechanism itself is "an active participant in the process, and it has a certain range of freedom of action" (1949: 201). In discussing the randomness and directiveness of behavior, the physiologist Lillie states that "whatever its special origin may be, directiveness in living organisms is a general fact of observation which typically has its physiological basis in activities carried out under the control of definitely organized structure" (1948a: 8). He also writes that "the production of novelty, or what is now called emergence, is a constant feature of natural process" (p. 15). Lillie suggests that "intranuclear directive action would be ultra-microscopic and ultimately intra-atomic, i.e., internal rather than external in its origin. Transition from a microphysical to a macrophysical mode of causation would constitute the essential physical feature of the conditions underlying the directive control" (1948b: 133). Coghill concluded that man is "a mechanism which, within his limitations of life, sensitivity and growth, is creating and operating himself" (Herrick 1949: 222).

Such a concept of "mechanism" and indeterminancy may appear today almost as incomprehensible as Newton's concepts were to most people in his time. It is not relevant to our major purpose here to pursue these leads in any detail or to take sides in any current controversy. All we want to do is to indicate that it is in the spirit of scientific inquiry never to advance a metaphysical or supranatural explanation if some physical explanation is even conceivable. As Simpson has pointed out, "The materialistic view is not abandoned when life is seen as a process and organization in which the behavior of matter is different from that in its nonliving state . . . the distinctive claim of materialism is not stupid denial of special attributes to life, but the view that the substances and the principles involved in organic evolution are those universal in the material world and that the distinctive attributes and activities of life are inherent in its organization only" (1949: 125f.).

I am merely indicating here that competent scientists hold out hope that eventually the gap now existing between experience as introspectively known and the materialistic processes collateral with this experience may eventually be brought within the range of scientific investigation. Whatever the exact organization of the machinery may prove to be that accomplishes this marvelous result, it involves taking into account many, many factors of past experience, weighing or evaluating them on the basis of the probability that a certain reaction to a certain set of circumstances will be a good bet, and then acting accordingly. The process involves all that Weiner has described under the heading of Cybernetics; and it involves a good deal more. The end result of this process is that the experiencing individual feels that he has an idea of sufficient reliability so that he can act to carry out his purposes.

The emergent characteristics of man are related to the development of his capacity to create artifacts, that is, his ability to produce things such as tools, buildings, and machines. This capacity is related to the development and application of man's capacity to inquire and figure out how and why things are as they are and happen as they do. In turn this capacity is connected to man's ability to intellectualize, to make intellectual judgments and to use abstractions which will give him greater reliability in judging the probable effectiveness of action. Finally, these capacities are related to the development and exercise of man's ability to make value judgments, to weigh and integrate a multitude of factors swiftly and unconsciously as he faces new problem situations. But we do not have time here to follow through these cross-relationships and indicate how each one apparently depends on all others for its very existence.

We certainly are far from understanding at present what the natural processes are that operate concomitantly to man's sense of the value attributes in experience. But as scientists we can take comfort from the fact that what is going on in our experience may eventually be better understood and that the processes involved certainly will be of a different order of complexity than psychologists deal with when they attempt to explain the push behind man's behavior in terms of reflexes, instincts, needs, or physiological tensions. Above all, the subtleties of man's experience must never be compromised for the sake of any explanation in the relatively crude terms natural scientists may be rather sure of so far.

Notes

1. The point of view sketched here was originally stimulated by considerations of the nature and function of perception with Adelbert Ames, Jr. I should also like

to acknowledge the contributions and clarifications to the formulation expressed that came from discussions with Albert Hastorf, William Ittelson, F.P. Kilpatrick, Andie Knutson, and Merle Lawrence.

References

Bridgman, P.W. 1950. Philosophical implications of physics. *Bull. Amer. Acad. Arts & Sci.* (Feb.)

Dewey, J., and Bentley, A.F. 1949. *Knowing and the known.* Boston: Beacon Press.

Einstein, A., and Infeld, L. 1942. *The evolution of physics.* New York: Simon & Schuster.

Hall, G. Stanley. 1894. On the history of American college textbooks. *Amer. Antiquarian Soc.* 9: 160-1.

Herrick, C.J. 1946. World federation in embryo. *Humanist* 6: 40-2.

_____. 1947. Seeing and believing. *Sci. Mon., N.Y.* 64: 253-60.

_____. 1949. *George Ellett Coghill.* Chicago: University of Chicago Press.

Korzybski, A. 1949. *Manhood of humanity.* 2d ed. Lakeville, Conn.: International Non-Aristotelian Publishing Co..

Lillie, R.S. 1948a. Randomness and directiveness in the evolution and activity of living organisms. *Amer. Nat.* 82: 5-25.

_____. 1948b. Some aspects of theoretical biology. *Phil. Sci.* 15: 118-34.

Rogers, C.R. 1948. Divergent trends in methods of improving adjustment. *Harvard Educ. Rev.* 18, no. 4: 209-19.

Schrödinger, E. 1946. *What is life?* New York: Macmillan.

Simpson, G.G. 1949. *Meaning of evolution.* New Haven: Yale University Press.

Steinbeck, J. 1947. *The pearl.* New York: Viking.

Stern, W. 1930. *Psychology of early childhood.* New York: Holt.

Whitehead, A.N. 1927. *Symbolism: its meaning and effect.* New York: Macmillan.

5

The qualities of being human

In his letter of May 14, 1743, Benjamin Franklin enumerated a number of subjects that might be discussed by members of an American Philosophical Society, the creation of which he was then proposing. Along with such topics as exchanges of information concerning "improvements of vegetable juices," "inventions for saving labour," and the "course and junctions of rivers," he included as a final aim the consideration of "all philosophical experiments that let light into the nature of things."

A year and a half later Franklin wrote from Philadelphia to one of his friends that "the members [of the society] here are very idle gentlemen." But as we all know, those who have taken it upon themselves to investigate "into the nature of things" have not been completely idle and have let considerable light in during the past 200 years.

Yet as a psychologist accepts the challenge of beginning discussions on "A Portrait of Western Man" and reviews the accumulated data of his discipline, he must in all honesty confess at the outset that in the brief history of his science the subject of man as a living, striving, anxious, hopeful, curious, valuing, prayerful organism has been somewhat neglected.

I have often wondered if Whitehead did not have psychologists particularly in mind when he wrote that "the intimate timidity of professional scholarship circumscribes reason by reducing its topics to triviality, for example, to bare sensa and to tautologies. It then frees itself from criticism by dogmatically handing over the remainder of experience to an animal faith or a religious mysticism, incapable of rationalization" (1933: 151).

The kind of scientific inquiry that has so far largely characterized West-

Originally presented as the opening lecture at the Benjamin Franklin Lectures for 1953, sponsored by the University of Pennsylvania under the general heading "A Portrait of Western Man." Reprinted by permission from *American Quarterly* 6, no. 1 (Spring 1954): 3-18. Copyright 1954, Trustees of the University of Pennsylvania.

ern Man's probing of his own nature has been traced back to Descartes by René Fülöp-Miller in his book *Science and Faith in the Crisis of Our Time* (1953). In this book we learn of an incident in Descartes' life which still seems to haunt many of today's investigations. It appears that one time when Descartes was visiting the King, he was impressed by an elaborate automaton set up in the King's garden according to the fashion of the times. A figure of the Goddess Diana adorned a fountain and when a hydraulic mechanism was released, the figure left the fountain, bathed in the surrounding pool of water, hid briefly in the adjoining shrubbery, and then resumed her position on the fountain. A very complicated machine indeed; and Descartes, so the story goes, decided that if this tin girl could do all of these things, then really the human being himself was nothing more than a machine, only infinitely more complicated.

Since then, many investigations concerning the nature of man have been saddled with Descartes' conception of a mechanistic determinism. But a quick glance at some of the conclusions of modern science—or what the philosopher would call some of its most general specifications—justifies our hope that the study of man *can* be approached from a new perspective. These conclusions of modern science have enabled us to expand the base of what we call scientific inquiry so that the very qualities of being human are not ruled out as variables for our study.

Modern physics, dealing with the inanimate aspects of nature, teaches us that our traditional conceptions of matter must be seriously revised. For the physicist today, matter does not exist. All that does exist is activity—an activity constantly changing into new forms and never repeating. The modern physicist denies the existence of a complete determinism. He speaks of the "principle of indeterminism." He further recognizes that man's knowledge of inanimate nature is limited by man's own limited point of view as a particular kind of living organism.

Modern biology recognizes the invariability of certain basic characteristics of organic nature which remain relatively stable in biological time in spite of the ever-changing characteristics of the inorganic world. The biologist points out that these characteristics are stored in every living organism which acts as a carrier into the future. The biologist recognizes that every human being is unique in terms of his own chromosome structure and in terms of his own life experiences. The biologist recognizes that every human being is also different from every other human being in any particular occasion of life, and, furthermore, that in every occasion of living an individual is different from what he was before or what he will be after the occasion.

From modern psychology we learn that there is no rigid dichotomy between what has been called "subjective" and what has been called "objective." What we experience as "out there," as "outside of ourselves," does not exist in its own right with certain inherent characteristics which are somehow "disclosed" to us without our own participation as experiencing organisms. We know from modern psychology that what we experience "out there" in our environment is not permanent or determined but varies in its characteristics with the subjective state of the organism. We know that the environment is uniquely different for every individual. We know that every act of behavior an individual participates in alters him uniquely at least in some small way.

This advance of science on many fronts in the past few decades has completely destroyed the myth which most Western men had held concerning permanence and stability—permanence and stability not only of their universe but of their moral codes and of themselves. Instead of this false certainty, modern science finds everywhere, as Julian Huxley has described it, a "self-transforming pattern and continuing process." There is ceaseless activity, with no one process ever repeating itself exactly. Permanence, John Dewey has pointed out, must be defined as change which takes place so slowly that we cannot observe it.

Now if we try to summarize in a very general way what all of this means in terms of a new perspective, we might say, simply, it means that what has happened *has* happened and is determined, unchangeable; it also means that what *will* happen, what is *going* to happen, is undisclosed, novel. It means further that what *is* happening in what we call "now" is that our experience of the present, like an ocean wave, is a fleeting transition, an aspect of a flowing process that connects the past with the future. Laotze noted centuries ago: "What is is the was of what shall be."

This view of things is consistent with the philosophy of history represented by Charles Beard. In a note on Beard as philosopher-historian, Horace Kallen has pointed out that for Beard "civilization is an idea of a course of events whose openness is intrinsic . . . civilization is not an existence either given or implied by the nature of things; it is a creation of the human spirit" (Kallen 1951: 243). Beard himself wrote that "the idea of civilization predicates a partial determinism, such as an irreversible and irrevocable historical heritage, and a partially open and dynamic world in which creative intelligence can and does work . . ."(Kallen 1951: 246).

From this perspective, then, let us re-examine some of those age-old problems associated with the qualities of being human.

The nature of "motivation"

We can begin this inquiry by proposing a working definition of life. We shall define living as a process in which an organism participates in the creation of an environment through which it can carry out its purposes. This definition, I believe, gives us a general specification applicable to the bird building its nest, the salmon returning to the river, as well as the human being, whether child or adult, participating in the multifarious transactions of living.

In this participation in which we human beings try to create an environment through which to carry out our purposes, our relationship with the undisclosed future is a relationship in which we are constantly making bets, following hunches, guessing at probabilities which we feel, on the basis of our past experience in similar situations, will lead us to action which will enable us to experience the consequences we desire.

For all human beings whom we could call normal, living is thus a constant flow from established form. There is in all "normal" human beings an apparent craving for novelty, a desire to escape boredom and ennui. The human being wants to test his assumptions in new instances. He wants to experience new qualities of satisfaction. He wants to break away from fixed forms. It seems to be a characteristic of man that he is never satisfied with his lot. And the more he becomes tied up with the routine and boredom of fixed forms, the greater is his desire for flow and change.

We see this in the case of children who have had little chance for new experience and who are therefore prone to insubordination. We see it in the sabotage that goes on in regimented industry or in police states. We see it when we read our history and realize that no despotism has ever survived.

Each of us can see how in our own lives we are motivated by the desire to experience qualities of value which we feel will somehow be more satisfying than those which constitute our living so far. Let me cite an example taken from Justice Douglas' book, *Of Men and Mountains*. Douglas tells how he had to hitch rides on freight trains in order to get himself from the Yakima Valley in Washington to the Columbia Law School in New York. As a moving freight train was going through the Chicago freight yards, Douglas was forced by a brakeman to jump off. He was scratched and bruised, had only a few dollars to his name. He was hungry, tired, and homesick. He reports his thoughts as follows:

Most of my friends and all the roots I had in life were in the Yakima Valley. There would be a job and a home awaiting me, and fishing trips and mountain climbs . . . it was a friendly place, not hard and cruel like these freight yards . . . I would be content and happy there. Then why this compulsion to leave the Valley? Why this drive, this impulse to leave the scenes I loved? To reach for unknown stars, to seek adventure, to abandon the convenience of home? And what of pride? What would I say if I returned? That I didn't have the guts to work my way East, to work my way through Law School, to live the hard way? [1950: 15]

Here we have an example of the quality of being human—the ceaseless striving for a more complete, a richer satisfaction in experience, the desire to experience new consequences of action we initiate.

Living, then, becomes a continuous series of transactions and for the human being is made up of an infinite variety and pattern of awarenesses, including such experiences as grief, surprise, anxiety, humor, accomplishment, joy, love, fear, and devotion, to mention only a few.

For the purpose of understanding the nature of these transactions it may be of use to us if we abstract them into different aspects. We must, of course, remember that this is an arbitrary differentiation and that each aspect is interrelated with every other; that no one aspect of experience functions except for the function it has served, now serves, and will continue to serve all other aspects.

One of these aspects of man's experience is what we might call "perceiving," that is, the bets we make of *what* the things are which we have learned to discriminate in our environment and of *where* these things are. These perceptions of ours become our directives for potential action relative to objects which we are able to separate out of the total environment in and through which we are carrying out our purposes.

Another aspect involves our sense of surety that certain consequences will follow certain events, that if one event takes place we can predict certain following events will occur. We can label this a "sequential" aspect—the assumptions we build up through experience and knowledge that one event is a sequence of another.

Then there is an aspect of experience involving our prediction of what kind of action will lead to the desired consequences. We make choices between the probable value satisfactions that will follow the pursuit of alternative types of behavior we might undertake. We can refer to this as the aspect of "purposeful action."

And permeating all these is that aspect of experience where we weigh or size up our potential behavior, consciously or unconsciously, in terms of its significance to our value standards. Obviously we seldom do anything just for the sake of doing it, we seldom accomplish a limited purpose just to accomplish that limited purpose. None of us gather together in a lecture situation just to participate in a lecture situation. We do what we do either because of the value satisfaction we experience in the doing, or because its accomplishment is of some importance to us as a step toward the fulfillment of further purposes involving still greater value satisfactions. We can label this the "valuing" aspect.

The outstanding quality of man's motivation, then, appears to be a desire to bring forth and to experience the value aspects latent in every concrete behavior situation. I hardly need point out that this is a very different perspective than we get when we take the usual impersonal, "scientific," third-person approach. For then we conceive of behavior as entirely a homeostatic reaction to a stimulus which has fixed properties—as an attempt only to reduce some physiological tensions. Then we find all behavior is determined since it is only determined behavior we have allowed ourselves to look for.

We are proposing, instead, that the central quality of being human is the creative search for new value satisfactions which serve as the initiators of behavior. We propose that this can only be experienced by the behaving individual who is bringing the determined of his own unique past to the undisclosed of his own unique present. This is not a flight into any form of vitalism, supernaturalism, or solipsism.

The nature of environment

In creating an environment through which to carry out his unique purposes, the human being has an amazing capacity to differentiate a variety of aspects out of the world which surrounds him. Among other things, man can learn the significance of certain sounds which he calls words, he learns the significance of a variety of organisms including other human beings, he learns the significance of ideas, of complicated symbols, of ideologies. He has the capacity to register these significances so he can use them at appropriate times.

Man is constantly making his environment more "human" by extending his understanding of the significances of events or happenings. The extent to which any one of us is aware of his environment is proportional to the extent to which he has been able to humanize it. From this point of view, we might say that instead of "conquering" nature, man essentially "humanizes" nature. A characteristic of man as an organism is that he is able to assign repeatability, significance, or meaning to a wider and more inclusive range of happenings than any other organism.

This view seems consistent with modern physics. In an article on "The Operational Aspect of Meaning," P.W. Bridgman concludes that

> in seeking the precision demanded by scientific use we have thus been led to discard the common sense method of handling our environment in terms of objects with properties, and have substituted for it a point of view that regards a reduction to activities or operations as a safer and better method of analysis. . . . What we are in effect doing in thus preferring the operational attack is to say what we *do* in meeting new physical situations has a greater stability than the situations themselves, and that we can go further without revising our operations than we can without revising our picture of the prop-

erties of objects. ... Our methods of handling the external world have a greater stability than the external world itself.[1950–1: 255–7]

Just as we differentiate our environment into various objects because of the relationship they have to our purposeful activity, so too we differentiate people according to the potential significance they have for us—i.e., we call people farmers, bakers, bachelors, friends or enemies, etc. This is a quick and useful step we make for separation and classification.

A most important difference, however, between classifying objects and classifying people is that we have an awareness that people, unlike objects, have purposes and values that exist in their own right. Hence people become qualitatively vastly different from "objects"—people are sensed as more "real," as more "valueful." While we do not hesitate to destroy objects, we believe "thou shalt not kill."

Analysis of concrete behavioral situations from this general point of view enables us to get a somewhat better understanding of what really is involved in situations we characterize as "social" and that play so large a role in man's behavior. A person is "social" insofar as he experiences significances to events that other people are also experiencing as significances. This sharing of the significances of events provides the links except for which a social event would not be experienced and actually would not exist. The links that the sharing of significances provide and which operationally make a social event possible are analogous to the forces of attraction that holds the parts of an atom together, keeping each part from following its independent, individual course.

It would appear that we are able to grasp the potential significances of events with others only insofar as we experience the same events in phase with them and humanize these events more or less similarly by "assigning" similar significances to them. Many of us have had the curious experience, for example, of attending a football or basketball game with a foreigner who does not understand the rules of the game and who therefore can assign no significances to the actions he observes. In such a situation, it is impossible to share experience and to enjoy the occurrences taking place on the field with the quality of feeling we would have if our companion also knew what it was all about.

If we are to have a full-bodied experience of social relationship with other people, it therefore becomes necessary for us to sense the potential significances that *they* experience in an event as well as the significances *we* experience in the same events.

These significances we attach to other people, to symbols, or to ideologies, we label "attitudes" or "opinions." And if we have never tested these potential significances through our own action, then we are likely to be more or less anxious, to lack surety and confidence in our opinions. This was nicely illustrated in a recent account of the conversations and speculations that took place on a ship bringing a number of elderly Italian people to begin life anew in America. Their journeys and immigrations were being sponsored largely by young relatives and friends already here. In reporting what he overheard among these people, the journalist wrote,

> . . . And the word that turned up most frequently in their conversation was "America." In colloquial Italian, "America" has come to mean something more than a geographical place. It is, by extension, any deposit of hopes, any tabernacle where all things too big, too difficult, too far beyond one's grasp take shape and become true—so true that all one needs in order to touch them is a ship that will take one there. "America" is, again, something one finds or makes, a stepping stone, a rung in the ladder that allows one to climb a little higher—not, of course, in the country called America but back home. "America" also means the treasure one finds when "America" (the rung in the ladder) is steadily under one's feet. Inevitably, the question that the old people asked one another, over and over, was "Is America *America?*"[Tucci 1951: 24]

We can regard man's customs, rituals, mores, and laws as significances which man has registered and preserved so that more people may share the meanings of more events more continuously and more extensively. Thus they provide more permanent links to the social matrix. For example, in nearly every culture of the world when a young man and woman fall in love with each other and decide they would like to spend the rest of their lives together, they go through the ritual we call "marriage." This wedding ceremony in nearly every culture is attended with some sort of unusual festivity, glamour, pomp, or circumstance. People have recognized for centuries that this new relationship between the two individuals is a novel value experience for both of them which can take on greater value for the two direct participants, acquire greater meaning for them, and make for greater social stability if it is somehow solemnized. Furthermore, the marriage ritual also enables friends and relatives to share in this value experience.

The function of our modern mass media and a reason they spread so rapidly is obviously because they enable more people to share more experiences concurrently. Since this is the role we expect radio and television especially to play, we are apt to feel cheated if we learn that some of the things we hear or view turn out to be "canned."

As we go about the process of living, we seek out the participation of other people according to our assumptions of what events and aspects of the environment have become humanized and significant for them and will, therefore, be potentially available to us if we participate with them to carry out our own purposes. Thus if we are lost in strange territory, we will seek out a native to get our bearings; or if, as a research man, we are looking for the answer to a technical question, we will seek out a scientific colleague. On the other hand, if we are temporarily "lost" in knowing what is the right or the good thing to do—if we are lost in the value matrix—we will seek the advice of a trusted friend, of our spouse, or of a person whom we call wise.

From this point of view, the important role played by the humanities may be somewhat better understood. For when we are searching for the value significances *others* have experienced and that may provide *us* with more reliable guesses as to how to act, it is often completely irrelevant whether or not such individuals are contemporary with us. This is particularly true in the value aspect of experience. Through the boundaries of time and space, it is possible for us to commune with others concerning the potential value significances we are sensing as we go along in the process of living. Hence we may turn to the classics, to our favorite poets or composers, to our New Testament, when our standards of value need freshening or sharpening up, or when we have an overpowering sense of loneliness.

All of our loyalties and allegiances to others seem to be formed because of the demonstrated usefulness these other people have for us as we participate with them. This holds with the member of a family, a member of the union, a person who aligns himself with a certain political party, or with a certain church. When we cease to experience from our association with others a confirmation or extension of some aspect of our own world of experience, then we are likely to give up our participation, or, if it does continue for some reason, it becomes formal and empty.

The nature of choice

Now we come to the problem of choice. If we are to understand the qualities of being human, we must inquire briefly about the ancient question of "free will," about man's capacity to choose.

Our awareness is made up of kaleidoscopic patterns of significances. If we take the impersonal, third-person point of view, we accept the conclusion that our awarenesses in any "now" are solely the result of the determinism of the past. But if we take the first-person point of view proposed here, where the determinism from the past functions with the undisclosed of the present, then our awareness must somehow be concerned with the problem of choice.

Human beings have the capacity to choose. And the opportunity to exercise this capacity of choice cannot be denied man without violating his very nature. This is a fact about human beings which cannot be liquidated. Since the outstanding quality of human beings appears to be their capacity to participate in the creation of more satisfying value experiences, it is most important to recognize that in the process of choosing, the top criterion for choice is the probability of greater value satisfaction through actions that follow choice.

Man appears to make choices in all occasions of living except those that have become reflexive and habitual because of their high reliability from past performance. Choice plays a role in all of those situations where we face alternatives, where we have a sense of inadequacy, where we have made mistakes, or where we have failed to derive from our experience the satisfaction desired. Most of the choices we make are not what we could describe as rational, intellectual, or logical. In most choice situations we do not reason out a decision to ourselves in any step-by-step fashion. Rather we exercise what Kallen terms our "ineffable intuition."

An uncertainty as to what choice to make or the fear of making any choice at all can lead to individual psychoses and to mass collectivism and give the individual or the group a sense of loss of freedom or a sense of freedom from freedom. But there is probably no such thing as freedom from freedom if men are to be themselves and to develop as nature has prescribed. This proposition is basic in our Western-Christian-Democratic heritage.

Freedom is, of course, not an end in itself. The quality of freedom is measured by what a person does with it. What he does with his freedom, that is, the quality of his actions, depends on the quality of his purposes. Hence freedom always involves great personal responsibility; it is not license but the responsibility for the realization of human values through purposeful behavior.

All of us have a conviction that when we are deciding to do one thing rather than another, our choice is our own decision and no one else's. To deny a human being his right to exercise his capacity of choice thus becomes a cardinal sin. The concept of guilt found in the legal systems of most cultures—as well as the experience of guilt nearly all "normal" individuals have at times—is evidence of the human being's belief in the efficacy of personal choice with its accompanying sense of personal responsibility.

Among the variety of difficulties we encounter, where we must exercise choice, two types deserve special consideration in order to understand the qualities of being human.

When we ask ourselves the question, "What shall I do?", we may really be asking ourselves the question, "*How* should I do a particular thing?" On the other hand, the question, "What shall I do?", may mean "Why should I do a particular thing?"

From the long view of evolutionary history it would apear that two of the great steps made in the course of development were, first, when organisms developed the capacity to choose *how* to do a certain thing, as contrasted to automatic, tropistic, or reflex action; and second, when organisms developed the capacity to choose *why* to do a certain thing.

A "how-to-do" difficulty is encountered when we are not sure of the way to achieve a desired end. Here is a simple example. Suppose you want to drive to a certain town to see an old friend. Suppose you have never driven to this town before from your home. You approach a crossroad and don't know which way to go. You consult your road map, you look for a road sign, or you ask directions. In this case, you know *what* you want to do, but you don't know *how* to do it.

Now a hitch on the why or the "*what for*" level involves a decision concerning the goal to be achieved. Here is an example. Again, suppose you are driving along a highway. You approach a pedestrian who is thumbing a ride. You have to decide whether to stop and give him a lift, or to keep on driving. You can do either quite easily. There is no problem of *how* to accomplish whatever you decide to do. But you must decide *why* you should act in one way or another. In this situation, if you decide against giving the pedestrian a lift, to drive on is just as positive an action as to stop.

When you meet a difficulty on the "how-to-do" level and feel that you are unable to act in some way which will effectively accomplish a definite end, you analyze the situation. You use rational inquiry. You ask questions of others, you read directions, you examine the situation and try to understand it. In all these pursuits, you are essentially trying to discover what action will offer a fair probability of achieving a goal. This means that the particular directives useful in your inquiry must refer to, and be limited by, the situation of which you are now a part. You can act only from your own particular standpoint in time and space.

Modern scientific inquiry is the outstanding example of the process arising from encountering this type of difficulty. The intellectual formulations of science give more precision to our understanding of the relatively determined relationships of particular space-time frames of reference. The role of pure science is essentially that of extending man's awareness and knowledge of the heretofore unrecognized sequential phenomena of nature; while applied science extends the range of man's sequential behavior, his how-to-do's, through the creation of artifacts. The contributions of science, it should be noted, are contributions confined largely to the sequential matrix.

While knowledge and rational inquiry are sometimes useful in helping us extend the range of the cues we can take into account in deciding *what* goals to pursue and in anticipating the consequences of different courses of action, no amount of knowledge or of rational inquiry *alone* can throw any light on the nature of the end or purpose we are attempting to achieve. That is, knowledge and rational inquiry in and of themselves can give us no understanding of *why* we are doing what we are doing, of what we are doing something *for*.

When we try to decide *why* we should do one thing rather than another, we also go into a kind of "inquiry." But the process involved in such inquiry is totally different from the processes involved in the inquiries necessary for solving procedural difficulties. If we are in a situation where a difficulty is encountered in deciding *why* we should do one thing or another—or possibly why we should do anything at all—the process of inquiry can be described vaguely as "meditation," "contemplation," "communion with one's self," and the like. Inquiry here is a value inquiry. And value inquiry is intensely personal and unique. It involves what is the "me" built up from the past facing the transition of the present into the future as "I."

The function of this value inquiry is to provide us with a value judgment that will serve as a compass, a directive for action. In value inquiry we are seeking standards of rightness, wrongness, goodness, badness, beauty, decency, and the like, which will serve as signs indicating to us the nature of the probable value satisfactions we will experience by following a particular course of action. The standards we use and question in value inquiry concern our duties, our loyalties, our responsibilities. Hence the value judgments we reach through value inquiry involve "conscience," "charity," "humility," "love." The role of value inquiry is symbolized by the Hindu custom of marking one's self between the brows with ashes each day in order to be reminded of the "inner vision" provided by a "third eye"; it is reflected in our Western hymn which says, "Lead, kindly light, amid the encircling gloom."

Christ and Gandhi may be taken as examples of individuals who were trying to create an environment in order to act on the "what for" value judgments emerging from their value inquiry. In order to indulge in the necessary value inquiry, Christ went to the top of the mountain and Gandhi had his day of silence.

We find in reading Gandhi's revealing autobiography that the function of prayer for him and a function of some of his fasts was to sensitize himself to cues that could be taken into account in the process of value inquiry in order to achieve the most reliable and satisfying value judgment. He was trying to take into account a synthesized phenomenon which he could feel, rather than abstracted aspects of a phenomenon he could grasp intellectually. And, as he says, it was only *after* what he calls his "instinct" had shown him a course of action was right that he tried to determine intellectually why it was right. Louis Fischer writes that "Gandhi always kept his eye on his objective, and when he could not see it he kept his eye on the spot where he thought it would appear" (1950: 221).

While most of us do not indulge in days of silence or prolonged fasts, certainly at times we have wanted to be alone so that we could mull things over. We apparently need to insulate ourselves in this way from immediate here-and-now conditions as we weight those standards that are not bounded by time-and-space consideration. Such insulation allows our conscious and subconscious processes the widest possible range.

A problem for every individual and a problem for every group or society or ideology appears to be the problem of clarifying purposes and simplifying means. For it would appear that only insofar as an individual raises the level of his purposes can he minimize the annoyances of his life and "carry on" most satisfyingly. Only then can discrimination be improved and means become simplified by being judged in terms of more inclusive purposes. In the *Bhagavad-Gita* there is a verse: "The wise should perform tasks without attachment, yet with as much ardor as the foolish, who are bound up in the results of their deeds—thus to the world shall they set an example."

Many people in Western society today do not recognize that knowledge and rational inquiry alone cannot give the answers to questions of why and what for. And the failure to make such a distinction may be one of the basic sources of Western man's bewilderment. We in America tend to think that if we are busy, we are effective; that we must always be doing something; that we must not "waste time." The Soviet citizen is systematically and officially discouraged from making a distinction between "how" and "why" by such devices as "organized leisure," which prevent the Russian people from having the time to ask, "What is all this really for, anyway?"

While we in the West do appear to be ahead today in the area of rational inquiry, the people in the Far East seem to be ahead on inquiry concerning motives and directional insights. But it would also appear to be a somewhat fair generalization to say that the people in the East have traditionally sought their answer in a nonemergent world by substituting abstractions for concreteness, thinking that the answer could be found in contemplating or pursuing the abstraction itself without bringing it to life through action.

The nature of faith

There is a final characteristic of man to consider before our portrait of man can be at all complete. I refer to man's need for faith and man's capacity for faith.

Let me introduce the problem with an incident reported by Carl Sandburg in his book, *Always the Young Strangers.*

I have always enjoyed riding up front in a smoking car, in a seat back of the "deadheads," the railroaders going back to the home base. Their talk about each other runs free. . . . Once I saw a young fireman in overalls take a seat and slouch down easy and comfortable. After a while a brakeman in blue uniform came along and planted himself alongside the fireman. They didn't say anything. The train ran along. The two of them didn't even look at each other. Then the brakeman, looking straight ahead, was saying, "Well, what do you know today?" and kept on looking straight ahead till suddenly he turned and stared the fireman in the face, adding, "For sure." I thought it was a keen and intelligent question. "What do you know today—*for sure?*" I remember the answer. It came slow and honest. The fireman made it plain what he knew that day for sure: "Not a damn thing! . . ."[1952: 145f.]

This story nicely illustrates the point made earlier: that in the process of living we are constantly making bets, weighing probabilities, guessing at significances. We have to do this in a world where there is constant change and emergence, in a world where the nature of future activity is not entirely determined, in a course of events where civilization is an open system.

While we may realize intellectually as scientists and psychologists that the happenings around us and our own perceptions, prehensions, actions, and valuings are only probabilities, still we must behave in our everyday life as *if* some probable happenings were certainties. For we couldn't *act*, we couldn't survive if we did not make some definite fixed assumptions. For example, in carrying on the process of living, we have to assume as we are crossing a street, that what we perceive as an oncoming car *is* an oncoming car; we *have* to assume that certain friends *are* loyal, that certain people *are* honest; we *have* to assume that certain things *are* the right things to do, and that certain things *are* wrong.

Hence we tend to make absolutes out of probabilities in order to act effectively. Those repeatable happenings and relationships that we have found from our past experience can be relied upon we might call "*functional absolutes.*" On the value level, these functional absolutes provide the sustaining power which keeps us going—our faith that we *will* experience certain consequences and value satisfactions if we act in certain ways. We lose this faith when our action on the basis of these absolutes fails to give us the anticipated value satisfactions or goes counter to our experiences and observations. And when value standards are lost, then *we* feel lost.

Faith, then, becomes a sense of certainty concerning some significance we assign. It is not intellectualized and rationalized in our minds. It is more of a sensed awareness, a feeling. Hence it is generally expressed through poetry, music, prayer, or meditation.

These "functional absolutes" we cling to as tested guides of our own experience might usefully be contrasted to another kind of absolute: what we shall call "*abstracted absolutes*." These abstracted absolutes are intellectual abstractions. We refer to them by such words as "law," "truth," "nature," or "God." They become meaningless in our own everyday lives, from our own personal behavioral centers, unless they consistently prove to be guides to effective action, that is, action which leads to value satisfaction. Any political or religious system is bound to fail sooner or later insofar as it must prop itself up by abstracted absolutes which people find it impossible to use in living.

A functional absolute is never an end in itself but a goal which, once achieved, points to further emerging value satisfactions. A few days before his death, John Dewey said, "A goal is a sign post."[2] Quite a thing to be able to say when one is over ninety years of age.

I like to think that it was some such distinction as this between abstracted absolutes and functional absolutes that Jesus had in mind when he said, "The Kingdom of God cometh not with observation: neither shall they say, 'lo, here' or 'lo, there,' for behold, the Kingdom of God is within you."

In summary

We have briefly sketched here four of the outstanding qualities of human beings. First, the unique qualities of their value experience as they participate in occasions of living and as they try through these occasions to make experience ever more satisfying.

Second, the unique capacity of human beings to create a world of meaning and significance as they humanize an otherwise neutral and undifferentiated environment.

Third, their amazing capacity to meet the indeterminism of living by making choices that range from simple motor adjustments to the highest ethical decisions.

And, fourth, the remarkable capacity of most human beings to sustain themselves through hardship, failure, uncertainties, and the stresses of life by sensing that only insofar as they keep plugged into the stream of events can they experience the good, the true, and the beautiful.

The personal and social problem of Western man, then, seems to be to discover for himself in terms of his own experience what value assumptions, what code of ethics, he can take as moral certainties and use as his functional absolutes in the changing world of today. It is the old question, "What faith shall we live by?" facing us in our unique situation in history.

In a Socratic dialogue, Benjamin Franklin wrote in his newspaper in 1730, "As the happiness or real good of men consists in right action, and right action cannot be produced without right opinion, it behooves us, above all things in this world, to take care that our opinions of things be according to the nature of things (Van Doren 1938: 87).

Notes

1. The point of view sketched here has been developed in the course of research and communion especially with Adelbert Ames, Jr., and also with W.H. Ittelson, F.P. Kilpatrick, C.H. Bumstead, and Earl Kelley.
2. Communication from Earl Kelley concerning his last conversation with John Dewey.

References

Bridgman, P.W. 1950-1. The operational aspect of meaning. *Synthese* 8: 255-7.

Douglas, W.O. 1950. *Of men and mountains*. New York: Harper.

Fischer, L. 1950. *The life of Mahatma Gandhi*. New York: Harper.

Fülöp-Miller, R. 1953. *Science and faith in the crisis of our time*. New York: Scribner.

Kallen, H. 1951. In remembrance of Charles Beard, philosopher-historian. *Soc. Res.* 18: 243-9.

Sandburg, C. 1952. *Always the young strangers*. New York: Harcourt Brace.

Tucci, N. 1951. The underground settlers. *New Yorker* 27: (Aug. 4): 24.

Van Doren,C. 1938. *Benjamin Franklin*. New York: Viking.

Whitehead, A.N. 1933. *Adventures of ideas*. Cambridge: Cambridge University Press.

6

Toward a humanistic psychology

In his article "The Task Before Us," the physicist P.W. Bridgman has lamented the humanistic interest of many American universities as merely a "return to" without any "notable revitalization of these humanities themselves in the light of our recent intellectual experiences." Bridgman continues, "It seems to me that in this cry for a 'return' there is grave danger that we shall turn our backs on a job which not only is not finished but which is hardly begun. This job is to assimilate into our whole intellectual outlook, and in particular into our relation to social problems, the lesson implicit in scientific experience" (1954: 98). We should perhaps bear in mind throughout this essay an important differentiation between the humanistic and scientific approaches: that the latter is developmental and additive, attempting to build on increasing data to reach more adequate conceptualizations. But just because of this, there is no reason why the "humanist" need feel apologetic, modest, or in any way be on the defensive for his insights and expressions.[1]

The problem is nicely posed in the *Dialogues of Alfred North Whitehead* as recorded by Lucien Price. Whitehead is asked the question, "Why should science be able to take such leaps, as it has done in the last century, even the last forty years, when the humanities advance so slowly? Are we really much ahead of Plato and Aristotle there?" To which Whitehead's reply was, "In the eighteenth century (I speak of England where I know what I am talking about) you could follow Rome and Greece of their best ages. The social structures were similar enough for historical precedents to be of some practical value: you still had the mob and the aristocrats. If it

Originally prepared at the invitation of Dr. Carsten Høeg for use during the II International Congress of Classical Studies, which met in Copenhagen in 1954. It was published with slight revisions in *ETC.: A Review of General Semantics* 12, no. 4 (Summer 1955): 278-98, from which it is reprinted here by permission of the International Society of General Semantics.

was a question of governing a colonial empire, India, you could still follow your Roman model; if a colonial governor was brought to trial for maladministration—Warren Hastings—you had Cicero's orations against Verres for his rapacious governship in Sicily. . . . Even in the nineteenth century the Graeco-Roman model would still be fairly closely patterned after. But now, in the twentieth, this new technology has so altered the moral values, or the social relationships, that a much more searching and subtle readjustment of the traditional classic models to modern needs is wanted. . . . We are sending out as colonial administrators men trained not in the old humanistic tradition, but products of the scientific schooling. They are just as good intellects, but is their training as happy? I doubt if they will bring as sensitive an understanding to the emotional set-up of the peoples they must rule" (Price 1954: 127f.).

I should like to take the liberty here to spell out a point of view which a group of us are developing and which we have labeled "Transactional Psychology," borrowing the term "transaction" from John Dewey. It is my hope that a brief discussion of the main premise of this point of view may serve as a catalyst for discussion among general semanticists. For it does seem to me that the way in which we are now trying to look at "experience" and "behavior" includes the possibility, indeed the necessity, of taking into account in any psychology that pretends to be adequate those problems which are common problems to the humanist and the true scientist.

The ultimate goal of psychology is the understanding of human living so that individuals can live more effectively. The psychologist's aim is that of formulating a set of constructs which will enable him conceptually to "understand," "explain," and "predict" the activities and experiences of the functional union we call a behaving person.

A prerequisite for psychological research is an understanding of what an individual is aware of from his unique behavioral center in any occasion of living. The word "center" is used here in the dictionary sense of "the point toward which any force, feeling or action tends or from which any force, or influence takes its origin; as a storm center" (*Webster's Collegiate*, 5th ed.).

The psychologist interested in understanding the process of living must start from naive experience in the phenomenal area. For only then will he be able to undertake investigations that will disclose the nature of the processes playing a role in behavior which the experiencing individual is taking into account. The words "experience" and "behavior" are used here as *interdependent* abstractions man has created, neither of which would be meaningful except for the other.

As anyone knows, the task of starting with naive experience and formulating systematic constructs on the basis of naive experience is a particularly difficult undertaking. For the very essence of living is its unity and flow. Yet in order to get any grasp of his most complicated subject matter and to communicate his understanding to others, the psychologist is forced to break up into distinguishable parts what really constitutes an indivisible, functional aggregate; he is forced to consider separately the various aspects of living which are all interrelated and interdependent and none of which would function as they do except for all the others. The various aspects of living that are experienced are never separate from each other but fuse together to form this living. And the psychologist must try to orchestrate into a single symphony the harmonious or discordant sounds with motifs, themes, phrases, accents, and repetitions related to the separate notes played by the many instruments.

If the psychologist, then, is to be faithful to his subject matter, he must always bear in mind that living is an orchestration of ongoing processes and that any process he may choose to differentiate out of this aggregate of ongoing processes of living can be understood only if it is recognized as referring to a phase of man's orchestrated functioning. It is, for example, a commonplace of philosophical and psychological thinking that "cognitive" and "motor" processes are themselves distinctions that can be misleading unless there is full cognizance of the fact that there can be no "knowing" without "doing," just as there can be no "person" except for an "environment," nothing "subjective" except for what is "objective," nothing "personal" except for what is "social," nothing experienced as existing "out there in its own right" except for the organizations and significances to an individual of the happenings going on in the world around him which he associated with light waves, sound waves, etc., as instruments of explanation.[2]

It is important in any consideration of "moral ideas" to reemphasize this point, to indicate some of the different experiential aspects into which the process of living may be abstracted, to show how each aspect plays a functional role in the congregation of experience and cannot be regarded as a single mechanistically-caused variable.

A necessary part of our consideration is, of course, that the conceptual abstractions we use are several steps removed from our primary data, namely, naive experience. In order to bridge the gap between naive experience and conceptual abstractions, the psychologist must consider areas of complexity and abstraction that become progressively further removed from his first-order data. It is imperative that any investigator be aware of the level of abstraction at which he operates. For there is always the danger that anyone, especially the scientist, may tend to mistake the conceptual abstraction for what it refers to, embrace it eagerly because of the feeling of security it affords, forget that it obscures uniqueness and differences, that it is a function of some human purpose and is at best partial and tentative.

Any such approach to the study of man's values and ideas is automatically denied us if we follow certain current "schools" of psychology which, stemming from the scientific tradition set by Descartes, attempt to explain the nature of man entirely in terms of a mechanistic determinism. This does not in the least, of course, imply that we turn out backs on the results of rigid scientific experimentation. Indeed, the most rigorous of these as found in modern physics support the conclusion that our traditional conceptions of matter are due for serious revision and, further and more important for us here, the conclusions of modern physics as well as modern biology deny any complete determinism and indicate that what makes up the universe, including man, is ceaseless activity, continual flow from form where the spirit of man plays a creative role.

Different ways of viewing experience

It may be helpful for us in setting the stage if we differentiate between four different ways in which experience may be viewed, four differentiable areas of complexity.

Ongoing, naive experience

This is the level of immediate, "pure" experience as experienced—unanalyzed, unconceptualized, unmediated, and with no concern on the part of the experiencing individual to describe, analyze, conceptualize, or communicate his experience. This ongoing, naive experience is what Korzybski called "first-order" or "objective level" or "un-speakable" experience. He writes: "Thus we *handle* what we call a pencil. Whatever we *handle* is unspeakable; yet we *say* 'this *is* a pencil,' which statement is unconditionally false to facts, because the object appears as an absolute individual and *is not* words" (1948: 35). This is perhaps what the poet Wordsworth had in mind when he said, "We murder to dissect."

As has been frequently pointed out, any attempt to describe or analyze experience immediately alters that experience. When we are trying to describe or analyze experience or any aspect of it, we are functionally organized quite differently than when we are participating in a process of living and are not describing or analyzing it. Our experiences in the occasions of living are dependent upon and characterized by processes involving, for example, overtones of satisfaction or dissatisfaction, a sense of involvement and responsibility, a sense of intent or aim, commitment through activity, a sense of worry, frustration, or urgency, a sense of despair, hope, or faith, etc., depending upon the particular orchestration going on in a particular unique occasion of living. The obvious complexity of the orchestration that any ongoing experience *is* makes the process of isolating aspects of it particularly difficult. But if the psychologist ignores any significant aspects of experience in an attempt to isolate easily manipulable variables, he is bound to fail in his attempt to understand that experience.

Description

Verbalization and communication, either retrospectively or simultaneously with the occurrence of some experience, may be distinguished methodologically from naive experience itself because of a form of awareness on selected aspects of experience. For some focusing, categorization, and coding are operating in the process of dealing consciously or verbally with any selected experiential aggregate. It is as if with any such focusing, awareness is shifted from the full orchestration as a whole to the role of a particular instrument in the orchestra.

As stated by Korzybski: "Animals may 'feel,' and 'suffer,' but they cannot *describe*. Humans differ in this respect; the given person may feel pain, the pain is very *objective* to the given individual, but it is *not words (objective level)*; but we can describe it, this description being valid on the *descriptive level*, a higher order abstraction than the objective level (which is unspeakable for the given individual). If we *ascribe* this process to others, this is no longer a description but an inference, or a still higher order abstraction . . ."(1948: 359).

It is important for psychologists using descriptive material of any kind never to lose sight of the fact that reports of experience are not to be equated with experience itself. Such "protocol" data, however, do provide the psychologist with valuable raw material. This is not limited to introspective reports obtained in the laboratory or to clinical material. Some of the most penetrating descriptions of experience have been given us by poets, novelists, composers, and religious prophets. From this point of view, the psychologist concerned with an understanding of the full range of human experience can enormously benefit by sensitizing himself to the insights found in the "humanities."[3] The humanists, on the other hand, as already indicated, should be able to profit by keeping in touch with the psychologist who, in his self-appointed capacity as scientist, must try to systematize the intuitive portrayals of humanists and formulate constructs of general validity.

Focused analysis and conceptualization

Instead of focusing on a selected phenomenon in an experience of living we may, in the midst of that living, try to "figure out" conceptually what is going on. We do so for some purpose. Perhaps we are trying to resolve some personal problem, perhaps we are delving into our own experience in the hope of discovering hunches or clues that will provide us with some hypothesis, or perhaps we are only obeying the instructions of some experimenter in the psychological laboratory. Analysis of any occurrence for whatever purpose is a very different experiential aggregate than purposive behavior itself or focused aspects of it.

This area of complexity described as "focused analysis and conceptualization" also includes our attempt to understand the behavior and purposes of other people as we try to carry out our own purposes in social situations. Such understanding will usually be successful insofar as we are able to bring to an occasion appropriate sets of abstractions derived from our own experience. Our ability to "put ourselves into another's position" and to "share" his experience vicariously seems generally to depend upon the similarity of our experiential backgrounds, our purposes, our standards for sensing satisfaction, our values, etc. In other instances, where there may be little similarity of experiential background, our understanding of others may increase if the situation is such that we develop with those others some community of interest through the repeated sharing of new experiences.

No matter how close the correspondence may be between all the factors involved in giving us an awareness of another person's experience under certain circumstances, we still have to interpret their experiences in terms of our own experience. And no matter how closely knit the person may feel in the social group, no matter how great the correspondence may be between his experiential background, his needs, his purposes or values, and those of other members of the group, his experience of participation with the group is still uniquely his own. Complete understanding of another person is an unobtainable ideal.

Yet our understanding of another person (or his understanding of us) may be more accurate than his own understanding of himself since our "explanation" of his behavior may be taking more factors into account, may give very different priorities to different aspects that constitute the aggregate experience, may differentiate or abstract out of his process of living as we observe it more intrinsically reasonable aspects so that we are more aware of the processes playing a role in his behavior than he is himself. Thus an experienced physician will be able to tell us why we are tired or suffer certain aches or pains; an experienced psychiatrist may be able to point out to us what purposes that we are unaware of seem to be guiding our actions; a wise friend may be able to point out contradictions in our value standards, etc.

Abstracting for scientific specification

The scientist's attempt to understand the nature of human living is ultimately an attempt to distinguish components, to choose those by means of which he will be able to define and interpret the significance of any process of living, and to describe the variables on which the singularity of any process depends. If the abstracting a scientist makes can be effectively related to his presuppositions, then he will have an instrument to render communication more accurate and to enable others to understand the abstractions without reference to any particular item of behavior that might illustrate it. This point is discussed at length by Korzybski in his treatment of "higher inferential levels" in his chapters "On Abstracting," "On the Structural Differential," and "On 'Consciousness' and Consciousness of Abstracting" (1948: chaps. 24–6).

Such scientific abstractions are not affected by individual behavior and are not altered when conceptualized from the point of view of different persons. If they were so affected or altered, they would prove useless; it is their static quality that gives them the utility they have in understanding the significance of concrete behavioral situations. This does not mean, of course, that such scientific abstractions never change. They are, on the other hand, constantly evolving and being modified by scientists themselves to increase their usefulness. The creative scientist tests his abstractions by their performance, not by their consistency, realizing that any abstraction is highly tentative. In describing William James, Whitehead wrote, "His intellectual life was one protest against the dismissal of experience in the interest of system" (1938: 4). What we mean by the "static quality" of an abstraction is simply that scientific abstractions would be operationally useless if their significances were not "fixed."

But it should be emphasized again that when we are dealing with this fourth area of complexity which makes scientific communication possible, we are necessarily violating phenomenal data. The psychologist's awareness of this fact and of some of the omissions involved in operating in this area should help give him perspective to increase the usefulness of his abstractions.

Two points should be noted in passing with respect to this four-fold differentiation: (1) Whichever way a process of living is considered will depend upon one's purposes, and, (2) no matter which way a process of living is considered, the consideration is still yours, is still a process in which you cannot be detached, is still a transaction involving what Bridgman has called the "personal equation" from which no scientist can escape. All experiences are from a personal behavioral center.

A major task, then, for anyone trying to work through an adequate understanding of human nature is to describe what a transaction of living *is* in all of its aspects from any personal behavioral center. Since experience is "real" only insofar as it is "yours," we must try to make an approximate description of a transaction of living that will appear intrinsically reasonable and verifiable in terms of your own experience and behavior. Such a description, of course, must be derived from an analysis of your own experience and behavior, which is all you have to base it on. This means that we must work out from what is given in a transaction of living rather than work in toward a transaction of living from some arbitrary outside starting point, such as any preestablished abstractions or any preestablished methods borrowed from another discipline.

The psychologist cannot avoid his responsibilities merely by becoming insensitive to the compelling aspects of human experience which defy neat systematization or the use of picturesque models which can be quantitatively described. If, for example, we take the more traditional, "scientific" point of view alone and try to account for another person's experience and behavior, we are likely to overemphasize the aspects of any transaction of living which have been determined in the past. For from this point of view—for example, from the past—since we are *outside* the personal behavioral center which is our object of understanding, we ourselves cannot possibly participate as another individual is himself participating in what is to him a "now" or "present" where *he* must make *his* choices in order to carry out *his* purposes in a situation that impinges upon *him* and in which he initiates some action that is, in part, pushed by a determined, repeatable past and in part pulled by an undisclosed, uncertain future. Likewise, from the "objective," "outside" point of view we may entirely neglect the experiential background and the past interpersonal relationships that bring to an occasion of living a determined set which affects the direction that occasion of living will take. We then land in the complete situational determinism "outside of us," a metaphoric "field" theory and cannot account for the consistency of behavior, the apparently directed flow of living, or the value overtones without which any transaction of living would not be what it is.

It is perhaps especially worth noting in a discussion of the ways in which "experience" can be viewed that, as William James long ago emphasized, the range of our awareness is most restricted. Your awareness is an attribute of a transaction of living which refers to a very limited and particular range of "things" (objects, people, happenings, ideas, etc.) at any time. Your awareness is of what "concerns you now" together with the sense of obligation or responsibility you experience at any given time as related to what concerns you at that time. You are by no means aware of all the determinants of your awareness—that is, all the aspects involved in a total transaction of living except for which you would not have the awareness you do.

You can become intellectually aware that your experience at any time is an almost infinitesimal drop in the bucket of what you might be potentially aware of and is even more limited with respect to all the happenings and stimulus-excitations going on within and around you—what Harry Stack Sullivan labeled "selective inattention." Through analysis you can see that what you are aware of at any given time, that your "selection" of possibilities for awarenesses is made on the basis of what is of importance, worth, or value to you relative to your immediate purposes whether these concern the retention of your psychological "form," structure, or set; or the effective participation in novel situations, or both. You can become intellectually aware that there is no *at*tention without *in*tention. As expressed by Horace Kallen, "Consciousness is attention between divergencies which decision temporarily relieves by bringing one to dominance" (1953: 32).

To state the matter somewhat differently, you can understand intellectually the difference between what you are "aware of" and what you are "taking into account" in any transaction of living. This was expressed by Mr. Justice Holmes as "an intuition of experience which outruns analyses and sums up many unnamed entangled impressions which may be beneath consciousness without losing their worth" (Frank 1953: 77). You can understand intellectually that you become aware of certain factors you are now taking into account, but had previously been unaware of when your behavior was incomplete, because you had not experienced the consequences you expected from your behavior—that is, as when a front tire on your car blows out and you suddenly swerve; when you go up in a fast elevator and become aware of your gravitational adjustment; when you underestimate the magnitude of some task you have set out to accomplish; when a trusted friend disappoints you; when some institution or ideology "fails" to give you expected satisfactions, etc. You can be intellectually aware of the legal concept that a person is guilty only if he had a certain "intent" in his awareness at the time the particular act was committed.

At any one time, then, there is a multiplicity of happenings potentially available for awareness, together with a multiplicity of previous happenings available for recall and a multiplicity of possible future happenings available for expectancies. Of all the phenomenal aspects of any transaction of living which we are taking into account during that transaction of living, we are aware only of those aspects which we are in the process of giving meaning or significance to in order to experience the consequences of the purposeful behavior we are trying to participate in or trying to initiate.

From the psychologist's point of view, then, "awareness" as a quality of any transaction of living is not merely an adornment of nature but itself plays a functional role.

From the point of view of our present discussion, this fact must be especially borne in mind since our behavior in everyday life seems to involve an implicit adherence to value and moral standards of some kind which basically pattern our behavior.

Differentiation of the significances we experience

In order better to understand where valuings and moral ideas fit into the total orchestration of human experience, it may be helpful to differentiate between what we might term various *matrices* of experience. In making such differentiation, however, we must recall that each matrix is dependent upon all other matrices and that no one would exist except for the others.

Our perception of the world around us

By "our perception of the world around us," we refer to our experience of objects and people as these seem to exist in a world outside of ourselves and seem to have attributes and characteristics of their own that can be placed in the space–time continuum. It can be demonstrated that the attributes which we assign to the "things" outside of ourselves—whether objects, people, or societies—are significances which we build up in the course of our experience, are learned. Insofar as our subjective perceptual experience corresponds to what we encounter in the environmental situation, then our perceptions are judged by us as correct or accurate. From this point of view we may say that the world as we experience it is the creation of our perception and not the cause of it. "Naked sense impressions simply do not occur, and the traditional analysis of our conscious experience into naked sensations as building blocks is palpably bad description" (Bridgman 1954: 194). This does not imply, of course, any variety of solipsism since we would not have our normal perceptions except for impingements from the outside environment. It should be particularly stressed that from this point of view our perceptual awarenesses are only probabilities—guesses or hunches that we make, based on our previous experience, as to what the attributes of "things" are. This parallels Korzybski's conception that there is no such thing as a raw "reality" but only that which we evaluate in terms of our values–fears–past–history, etc. (1948: chap. 2).

Our awareness of sequential significances

By "our awareness of sequential significances," we refer to our assumptions that a certain event will be followed by another event, that events take place in sequences. When we are able to predict with considerable reliability what the sequential order of events will be, we experience a sense of surety. On the other hand, we become apprehensive when we cannot predict consequences.

From the point of view of the relationship between the sciences and the humanities, it is important to stress that all of man's scientific inquiry and the ingenious applications man makes from this inquiry are concerned either with extending the range of man's perceptual and motor processes (radar, television, airplanes, etc.) or with improving the reliability with which he will be able to predict and manipulate sequential events. Man has already created a bewildering variety of artifacts which he seems to have designed for the purpose of insuring that certain sequential events will follow other events in a direction which he can reliably predict. The important point to bear in mind here and to be elaborated later is that scientific inquiry as such does *not* concern itself with the problem of rightness or wrongness, the goodness or badness, of these sequential events which the scientist tries to understand and to control.

We stated above that our perception is only a probability. It is a probability for *action* or some potential action which we might undertake. Perception, then, has reference to the future as well as to the past. We act in order to experience some consequence from our actions, in order to achieve what we call some "purpose." The purpose which we intend to achieve may be immediate or it may be a long-range goal.

The purpose which we set out to achieve, the consequence which we hope will result from our action, is obviously not a purpose that exists in a vacuum or that is determined entirely by whim or the circumstances of the moment. Purposive action seems to have as its ultimate goal the experience of *value satisfaction*, which may take the form of the rudimentary attempts to preserve our physiological organism or, particularly characteristic of human beings, the more basic and ultimate satisfaction of experiencing some *emergence*, some novelty.that we characterize as "richer," "higher," "better." As I have stated elsewhere, "the outstanding characteristic of man is his capacity to participate in the creation of emergent value attributes which enrich the quality of his experience" (1950: 159). It would appear that if we do not root our conceptual scheme in this value matrix characteristic of man, then all the other matrices tumble since their function appears to be to *serve* man in his ceaseless striving for value satisfactions.

Some inferences related to humanistic inquiry

I have taken the liberty to outline the point of view expressed above in the hope that it will provide in bold relief a background against which to consider what seem to me important aspects involved in the development and function of moral ideas. The genetic development of moral ideas has been brilliantly traced by Jean Piaget, as well as by numerous psychologists and social scientists in the United States and England. From the data so far gathered by these investigators and from our own analysis of what seems to be an intrinsically reasonable account, I should like to call attention here to at least five aspects or characteristics of human experience that are related to the development and function of man's moral ideas: purposive behavior, hitches or obstructions, choice, inquiry, and the reality of faith.

Purpose

When you do something, you nearly always do it because of some intent, aim, or purpose. You are generally only aware of a single intent, aim, or purpose. And in doing this something—for example, reading this paper—you sense that "you" are involved in directing the doing because of "your" decision or intuition as to what will be the best thing to do under the particular circumstances, what will bring about a sense of worthwhileness and satisfaction, or, in other instances, what it is necessary to do in order to maintain life, to carry on, etc. The intent, aim, or purpose you have in mind when you do something is experienced with varying degrees of conflict or lack of conflict concerning its "goodness," "rightness," "efficacy," etc.

You can realize intellectually that while your naive, ongoing, unanalyzed experience is of some single and particular purpose—that is, a desire for the coming-about in your awareness of some particular consequence—if this purpose is to be carried out, a number of intermediate purposes will also be involved. For example, while your purpose at the moment may be to read this, you are also involved in the intermediate purposes of maintaining your equilibrium in a chair, holding this paper, focusing your eyes, etc. Furthermore, you are not reading this simply for the purpose of reading it but because such reading is presumably related to other, "higher" valueful purposes having to do with your basic standards of what is worthwhile and what will bring about a sense of personal satisfaction, development, etc.

In any transaction of living there is a multiplicity of purposes involved. These require differentiation and a choice of the satisfactions to be derived from various possibilities of what behavior is *for* anyway, what the value standards for this behavior "should" be. An individual's "sensed values"— this is, his own feeling of what is "important," "worthwhile," or "satisfying," are ultimately the impelling aspects of living that lead to any behavior at all. In any transaction of living it appears that the purposeful aspect of the transaction can be further differentiated into three factors: the first involving and insuring the preservation of physiological and psychological processes, the second "directing" action and sensed as the "purposive" accent in experience, the third involving a sense of the consequences the action will have once it is initiated. Each of these three factors has its own felt significance and no one of them would be experienced except for the felt importances of the other aspects. A "purpose" therefore becomes a weighted average of multiple purposes.

Hitches or obstructions

The process of living involves participation in situations which you do not by any means sail through without experiencing some obstruction, some obstacle, or some problem. You experience some sense of frustration, which may be great or small, ephemeral or relatively enduring. This frustration may come about either from a difficulty in carrying out effective behavior that will lead to some predetermined goal, or it may result from your concern as to what goal is the proper one for you to pursue anyway. Your sense of frustration in these respects is characterized by what you call "worry," "inferiority," "guilt," "struggle," "indecision," "anxiety," etc., depending upon the circumstances of the particular occasion.

On analysis you can be aware of the fact that no matter how annoying or upsetting the hitches or problems you encounter may be, these are almost inevitable aspects of living in a cosmos where the future is undisclosed and where you, as a participant, must play a role in determining that future. Furthermore, you can become intellectually aware that it is only insofar as you encounter illusions, surprises, disappointments, or other varieties of obstacles and problems that you yourself "learn" something, that you yourself have an opportunity to test out new choices, hunches, and formulations by experiencing the consequences they lead to in action. Problems of "how" to achieve a predetermined end challenge and hold the possibility of clarifying and enlarging your value standards, that is, your own code of ethics, morality, or worthwhileness.

A transaction of living involves in more or less degree a set of conditions that present a problem for choice or action. The ability to meet the problem depends upon the adequacy and appropriateness of the pattern of assumptions we bring to bear on the occasion, and only by "working through" the problems can we build up more inclusive and more appropriate assumptions for future occasions.

Choice

You sense, sometimes vaguely, sometimes intensely, that what you do involves the choice you make of alternatives and possibilities; the hunch you have that your intended actions will result in the intended consequences with their intended satisfactions. You have a sense of greater or less surety concerning the probable effectiveness of your choice; a sense of more or less conflict between alternatives involved in making your choice. And in the process of choosing and carrying out selected behavior resulting from choice, you have a sense of more or less personal responsibility.

You can be intellectually aware that you have no absolute control over future occurrences and that chance is likely to play a greater or lesser role in your behavior. You can become intellectually aware of many of the factors you are taking into account in the process of choosing. You can observe that many of your choices concerned with long-range goals involve the selection of alternatives and possibilities which you feel will lead to further alternatives and possibilities that will make future choices more effective.

Since what we call the "future" is made up of nonrepeatable, undisclosed happenings, a transaction of living involves in some degree the aspect of choice with the corollary aspects of personal responsibility and anxiety concerning the consequences of that choice. "Choosings are seen to be process of the normal consciousness, each a present passage to an anticipated future having no guarantees and contingent on 'faith' and 'fortune' as well as on the energies and intellect of the chooser" (Kallen 1953: 33).

Inquiry

As you participate in a transaction of living, you sense that you are more or less figuring out how to do what you want to do, or that you are making some evaluation of what is most worthwhile doing, what you "should be" doing.

On analysis, we can become intellectually aware that insofar as our behavior is completely reliable, certain, and effective we will go on to further behavior which will lead us to further desired consequences, but that when we run up against some obstacle, some difficulty, some sense of inadequacy, we become aware of this and must undertake some inquiry. If the difficulty encountered is one of *how* to achieve a predetermined goal, we make use of rational, logical inquiry involving conceptual abstractions which in its most highly developed form can be labeled "scientific inquiry." On the other hand, if a difficulty involves a choice of goals, a lack of surety with respect to *what* goals we "should" pursue, then we undertake a different kind of inquiry: Instead of indulging in rational and intellectual processes alone, we undertake what we refer to as "mulling things over," "reflecting," "meditating," in which we try to weigh the reliability of different value standards. We can sense that associated with inquiry of the former type is the collection of facts, the accumulation of knowledge, the attainment of skills, the use and development of artifacts, the development of "know how," the proper use of scientific method, etc. Associated with the latter type of inquiry are the less tangible but equally "real" experiences concerned with the development of faith, the acceptance of things past, the cultivation of charity, the broadening of love, etc.

In any transaction of living there is a multiplicity of alternative possibilities with respect to what goals an individual may pursue and a multiplicity of alternative possibilities with respect to how he may best realize any intended goal.

It is with respect to the form of inquiry involved when we must decide *why* we should do one thing rather than another (or possibly why we should do anything at all) that the psychologist still has to create some method of investigation. And it is in this area especially where he can learn from the humanists, skilled in description or portrayal, how individuals have learned to sensitize themselves to value inquiry. For, as already stated, the process involved in such value inquiry is totally different from the processes involved in the inquiries necessary for solving procedural difficulties. We remember that Aristotle said in his *Ethics*, "The end cannot be a subject of deliberation." Value inquiry is intensely personal and unique. You always feel it as yours. It involves what is the "me" built up from the past facing the transition of the present into the future as "I."

The function of this "value inquiry" is to provide us with a value judgment that will serve as a compass, a directive for action. In "value inquiry" we are seeking standards of rightness, wrongness, more right than, goodness, badness, beauty, ugliness, etc., which will serve as signs or clues and which will indicate to us the nature of the probable consequences we will experience by following a particular course of action. The standards we use and question in "value inquiry" concern our duties, loyalties, and responsibilities. Hence the value judgments we reach through "value inquiry" involve "conscience," "charity," "humility," etc.

The role of "value inquiry" is symbolized by the Hindu custom of marking one's self between the brows with ashes each day in order to be reminded of the "inner vision" provided by a "third eye"; it is reflected in the hymn which says, "Lead, kindly light, amid the encircling gloom."

Descriptions of value inquiry are almost necessarily best given us by poets. A revealing description by a modern poet is found in Christopher Fry's *The Lady's Not for Burning*. In the excerpts which follow, Jennet, who had been accused of being a witch and is to be burned the next day, is wondering whether or not to accede to the request of Humphreys that he enter her cell at night and sleep with her, in return for which favor Humphreys will have her sentence revoked because of his official position. Her decision not to accede to his request is a value judgment. Jennet soliloquizes:

> *Don't speak, contemptible boy,*
> *I'll tell you: I am not. We have*
> *To look elsewhere—for instance, into my heart*
> *Where recently I heard begin*
> *A bell of longing which calls no one to church.*
> *But need that, ringing anyway in vain,*
> *Drown the milkmaid singing in my blood*
> *And freeze into the tolling of my knell?*
> *That would be pretty, indeed, but unproductive,*
> *No, its not that . . .*
>
> *I am interested*
> *In my feelings. I seem to wish to have some importance*
> *In the play of time. If not,*
> *Then sad was my mother's pain, sad my breath,*
> *Sad the articulation of my bones,*
> *Sad, Sad my alacritous web of nerves,*
> *Woefully, woefully sad my wondering brain,*
> *To be shaped and sharpened into such tendrils*
> *Of anticipation, to feed the swamp of space.*
> *What is deep, as love is deep, I'll have*
> *Deeply. What is good, as love is good,*
> *I'll have well. Then if time and space*
> *Have any purpose, I shall belong to it.*
> *If not, if all is pretty fiction*
> *To distract the cherubim and seraphim*
> *Who so continually do cry, the least*
> *I can do is to fill the curled shell of the world*
> *With human deep-sea sound, and hold it to*
> *The ear of God, until he has appetite*
> *To taste our salt sorrow on his lips.*
> *And so you see it might be better to die.*
> *Though, on the other hand, I admit it might*
> *Be immensely foolish. [Fry 1950: 82ff]*[4]

Christ and Gandhi may be taken as examples of individuals who were trying to create an environment in order to act on the "what for" value judgments emerging from their value inquiry. In order to indulge in the necessary value inquiry, Christ went to the top of the mountain and Gandhi had his day of silence.

Most of us, at times, have wanted to be alone so that we could "mull things over." We apparently need to insulate ourselves in this way from immediate here-and-now conditions as we weigh those standards that are not bounded by time-and-space considerations. Such insulation allows our conscious and subconscious processes of mentation and feeling the widest possible range.

And some such insulation also allows us to make a more accurate distinction between (1) those feelings and emotions related to our physiological bodily activity and the conditions at the moment of which we are a part and (2) those overtones of feeling which derive from the standards for value that have become a part of our assumptive world and that are not dependent on a specific set of conditions or actions in the here and now. It is these value standards that sustain us between one doing and the next. Insofar as we feel sure of these value standards, we can weather frustration and deprivations; if we have no such value standards, then we feel lost.

We use our value standards to give us the most reliable bets for obtaining a repetition of some experience that has been satisfying. And it is especially characteristic of human beings also to use value standards as springboards for obtaining some new satisfactions they feel will emerge in the flow of the present from the past into the future.

The value standards each of us uses are the consequences of our action in the past that have been registered, and have become a part of our assumptive world insofar as they have proved to be good bets for further judgment and action. This registration is not of an intellectual nature. It is a change, a confirmation, or a denial of the weight to be given different assumptions concerning the "worthwhileness," the "goodness," the "rightness" of any action. Thus our complex of standards serves both as our criterion of satisfaction and as our best guide for effective action.

The process involved in "value inquiry" is one of trying to expand the range of the cues we can include. We attempt to increase our value specifications. These are bounded neither by the space-time considerations of any immediate situation nor by conceptual specifications. Hence, if a person accepts as absolute and inviolable any variety of ideology, the clues he uses in his value inquiry will be restricted, and the directive for action indicated by his inquiry will lack the reliability it might otherwise have. For the reliability of the directives reached through value inquiry is directly related to the adequacy of the cues taken into account. The point was made by Hayakawa: "People who are not accustomed to distinguishing between attitudes institutionally arrived at and those extensionally arrived at are capable of real self-deception. In a real sense, they don't know which of their opinions are simply a parrot-like repetition of institutional opinions, and which are the result of their own experience and their own thinking. Lacking that self-insight, they are unable to arrive at realistic self-concepts; they are unable to map accurately the territory of their own personalities" (1949: 304).

In cases where we have resolved a "what for" hitch and have arrived at a value judgment or decision, we may conceptualize this decision to ourselves or feel emotionally that it is good and proper. However, it is important to bear in mind that this conceptualization or feeling can be experienced only because of a large background of value standards which constitute an important aspect of each of our assumptive form worlds.

If this is not recognized, we are apt to make the mistake of believing that our purposive decision in and of itself is of a final or ultimate nature and justifies any action that may lead to its accomplishment. Furthermore, these value standards are largely on the silent, nonverbal level. By and large we are quite unaware of them and, except in rare cases, have never "thought them through" or systematized them. Yet they are the standards against which we measure our feelings of pleasure, happiness, our sense of well-being, our sense of self- esteem, our "ought I" judgments.

Thus it becomes "wrong" to act on the basis of the adage, "The end justifies the means" insofar as the consequences of our actions will not ultimately lead to what we expected. The glib rationalizations and conceptualizations of a particular "end," together with the action we take to achieve it, may prevent the realization of those unconceptualized, unconscious value standards without which the specific end we have in mind would not exist. There is a marked contrast between the ease with which most of us can rationalize why we have set a particular goal and the tortuous, soul-searching type of rationalization in which Lincoln indulged.

Rational inquiry, while not excluded in the resolution of difficulties on the *why* level, is only of secondary importance. In "what for" purposive inquiry, we keep expanding our reference base. This extension cannot go on freely, as indicated before, if an individual is disturbed by impingements from his senses. Apparently the function of our senses is to give us a standpoint in time and space so that we *can* act *after* we have decided *why* we should act.

Thus to return to Gandhi as an example, the function of prayer for him, and one of the functions of some of his fasts, was to sensitize himself to cues that could be taken into account in the process of value inquiry in order to achieve the most reliable and satisfying value judgment. He was trying to take into account a synthesized phenomenon which he could feel, rather than abstracted aspects of a phenomenon he could grasp intellectually. It was only *after* what Gandhi called his "instinct" had shown him a course of action was right that he tried to determine intellectually why it was right.

The resolution of a difficulty encountered on the *why* or *what for* level, and the consequences of action that follow, more likely than not involve some modification of our previous assumptions, some revision of our assumptive form world. Decisions involving purpose are peculiarly our own, since the value standards that compose so crucial a part of our assumptive form world constitute a complex of value assumptions unique to each of us. These decisions, therefore, involve both responsibility and opportunity. These interdependent responsibilities and opportunities are highly personal. They are products of our unique biological equipment participating in the culture unique to our own life history.

Judgments concerning *what for* and *why* are often disturbing or painful because the resolution of "what for" or "why" difficulties does involve a modification or revision of our assumptions. Hence, we may try to delay them or temporarily rationalize the dilemma away.

Practically all of us at times try to avoid—and usually unconsciously— many hitches on the purposive level of "what for." We do this by keeping ourselves busy, by pursuing only the means involved in earning a living, or by escape through overindulgence in entertainment, by overconcern with what we eat or wear, by escape through drink, or by rationalization. In some such cases, we are making the false assumption that solving hitches in the means will bring personal development. In other instances, we may be deliberately marking time in the hope that things will change and we can renew our pursuit of goals. Or in order to obtain some relief from the anguish of making such decisions, we may let other people make the decisions for us, possibly leaving the responsibility to God or to some charismatic leader. A prolonged inability of individuals to make these "what for" decisions themselves provides the psychiatrist with many of his patients and the political or religious leader with followers who are blindly devoted.

We get satisfaction in our experience only insofar as *we* are involved in *action* as well as in *judgment*. If there is no participation, no action on our part, there is no real satisfaction, no value attribute to our experience. It is our action only that can be registered in us and that can give some stability to or cause some revisions in our assumptive form world. And it is only through action that our value judgments have the possibility of being registered beyond ourselves, as was pointed out long ago in the parable of the Good Samaritan.

If our satisfaction is to be genuine, our action must be related to a "what for" reason. Otherwise, there is no assurance at all for the very existence of value standards. Real pioneers in any field seem to sense this. For example,

Charles Edison reports, "After an invention became a commercial success, father simply lost interest in it."

All our means of "how-to-do's" are related to some purpose, some "what for's," even though in many cases we may be quite unconscious of the purposive assumptions involved. It would seem that insofar as a person can obtain insight into the purposes that lie behind the means, he can experience what we label personal development, a "richer" life, emergent values.

If value standards are continually disregarded, then the means may become goals in themselves with a consequent "lowering" in the satisfyingness of experience, a "lowering" for which the experiencing individual may not be able to account. We can see examples of this in those who fish to win a prize, those who earn more money than they need to satisfy their wants simply in order to become rich, those who try to get a college degree for the sake of a degree, those who strive to live on a reputation after achieving some position that has prestige in their particular social group.

There is a submergence of an individual's capacity to make value decisions involving purposes insofar as he is coerced to do anything, insofar as force is a factor he must heed. Compulsion restricts the free flow of value inquiry. This necessarily means that the quality of satisfaction obtained in living will be "lower." Under compulsion a person is forced to worry about means, about "how-to-do's," and his consideration of purposes becomes dulled or restricted by fear, insecurity, intimidation, or the uncertainty that comes from being unable to test his own decisions in action.

As we have already said, value judgments are intensely personal and unique. Hence, freedom exists only insofar as an individual makes decisions on his own responsibility. This is an inalienable right, rooted in the very biological organization that characterizes human beings. If the possibility to make one's own choice does not exist, there is not true liberty but, rather, some degree of enslavement.

Also, insofar as an individual is freed from frustrations, for example by being protected by parents and others from encountering difficulties, he will be unable to experience personal growth in the sense of progressing from one value judgment to another value judgment that is more satisfying because it is more inclusive and provides a better bet for effective action in new situations.

A problem for every individual, or for every group or society or ideology, therefore, appears to be the problem of clarifying purposes and simplifying means. Clarification of purposes in terms of creating value standards that serve as effective and satisfying guides for action can be a never-ending process. And it is such for individuals who themselves surmount the continuing hitches or frustrations brought about by changing conditions. The process of value inquiry they engage in and test by action gives them increasingly adequate value judgments. Insofar as an individual becomes complacent and static in his own value judgments, then living becomes repetitious, loses its zest, and changing conditions bring increasing puzzlement or new searches for escape.

And it appears that only insofar as an individual "raises" the level of his purposes can he minimize the annoyances of life. Only then can discrimination be improved and means become simplified by being judged in terms of more inclusive purposes. In the *Bhagavad-Gita* there is a verse: "The wise should perform tasks without attachment, yet with as much ardor as the foolish, who are bound up in the results of their deeds—thus to the world shall they set an example."

The reality of faith

While it may be easy enough for us to realize intellectually that all of our own perceptions of objects and people, our prehension of the sequences which events may take, our purposes and our values, are only probabilities, in everyday life we cannot possibly act only on the basis of what might "probably" happen. We must, as Vaihinger noted, act *als ob*. We must make fixed assumptions, have certainties and beliefs. For example, as we carry on the process of living we have to assume that the chair which we are about to sit in *is* a chair; we have to assume that certain people *are* trustworthy; we have to assume that certain actions *are* the right actions to take. Throughout the whole process of living, then, we are continually engaged in the business of making certainties out of probabilities in order that we can act effectively to attain some value satisfactions. Thus objects and people become realities for us. Causal effects become realities for us. Purposive behavior becomes a reality for us. Our values and moral codes become realities for us. All of these become realities in concrete situations and must become such if we are to act at all. While our action in such concrete situations takes place in a milieu bounded by time and space, the values which carry us through this action transcend time and space. Yet they become real in our experience only insofar as we transact—as unique and responsible individuals endowed with the capacity to choose—within the environment around us.

In the same way, the symbols man has created to conceptualize his awarenesses and the behavioral patterns, such as rituals and ceremonies, that he sustains in order to "feel" value relationships, are realities from the point of view of the individual acting in his unique behavioral situation. Apart from the behaving individual acting in a concrete situation, these realities would not exist as such. But to deny them from the point of view of the experiencing person can lead only to chaos and ineffectual action.

The individual, then, becomes the focus of reality. And in creating our patterns of value and our moral codes, we seem constantly to be attempting to integrate more and more specific purposes which are themselves unconceptualized and undetermined.

Notes

1. I should like to acknowledge especially discussions with Adelbert Ames, Jr., Horace M. Kallen, C.H. Bumstead, and A.H. Hastorf in the develoment of the point of view expressed here. None of these men should, however, be held responsibile for this essay. I am also grateful to Dr. S.I. Hayakawa for his editorial suggestions.
2. This is, of course, by no means a new emphasis. It runs through William James and was clearly expressed by John Dewey in his memorable address in 1896: "The older dualism between sensation and idea is repeated in the current dualism of peripheral and central structures and functions; the older dualism of body and soul finds a distinct echo in the current dualism of stimulus and response. Instead of interpreting the character of sensation, idea and action from their place and function in the sensory motor circuit, we still incline to interpret the latter from our preconceived and preformulated ideas of rigid distinctions between sensations, thoughts and acts."

    In giving a list of ideas he rejects, Korzybski names, among others, "elementalism" which he defines as "the assumed sharp division of 'senses' *and* 'mind,' 'precept' *and* 'concept,' 'emotions' *and* 'intellect,' etc." (1948: 93). He proposes instead a "non-elementalistic theory of meanings" based on a "psycho-physiological theory of semantic reactions" of the "organism-as-a-whole" (pp. 107f., 189, 192, 243, 265 *passim*).

    The same point of view has been more recently elaborated by Dewey and Bentley (1949), who used the term "transactional" to refer to the relationship between the processes involved in human behavior in contradistinction to "interaction" and "self action" which have so affected much psychological thinking. While we have also used the term "transactional" as it is commonly employed in everyday life with reference to our interpersonal dealings, it is hardly inclusive enough for our purposes, chiefly because it leaves out the novel aspects of living. But for psychological description, however, the term "transactional" does seem useful in referring to the variables we describe below that are involved in the orchestration of man's experience and except for which there would be no real "transaction of living."
3. Henry A. Murray has pointed out: "Until theory has been much further developed we would be inclined to favour the use of clear literary language, despite the current tendency among American psychologists to become suspicious whenever there appears in the writings or speech of a fellow-scientist the slightest trace of aesthetic feeling. A psychologist who believes that he can tell the truth without being 'literary' has only to try writing a case history or biography, and then compare what he has done to a character sketch by any novelist of the first order. We academic psychologists have yet to discover how much can be learnt from the realists of literature. A little humility here would add to our stature" (1939: 608f.).
4. Quoted by permission of Oxford University Press.

References

Bridgman, P.W. 1954. The task before us. *Proc. Amer. Acad. Arts & Sci.* 83: 98.

Cantril, H. 1950. *The "why" of man's experience.* New York: Macmillan.

Dewey, J., and Bentley, A.F. 1949. *Knowing and the known.* Boston: Beacon Press.

Frank, J. 1953. Some tame reflections on some wild facts. In *Vision and action,* ed. S. Ratner, New Brunswick, N.J.: Rutgers University Press.

Fry, C. 1950. *The lady's not for burning.* New York: Oxford University Press.

Hayakawa, S.I. 1949. *Language in thought and action.* New York: Harcourt, Brace.

Kallen, H.M. 1953. Freedom, anxiety, and social process. In *Educational freedom in an age of anxiety,* ed. H.G. Hullfish. New York: Harper.

Korzybski, A. 1948. *Science and sanity: an introduction to non-Aristotelian systems and general semantics.* 3d ed. Lakeville, Conn.: Institute of General Semantics.

Murray, H.A. 1939. *Explorations in personality.* New York: Oxford University Press.

Price, L. 1954. *Dialogues of Alfred North Whitehead.* Boston: Little, Brown.

Whitehead, A.N. 1938. *Modes of thought.* New York: Macmillan.

7

The human design

With the mounting discussion of "existentialist" and "humanistic" psychology on both sides of the Atlantic, together with the search of political scientists for a psychological interpretation useful for their level of analysis, it seems appropriate to try to spell out what seem to be the demands human beings impose on any society or political culture because of their genetically build-in design. Furthermore, in bringing together recently in summary form the conclusions of a cross-national study of thirteen different countries, I kept realizing anew that in describing differences found among people, it is all too easy to neglect basic functional uniformities which take diverse forms and to leave the accounting or explanation at that level. Differences are often dramatic and easier to detect than the similarities they may obscure. Here I shall try to orchestrate the diversities of mankind found in different societies into some systematic unity.

The aspects of "human nature" differentiated here are those that seem to me to be pointed to by the data of psychology and by the observations sensitive observers have made of the way people live their lives in a variety of circumstances. I shall try to use a level of accounting appropriate both to an understanding of people and to an understanding of social and political systems. In doing this some of the absurdities may be avoided that result when a single man-made abstraction, usually devised to account for some single aspect of behavior, is the sole theme song. As the different characteristics of the human design are reviewed here, it must be recognized and emphasized that they all overlap, intertwine, and are interdependent. One must differentiate artificially in order to focus and describe.

1. *Man requires the satisfaction of his survival needs.* Any listing of the

This chapter is a somewhat revised version of the concluding chapter of H. Cantril, *The Pattern of Human Concerns* (New Brunswick, N.J.: Rutgers University Press, 1965). Reprinted by permission from the *Journal of Individual Psychology* 20 (Nov. 1964): 129-36.

characteristics of any living organism must begin here. Neurophysiologists have located and described in a most general way two built-in appetitive systems found in higher animals: one system propelling them to seek satisfying and pleasurable experiences, the other protecting them from threatening or unpleasant experiences (Cantril and Livingston 1963). These two systems together can be thought of as the basic forces contained within all human beings which not only keep them and the species alive as their simple survival needs for food, shelter, and sex are gratified, but that are involved in the desire for life itself.

These appetitive systems of course become enormously developed, refined, and conditioned, especially in man, as new ways are learned to achieve satisfactions and avoid dangers and discomforts. It has often been noted that unless the survival needs are satisfied, a person devotes himself almost exclusively to a continued attempt to fulfill them, a preoccupation which preempts his energies and repels any concern for other activities. Most people in the world today are still concerned with living a type of life that constitutes well-being on a relatively simple level with what amenities their cultures can provide.

2. *Man wants security both in its physical and its psychological meaning to protect gains already made and to assure a beachhead from which further advances may be staged.* Man wants some surety that one action can lead to another, some definite prehension which provides an orientation and integration through time. People invariably become embittered if they nurse a dream for what they regard as a long time with no signs of it becoming a reality.

In this connection it should be recalled that the story of evolution seems to tell us that members of every species stake out some territory for themselves within which they can provide for their needs and carry on their living, the extent of this territory being dependent on what is required for the survival of the species and being extended if it will contribute to such survival. In the present era the territories human beings stake out for themselves are largely bounded by the nation-state, a territorial unit rapidly replacing narrower geographical and psychological identifications but doing so just at the time when it is becoming more and more apparent that the concept of nation itself limits and threatens man's development in an age of increasing interdependence and highly developed weaponry.

3. *Man craves sufficient order and certainty in his life to enable him to judge with fair accuracy what will or will not occur if he does or does not act in certain ways.* People want sufficient form and pattern in life to be sure that certain satisfactions already enjoyed will be repeatable and will provide a secure springboard for takeoffs in new directions.

The conflict of old loyalties with emerging new loyalties in the case of developing people is bound to create uncertainties, doubts, and hesitations. If people become frustrated and anxious enough, they will do almost anything in a desperate attempt to put some order into apparent chaos or rally around new smbols and abstractions that enable them to identify with a new order that promises to alleviate the uncertainties experienced in the here and now.

In stressing process and change, the desire of people to preserve the status quo when it has proved satisfying and rewarding and to protect existing forms against alteration must never be overlooked. And the craving for certainty would include the satisfactions that come from the sense of stability provided by our habitual behavior—including much of our social and political behavior.

4. *Human beings continuously seek to enlarge the range and to enrich the quality of their satisfactions.* There is a ceaseless quest impelling man to extend the range and quality of his satisfactions through the exercise of his creative and inventive capacities. This is, of course, a basic reason why order of any kind is constantly being upset. Whitehead expressed the point eloquently and repeatedly, for example, in his statements "The essence of life is to be found in the frustrations of established order" (1938: 119) and "The art of progress is to preserve order amid change, and to preserve change amid order" (1929: 515).

The distinguished British philosopher John Macmurray has used the phrase *The Self as Agent* as the title of his book (1957) analyzing the role of action in man's constant search for value satisfactions. And in a companion volume he has noted that "Human behavior cannot be understood, but only caricatured, if it is represented as an adaptation to environment" (1961: 46). The search for an enlargement of satisfactions in the transactions of living can also be phrased as the *desire for development in a direction*, the desire to do something which will bring a sense of accomplishment as we experience the consequences of successfully carrying out some intention, and thereby have an occasional feeling that our lives are continuous creations in which we can take an active part. During a conversation in Beirut, a wise man once remarked to me that "people are hungry for new and good experiences."

It seems worthwhile to differentiate this search for value satisfactions into two varieties: *(a)* value satisfactions that are essentially new, different, more efficient, more reliable, more pleasurable, or more status-producing results of activity along familiar and tried dimensions, and *(b)* value satisfactions that are new in the sense of being emergent, a new quality a person discovers or creates himself for the first time as does the child who tries out and relishes new experiences as his own developmental pattern unfolds. The former variety, like the growth on the limb of a tree, builds people out and extends their range, while the latter, like the new growth at the top of the tree, lets them attain new heights and see new vistas. The satisfactions sought by a newly developing people are at first most likely to be of the former type.

The particular value satisfactions man acquires are the result of learning. Some of the values learned will serve as the operative ideals of a people, others will be chiefly instrumental. People in rich countries have learned to want and to expect many aspects of a good life that less favored people have not yet learned are possibilities. From this point of view one might say that the competition between social and political systems is a competition in teaching people what to want, what is potentially available to them, and then proving to them in their own private experience that these wants are best attainable under the system described.

5. *Human beings are creatures of hope and are not genetically designed to resign themselves.* This characteristic of man stems from the characteristic just described: that man is always likely to be dissatisfied and never fully "adapts" to his environment.

Man seems continually to hope that the world he encounters will correspond more and more to his vision of it as he acts within it to carry out his purposes, while the vision itself continuously unfolds in an irreversible direction. The whole process is a never-ending one. It is characteristic of man in his ongoing experience to ask himself "Where do I go from here?" Only in his more reflective moods does a person ask "Where did I come from?" or "How did I get this way?" Most of the time, most people who are plugged into the changing world around them are future-oriented in their concerns.

6. *Human beings have the capacity to make choices and the desire to exercise this capacity.* Any mechanical model of man constructed by a psychologist or by anyone else is bound to leave out the crucially important characteristic of man as an "appetitive-perceptive agency." Perceptions are learned and utilized by people to provide prognoses or bets of a variety of kinds to weigh alternative courses of action to achieve purposes. Consciously or without conscious awareness, people are trying to perceive the probable relation between their potential acts and the consequences of these acts to the intentions that constitute their goals.

The human nervous system, including the brain, has the capacity to police its input, to determine what is and what is not significant for it, and to pay attention to and to reinforce or otherwise modify its behavior as it transacts in the occasions of living (Cantril and Livingston 1963). In this sense, the human being is a participant in and producer of his own value satisfactions: People perceive only what is relevant to their purposes and make their choices accordingly.

7. *Human beings require freedom to exercise the choices they are capable*

of making. This characteristic of man related to freedom is deliberately worded as it is, rather than as a blanket statement that "Human beings require freedom," since the freedom people want is so relative to their desires and the stage of development they have attained. Human beings, incidentally, apparently require more freedom than other species of animals because of their much greater capacity to move about and to engage in a much wider variety of behavior.

While it seems true that maximum freedom is a necessary condition if a highly developed individual is to obtain maximum value satisfaction, it is equally true, as many people have pointed out, that too much freedom too soon can be an unbearable burden and a source of bondage if people, like children, are insufficiently developed to know what to do with it. For freedom clearly involves a learning of responsibility and an ability to take advantage of it wisely.

The concept of freedom is essentially a psychological and not a political concept. It describes the opportunity of an individual to make his own choices and act accordingly. Psychologically, freedom refers to the freedom to experience more of what is potentially available, the freedom to move about and ahead, to be and to become. Freedom is thus less and less determined and more of a reality as man evolves and develops; it emerges and flowers as people learn what it can mean to them in terms of resolving some frustrations under which they are living.

The authoritarian leadership sometimes required to bring about man's awakening and to start him on the road to his definition of progress appears to go against the grain of the human design once man is transformed into a self-conscious citizen who has the desire to exercise the capacity latent within him. The definition of freedom in the Soviet dictionary, *Ushakov*, as "the recognition of necessity" is limited to those periods in the life of an individual or a people when they are willing to let others define what is necessary and to submerge their own individuality.

8. *Human beings want to experience their own identity and integrity,* more properly referred to as the need for *personal dignity.* Every human being craves a sense of his own self-constancy, an assurance of the repeatability of experience in which he is a determining participant. He obtains this from the transactions he has with other individuals.

People develop significances they share with others in their membership and reference groups. If the satisfaction and significance of participation with others ceases to confirm assumptions or to enrich values, then a person's sense of self-constancy becomes shaken or insecure, his loyalties become formalized and empty or are given up altogether. He becomes alienated or seeks new significances, new loyalties that are more operationally real.

9. *People want to experience a sense of their own worthwhileness.* This

differentiation is made from the desire for personal identity and integrity to bring out the important relationship between this search for identity and the behavior and attitudes of others towards us. A human being wants to know he is valued by others and that others will somehow show through their behavior that his own behavior and its consequences make some sort of difference to them in ways that give him a sense of satisfaction. When this occurs, not only is a person's sense of identity confirmed, but he also experiences a sense of personal worth and self-respect. The process of extending the sense of Self both in space and in time appears also to involve the desire that one's "presence" shall not be limited merely to the here and now of existence but will extend into larger dimensions.

People acquire, maintain, and enrich their sense of worthwhileness only if they at least vaguely recognize the sources of what personal identity they have: from their family, their friends and neighbors, their associates or fellow workers, their group ties or their nations. The social, religious, intellectual, regional, or national loyalties formed play the important role of making it possible for individuals to extend themselves backward into the past, and forward into the future, and to identify themselves with others who live at more or less remote distances from them. This means the compounding of shared experiences into a bundle that can be conceptualized, felt, or somehow referred to in the here and now of daily living, thus making a person feel a functional part of a more enduring alliance. Man accomplishes such feats of self- extension largely through his capacity to create symbols, images, and myths which provide focal points for identification and self-expansion. After reviewing the lessons from history, Herbert Muller noted as one of the "forgotten simplicities" this fact: "Men have always been willing to sacrifice themselves for some larger cause, fighting and dying for their family, tribe, or community, with or without hope of eternal reward" (1954: 392).

10. *Human beings seek some value or system of beliefs to which they can commit themselves.* In the midst of the probabilities and uncertainties that surround them, people want some anchoring points, some certainties, some faith that will serve either as a beacon light to guide them or a balm to assuage them during the inevitable frustrations and anxieties living engenders.

People who have long been frustrated and who have searched for means to alleviate their situations are, of course, particularly susceptible to a commitment to a new system of beliefs or an ideology that they feel holds promise of effective action.

Beliefs are confirmed insofar as action based on them brings satisfying consequences and they are denied with growing skepticism if disastrous results consistently occur because they are followed.

Commitment to a value or belief system becomes more difficult among well-informed and sophisticated people who self-consciously try to reconcile what they believe with what they know and what they know with what they believe. In such circumstances, beliefs become more secular and less important as personal identifications.

11. *Human beings want a sense of surety and confidence that the society of which they are a part holds out a fair degree of hope that their aspirations will be fulfilled.* If people cannot experience the effectivity of social mechanisms to accomplish some of the potential goals they aspire to, then obviously their frustrations and anxieties mount, and they search for new means to accomplish aims. On the other hand, they make any sacrifice required to protect a society they feel is fulfilling their needs but appears seriously threatened.

It cannot be stressed too strongly that any people will become apathetic toward or anxious about ultimate goals they would like to achieve through social organizations if they continually sense a lack of reliability in the means provided to accomplish these goals. Obviously any society that is to be viable must satisfy basic survival needs, must provide security, must insure the repeatability of value satisfactions already attained, and, must provide for new and emerging satisfactions. The effective society is one that enables the individual to develop personal loyalties and aspirations which overlap with and are congenial to social values and loyalties, and which at the same time take full account of the wide range of individual differences that exist.

Such a social organization must, too, become the repository of values, must provide symbols for people's aspirations, must comprise and contain customs, institutions, laws, economic arrangements, and political forms which enable an individual in various ways to give concrete reference to his values in his day-to-day behavior. If the gap between what his society actually provides in terms of effective mechanisms for living and what it purports to provide becomes too great, the vacuum created will sooner or later engender the frustrations that urge people on to seek new social patterns and new symbols. Whitehead wrote:

> The major advances in civilization are processes which all but wreck the societies in which they occur—like unto an arrow in the hand of a child. The art of free society consists first in the maintenance of the symbolic code; and secondly in fearlessness of revision, to secure that the code serves those purposes which satisfy an enlightened reason. Those societies which cannot combine reverence to their symbols with freedom of revision, must ultimately decay either from anarchy, or from the slow atrophy of a life stifled by useless shadows. [1927: 88]

Every social and political system can be regarded as an experiment in the broad perspective of time. Whatever the experiment, the human design will in the long run force any experiment to accommodate it. This has been the case throughout human history. And few would deny that the varied patterns of experiments going on today hold out more promise of satisfying the human condition for a greater number of people than ever before.

References

Cantril, H., and Livingston, W.K. 1963. Concept of transaction in psychology and neurology. *J. Indiv. Psychol.* 19: 3-16.
Macmurray, J. 1957. *The self as agent.* New York: Harper.
_____. 1961. *Persons in relation.* London: Faber & Faber.
Muller, H.J. 1954. *The uses of the past.* New York: Mentor.
Whitehead, A.N. 1927. *Symbolism: its meaning and effect.* New York: Macmillan.
_____. 1929. *Process and reality.* New York: Macmillan.
_____. 1938. *Modes of thought.* New York: Macmillan.

III
Psychology in the humanistic realm

8

Toward a scientific morality

Many of us in the human sciences feel that we must assume our share of responsibility for the solution of problems we see reflected in the many varieties of group tension around us. Those of us who do feel this way are apt at the same time to feel frustrated because of our inability to make any demonstrable dent on the course of affairs. And many of us who share these feelings may not have adequately intellectualized to ourselves why it is that we believe we, as self-appointed experts on this thing called "human nature," are in a position to help decide what is "right" and what is "wrong."[1]

The psychologist who takes it upon himself to study man in his social environment may in part avoid a feeling of helpless frustration if he gains some perspective on his role in the current world scene. And if he is to act with any degree of surety he must have some plausible and valid rationale to justify his assumption that he has something to contribute. We shall be concerned here, then, with these two problems: gaining perspective and pointing to a systematic basis for judging what is "good" and "bad" for man's nature.

Man in evolutionary perspective

I can think of no better springboard for gaining some perspective on our own jobs as social scientist–citizens than to refer to the series of essays written by Julian Huxley. In his book *Evolution and Ethics*, he points out that "biological or organic evolution has at its upper end been merged into and largely succeeded by conscious or social evolution" (Huxley and Hux-

Originally presented in expanded form as "The Development of a Scientific Morality," presidential address, before the Society for the Psychological Study of Social Issues, Boston, Sept. 6, 1948. Reprinted by permission from *The Journal of Psychology* 27 (1949): 363-76.

ley 1947: 122). He continues that "there are grounds for suspecting that biological evolution has come to an end, so far as any sort of major advance is concerned" (123). The obvious conclusion, then, which this socially minded biologist draws is that "it is only through social evolution that the world-stuff can now realize radically new possibilities" (123).

Huxley goes on to point out what the comparative psychologist would confirm, that man alone is the only part of the "world-stuff" where mental conflict is a normal and important part of life. Translating the implications of this statement into psychological terms, I should like to venture again the thesis that while all organisms appear to have an urge to live and grow, man's unique set of conflicts basically derive from a unique, emergent pattern of growth subjectively characterized by a desire for development.

Even though this hypothesis may seem quite fanciful to many psychologists, it is comforting to discover that it does not appear completely outrageous to a number of outstanding biologists. For example, C. Judson Herrick has written "the thing that is most distinctive about man is the pattern of his growth and the instrumentation of it by a rationally directed desire for improvement."[2] This emergent characteristic of man is, of course, enormously instrumented by man's unique higher mental processes, his use of symbols and concepts, his ability for rational thinking, intuition, and foresight.

This unique pattern of man's growth constantly jeopardizes his security, creates frustration, and necessitates choice. I submit that one of the most common denominators that runs through all of man's choice is the conflict between what we may call "security" including physical well-being ("form") on the one hand, and "development" ("flow") on the other. "Development" in the sense I am using it is possible only with the attainment of security, of some "form" in social life, the pursuit of knowledge and all cultural activities. The desire for improvement requires first of all that the organism have security. For there can be no direction unless we have a base from which to get direction. In terms of the way "security" is obtained in our culture today, this means a secure job, a decent standard of living, health and old-age benefits, etc.

It is a relatively simple matter to describe psychologically the way men in different societies learn to satisfy in derived ways the instinctual urges and tension systems that make for security, including physical well-being. It is also a relatively simple matter to account for the enormously varied ways of obtaining this security to be found in different cultural groups.

Current attempts to account for man's motivation solely in terms of the "reduction of tension" seem to me completely inadequate if we are going to "explain" the many situations in which men's satisfactions and happiness are actually related to an increase, not a decrease, in the state of "tension," such as exists, for example, when one undertakes a new task or strives to meet new levels of aspiration. No matter how much such theories are strained and enlarged, they somehow fail to bring in the pull of expectancies as well as the push of the existing "tensions." The only way out, I think, is to jump to a different, a "higher," order of accounting which must include man's desire to develop and his capacity to experience value quality. Once this is done, "tension" can be understood; the "now" in which the organism finds itself can be seen as indissolubly related to the past and the future; and clarification of the reasons for actions which seem to increase, rather than decrease, "tensions" becomes possible.

This is not the place to discuss this particular thesis at length. I can only indicate here my current feeling that man's characteristic pattern of growth, as laid down in his chromosome activity, constantly forces him to choose between various alternative possible courses of action. And concomitant with the development of the higher mental processes characteristic of man, there emerges the possibility of increased conflict as well as the possibility of increased conscious choice. And, as Huxley points out, the fact that man alone among all organisms is subject to mental conflict as a normal factor in life means that "the existence of this conflict is the necessary basis or ground on which conscience, the moral sense, and our systems of ethics grow and develop" (Huxley and Huxley 1947: 2).

In other words, ethics and morality are emergent coproducts of life when seen from the long perspective of evolution.

We must remember, of course, that ethics and morality emerge not only with the human species as such, but emerge afresh in each specific individual human being and that the code of ethics a particular human being acquires is relative to the group loyalties to which he is exposed and is dependent on the situation in which the child or the adult finds himself.

The social scientist must also remember that a system of ethics and a code of morality are not only emergent coproducts of man's evolution but become themselves directive agencies in the evolutionary process itself. Huxley points out that "just as biological evolution was rendered both possible and inevitable when material organization became self-reproducing, so conscious evolution was rendered both possible and inevitable when social organization became self-reproducing" (Huxley and Huxley 1947: 122). When that portion of the "world-stuff" we know as "man" emerged with its capacity to use concepts, to manipulate symbols, to communicate over a distance, and to write its own history, then it also acquired the capacity to plan its own social and economic life for the future. It therefore acquired unique responsibility.

What this means, then, if we are to stick to a naturalistic explanation, is that a system of ethics, a code of morality, is not something based on a priori generalizations, on causal speculations, or on wish-fulfillments. It means that social scientists have a major responsibility in searching for the laws of the moral world just as physical scientists have searched for the laws of the physical world.

Causal relationships are inherent in all natural processes. If this were not so, then nature, including man and his social behavior, would be completely chaotic. Any system of ethics, any code of morality, can have a scientific basis only insofar as we can arrive at causal explanations. In this connection we must remember that because two phenomena are related to each other there is not necessarily a causal connection between them. Many relationships are not causal. In a causal relationship there is always some effect determined by the intrinsic organization of the situation under observation.

The psychologist and the social scientist must also constantly bear in mind the fact that the material they deal with—the human organism in its social environment—is infinitely more complex than the material dealt with by the physical scientist. For example, a neurologist has pointed out that "our bodies think as naturally as they breathe and if we do not yet understand *how* we understand, the thing to do is to try to find out" (Herrick 1946: 40).

> The human brain is the most complicated structural apparatus known to science. If all the equipment of the telegraph, telephone, and radio of the North American continent could be squeezed into a half-gallon cup, it would be less intricate than the three pints of brain that fill your skull and mine. More than half of this brain tissue is cerebral cortex and parts immediately dependent upon it. The most ungifted normal man has twice as much of this matter tissue as the most highly educated chimpanzee. [Herrick 1939: 107]

This fact can also comfort us for our lack of success as we grope always somewhat unsatisfactorily for causal explanations of human behavior. It is important to stress the complexity of the task facing the social scientist who searches for causal explanations, so he will be continually dissatisfied with any conceptual structure, any system of ethics, any code of morality, or any social organization based on any assumptions or condoning any practices which go against what facts we have to date about human nature and social relationships.

In other words, the multitude of factors inherent in any concrete human situation, insofar as they are known, must be taken into account and squarely faced by anyone who assumes the responsibility for molding social organizations or for making any pronouncements as to what is right and wrong, good or bad, for human beings. But as the statement issued by the Preparatory Commission of the International Congress on Mental

Health pointed out: "There is, however, all the difference between recognizing that a task has immense difficulties, and insisting that it is impossible" (International Congress on Mental Health 1948: 28).

So far we have pointed out that man seems to be the only organism in which conflict and choice in any moral sense are part of the normal processes of life. We have pointed out that man's mental capacities enormously increase the range of choice and at the same time impose on man the responsibility of guiding his own destiny. We have pointed out the possibility of creating a morality based on empirical evidence and that this is a job enormously complicated by the very nature of the material with which we deal. Our problem now is that of finding some toehold, some reference point, upon which we can begin to build a scientific morality.

Perception and value judgment

I submit that this reference point can be found in what we may call, for want of a better term, the phenomenon of value judgment. Although any such term may be rejected by those who think science should not use words that have a philosophical ring. I believe the history of science would indicate that when value judgments are excluded from science, any datum becomes inert and useless, any abstraction becomes futile and without functional significance.

From the point of view of the problem of morality we are considering here, it is noteworthy that biologists such as Huxley, Leo Loeb, J.B.S. Haldane, and others deliberately place values in the forefront of their thinking when they begin to discuss, as scientists, the implications of man's peculiar capacity for his continued social existence. To quote Huxley again: "We find values not merely emerging from the evolutionary process, but playing an active part in its latest phase; we know as an immediate and obvious fact that there are higher and lower values; we discover as a result of scientific analysis that there are more or less desirable or valuable directions in evolution" (Huxley and Huxley 1947: 32).

Whether we like to admit it or not, nearly all of our experiences are tinged with a value quality more or less intensely felt. Whether we like to admit it or not, the type of conflict that characterizes the human being is one he resolves by means of a value judgment. Whether the scientist likes to admit it or not, any interpretation he makes is a value judgment. And whether or not the psychologist likes to admit it, any psychology that does not include introspection and the analysis of one's own experience in making value judgments is helplessly inadequate.

It is because of my own value judgment that psychology has by now accumulated sufficient evidence relating to the nature of the process of value judgment that I dare to discuss the development of a scientific morality. For it does seem to me that the psychologist who studies the experiencing organism can now feel equipped in a very modest way to throw some light on the nature of value judgment and, through his knowledge of the process itself, reach certain conclusions as to what value judgments are "good," what value judgments are "bad." The psychologist, now, should be able to go a step further than do those who say that anything that promotes "higher values" such as knowledge, love, or beauty is ethically "right."

On the basis of evidence from experimental psychology, particularly the evidence from the phenomena revealed in the demonstrations of Adelbert Ames, Jr., of the Hanover Institute, I believe it is safe to say that every perception is in itself a value judgment process. For it appears that even the simplest perception, for example the perception of a star point, depends upon a whole host of indications that are weighed and integrated to give us our final awareness. In most of our perceptions, of course, this weighing process goes on quite unconsciously. And as the stimuli from outside become more and more complicated, running for example from star points to lines to three-dimensional objects to a newspaper headline or to participation in a race riot, the number of factors which must be integrated runs into many, many thousands. This weighing process is, of course, not only extremely complicated but it goes on in most cases with amazing rapidity.

The weighing process is the process of value judgment and the end result is our perception, our attitude, our interpretation, in brief, the value judgment we make.

It also seems to be a fact that perceptions are conceived and given birth to in purposeful action, that the weighing process, the process of value judgment, goes on for a purpose, whether that purpose is seeking food, crossing a street, accepting some political ideology, or satisfying in any other way our desire for emergence and improvement.

All of our perceptions have in them implicitly an awareness of the probable consequences the externality related to a stimulus might have on our purposes if we should act to carry out those purposes. We test out our hunch of what the externality related to a stimulus really is, what it really means, through action. For nearly any given perception can be created by an infinite variety of external stimuli and we must learn the reliability of a perception through experiencing its consequences in action.

If we don't act on our perceptions they become atrophied; if we do act on our perceptions, if our actions invariably meet with high success, they become enduring possibilities for choice. Perceptions which have given us a high prognosis for carrying out our purposes in the past provide us with a subjective feeling of surety; those which do not give us a high prognosis create lack of surety and anxiety.

The evidence from developmental, experimental, clinical, and social psychology indicates that one is only able to carry out his purposes by acquiring more accurate and effective perceptions through experiencing and resolving frustrations.

Value quality

An individual's own awareness as to whether a perception is "right" or "wrong" is the value quality[3] an experience has for him and for him alone. The sense of "higher" value quality of one perception over another is due to the more reliable prognosis of the perception with the "higher" value quality for carrying out a purpose. A hungry man may give up food that finally is within his grasp if, by so doing, he can relieve the hunger of a child; a research chemist may refuse a highly paid industrial position in favor of maintaining an academic position which he feels in the long run will further his own personal growth.

No amount of "logical reasoning" can act as a substitute for the judgment of what is "right" as given by the experienced value quality of a perception. For logical reasoning does not take into account nearly as many factors as does a value judgment. We are all aware, for example, of the difference in the behavior of someone whose good manners are "bred into him" and the behavior of someone who tries to do what is right by consciously following Emily Post.

Our world of assumptions

A perception may be defined as an implicit awareness of the probable consequence an action might have for us with respect to carrying out some purpose that has value for us. Every perception is based on assumptions. These assumptions are largely unconscious and nonintellectual. They come into being in the process of adjustment and development. When taken together they constitute a person's assumptive world.

It has been pointed out above that the accuracy and effectiveness of our perceptions are only improved when we experience and resolve a frustration which has resulted from the inadequacy of a perception in providing an effective guide to action. Since the adequacy of perceptions is also determined by the nature of the assumptions on which they are based, and since these assumptions are generally unconscious and nonintellectual, instances constantly arise when our perceptions prove to be unreliable and "wrong," due to inadequate assumptions. We therefore face the problem, usually without being aware of it, as to whether our assumptions really are unreliable and wrong or whether they may not be reliable after all in terms of our long-range purposes no matter how much we are temporarily frustrated, blocked, or disillusioned by specific experiences.

Here we are dealing essentially with a partial analysis of what is referred to as "faith." The greatness of individuals is known by history and less frequently by contemporaries in terms of their ability to weigh the ultimate reliability of these out-of-time-and-space assumptions against the momentary unreliability and reverses given by the here-and-now experiences. A common denominator of great political and religious leaders (a Lincoln or Lenin, Jesus or Gandhi) seems to be their capacity to make a value choice in which more weight is given to the soundness of long-range assumptions than to the frustration of immediate experience.

Social perception

Before considering the implications of this interpretation of perception for the development of a scientific morality, it is necessary to say a word about what has been called "social perception." This term, used by Woodworth over two decades ago, has recently become very popular. I believe the term "social perception" can be a useful term for psychologists *if* they do not employ it loosely as a mere analogy and *if* they remember that in making a distinction between "perception" and "social perception" there is no implication whatever of any inherent difference between the underlying psychological principles involved.

The essential characteristic in any perception we may label "social" is that the situation giving rise to the stimulus includes other organisms with purposes of their own which have the potentiality of affecting our purposes and being affected by us. Since this potentiality is our own awareness, this means that the adequacy of our perception is dependent on our capacity to perceive and be aware of the purpose of other organisms.

We can label as "social perceptions" all those perceptions where there is the possibility of a mutual interaction of purposes. And although a "social perception" as used here has nothing to do with the inherent nature of the source of the stimulus as such, nevertheless, for most of us, what we can label our "social perceptions" involve other people whose purposes have a potential influence on our purposes while the carrying-out of our purposes has a potential influence on others.

Since man's specific purposes are largely derived from the group loyalties he acquires, what may be "social perceptions" for some people are not "social perceptions" for others. Ethnology is filled with examples.

Because social perceptions in this sense involve a potential reciprocal reaction of purposes, they are especially characterized by affective or emotional overtones.

Since the functional activity giving rise to what we label a "social perception" has an important characteristic or attribute not part of a "nonsocial perception," the content of those perceptions we may call "social" is likely to be of vastly more significance and importance to the social scientist and to the individual in his daily life than is the content of most "nonsocial perceptions."[4] Something new has been added—the potential purposes of something else that we must take into account in the weighing process that results in a value judgment. This also means that a "social perception" generally has much greater complexity than a "nonsocial perception."

Judging what is "right"

From the point of view developed so far, any action can be called "right" if, through past experience, it has proved highly effective in carrying out a purpose, in checking a prognosis. It is imperative, however, to remember that because of the reciprocal influence of the purposes of one individual or group on the purposes of another individual or group, actions will prove effective in the long run only when the purposes common to individuals or individuals as members of groups are included in perception. Since perceptions are our own creations, we have the possibility and the opportunity of trying to make them efficient.

Although this is a pragmatic approach, it should be clear that this formulation so extends the consideration of what makes for effective action that it is by no means synonymous to the pragmatism of James. "Effectiveness" of the type considered here is based on the emergence of value quality which takes into account the community of human purposes. This completely rules out the effectiveness of a Mussolini, a Hitler, a ruthless (but "successful" in worldly terms) exploiter of human or natural resources.

If our actions consistently show that our perception is wrong, we may still, however, cling to these wrong perceptions, as we do with a prejudice or some other abstraction. The "right" perception, the one that gives higher prognosis, hasn't yet got "in" us—probably because the wrong perception hasn't sufficiently thwarted us in carrying out our purposes, or hasn't made us aware of the inadequacy of our underlying assumptions.

Sometimes these "wrong" perceptions actually appear to be helping us carry out some more deep-seated purposes—as with the anti-Semitism which was part of the Nazis' successful rise to power, the prejudices toward the Negroes of Southern whites who thereby maintain their position, etc.

But "wrong" perceptions such as these which may be useful from the short-time point of view are bound to prove themselves false and to create difficulty from the long-time point of view. Continued experience will show that such perceptions have not included enough factors (viz., the purposes of others) to make them reliable prognoses. Attempts to stamp out Communism by legal means only, while doing too little, too late to remedy the conditions upon which Communism thrives, is a case in point.

However, it is apparently true that in all such cases, these "wrong" perceptions prevent the emergence of higher value-inquiry judgments that experientially accompany more advanced development of the pattern of growth. And, when these "wrong" perceptions do not take into account the purposes of other human beings, history shows that they inevitably breed frustration and counteraction which eventually forces an alteration, a correction of the perception. We are all familiar with studies which show that prejudices are dropped only when conflicting purposes evaporate, that is, white troops during World War II were found to drop their Negro prejudices largely insofar as they fought side by side with Negro troops against a common enemy; there is a striking absence of labor management disputes in the TVA, etc. In such instances there are clear common purposes, neither group sees the other as a threat to its own purposes.

One reason for the decline of certain institutions, ideologies, or groups is that they gradually or suddenly fail to provide individuals with potentialities for effective action in carrying out purposes; they outlive the original functions they serve. For example, to the extent that the factor of action involved in the wisdom of the prophets is left out by organized and formalized religion, it fails to accomplish its professed purposes. And what is often described as the "poverty" of a civilization refers to that state of affairs where the values that characterize that civilization, the abstractions it sets as its goals or uses as its symbols, do not have the potentiality of being connected with action for carrying out the present emergent development. Likewise public "apathy" to problems experts may call "crucial" such, for example, as the control of atomic energy, can be accounted for by the fact that the average citizen even though quite aware of the dangers in the misuse of atomic power, sees no effective way in which he can act to do anything about the existing situation.

A criterion for social change should be that it provides the possibility of acquiring nonconflicting loyalties. For if individual purposes and group, class, or national purposes do not include the purposes of other individuals, groups, classes, or nations, conflict is inevitable. Hence all reform, social changes, artistic expressions, etc., that will prove to be springboards for further developments and not mere compromises, blind alleys, or cruel illusions will be those that provide the potentiality for development through action of all human beings, not for any one special group, race, nation, class, etc.

The "morality" or "ethical" nature—the correctness or rightness—of any action, then, is to be judged in terms of the degree to which it includes and integrates the purposes and provides for the potential development of those purposes of all other people concerned in the action or possibly affected by it. In this way, the "effectiveness" of an action and its inclusion of a common denominator of relevant purposes becomes inseparable. Emerging personal goals must be in harmony with emerging social goals while still emerging on the concrete individual level. From this point of view, the "rightness" or "morality" of an action becomes inseparable from its effectiveness. This is essentially the ethics of all great prophets with their emphasis on charity.

Individual liberty for men in any group or society, then, means that they must acquire overlapping rather than divergent or conflicting loyalties to those persons they are dependent on. For under modern conditions of living our independence increases with our interdependence.

But this does not imply blind tolerance. Tolerance is a virtue very likely to defeat itself. We are likely to be tolerant only when we are ignorant of what is the right thing to do. Tolerance must not be confused with charity, which is a willingness to take account of the other fellow's purposes. What I am saying, simply, is that "what is right" means what is right for man's nature. This is not compromise, which always involves some submergence, but growth through a nonconflicting interaction of purposes.

Change

We must also remember that no matter what code of morality we might work out today on the basis of all evidence at hand, this code should itself never be considered as static or fixed. There are no fixed prescriptions.

Many of you will remember the story of the ancient king who in his last years called together his three wise men and told them he wanted an epitaph that could be chiseled on his stone tomb and would consist of a statement which would forever be true. After long counsel the wise men reported back to their king with the recommendation that he have on his tomb the phrase "Everything changes." It is a most encouraging sign to see that the report of the Preparatory Commission of the International Mental Health Congress takes full cognizance of this fact.

Any viable system of ethics must be so designed that it will not only be sensitive to change but will provide for change. For to be set against change is to go against all the rules of nature and of human nature. Nothing in nature is static and least of all, apparently, anything man has any connection with. Through his discoveries and his technological improvements man is always transforming the world around him.

Anyone who argues for the return of the good old days or who expects life and the world to somehow settle down to a determined form is completely unrealistic, not plugged in to concreteness. Those prophets of doom whom we encounter in every generation are essentially people who are unable to accept the fact that the world is changing because the world created by their assumptions is a static one. What my Princeton predecessor, J.M. Baldwin, many years ago called "the dialectic of personal growth" is constantly going on with new emerging social conditions creating new value experiences for the individual and forcing him to new value judgments. It should also be pointed out that the process of evolution, including social evolution, is essentially a one-way street. There is no going back to an earlier set of conditions.

At the present time it is quite clear that we are in what Huxley has called "a rudimentary and make-shift stage of social evolution" (Huxley and Huxley 1947: 135f.). The assumptive worlds most of us live in are pragmatic approximations not necessarily consistent with effective long-range action. Hence they can retard the emergence of more adequate perceptions with a higher prognostic reliability and a higher, experiential value quality.

The role for the social scientist

There is no fundamental difference in the process of value judgment or interpretation between the physical scientist and the social scientist whether they deal with atoms, nerve conduction, or everyday social behavior. The difference between them is merely a difference in the complexity of the value judgment process required in reaching higher-order abstractions or explanations.

There can be no such thing as "impartiality" for any social scientist who is in the stream of things, any more than there can be pure "objectivity" for any scientist who is more than a recorder. Any interpretation is a value judgment and any pretense of impartiality is more than likely to lead only to social irresponsibility.

Since the social scientist is likely to be criticized by those whose purposes differ from his own, it is particularly essential for him to try to include his own purposes as well as the purposes of the people he is analyzing as conscious factors in his value judgments. And since it can be the responsibility of social scientists to make value judgments concerning what social action is "right" and what social action is "wrong," it must also be their responsibility as scientists to be as sure as they can that their value judgments are really based on all the knowledge of human nature available to them.

If this knowledge includes the facts concerning the nature of perception and value judgment, something more than mere amendments to present formulations will be required. The social scientist today, I believe, should try to accomplish a radical shift in his thinking. Real progress in any science comes not merely by "adding to" existing knowledge but by becoming aware of our assumptive worlds, conscious of their inadequacy, destroying and disintegrating them, and then rebuilding them in the constant search for more adequate formulations.

Notes

1. Some of the points stressed in this chapter were first published in Cantril 1941, 1947. I should like to express again here my indebtedness to Adelbert Ames, Jr., for stimulating discussions from which much included here emerged.
2. Communication to the author, 1947.
3. The very brief discussions of "value quality" and "our world of assumptions" are included here only to open up points of view that seem to have an intrinsic reasonableness in helping us understand social behavior. Although experimental work now in progress at The Hanover Institute and at Princeton seems to be turning up supporting scientific evidence for these formulations, the treatment here is in no sense meant to be inclusive or final.
4. If this formulation of the problem had been made in Külpe's time, I suspect we would be somewhat further along in our understanding of social behavior and might have been spared the artificial division that has so often separated "experimental" from "social" psychology and that has been reflected from time to time in a mutual lack of appreciation of the problem and research that constitute the other fellow's area.

References

Cantril, H. 1941. *Psychology of social movements*. New York: Wiley.
_____. 1947. *Understanding man's social behavior: Preliminary notes*. Princeton: Princeton University Office of Public Opinion Research.
_____. 1948. Nature of social perception. *Trans. N.Y. Acad. Sci.* 10: 142–53.
Herrick, C.J. 1939. *A neurologist makes up his mind*. Mellon Lecture. Pittsburgh: University of Pittsburgh School of Medicine.
_____. 1946. World federation in embryo. *The Humanist* 6: 40ff.
Huxley, J., and Huxley, T.H. 1947. *Evolution and ethics*. London: Pilot Press.
International Congress on Mental Health. 1948. Statement by International Preparatory Commission. London.

9

Ethical relativity from the transactional point of view

The invitation to prepare a paper for the consideration of professional philosophers is one a psychologist accepts only with utmost humility. At the same time, it is most encouraging if philosophers feel a psychologist might have something worthwhile to contribute to a problem so intimately related to the value aspect of human living. Perhaps psychology is beginning to break away from the mechanistic determinism which has so often fenced it in.

My consideration of the subject assigned must necessarily be from a point of view within psychology which seems to me most intrinsically reasonable.[1] I shall not, therefore, discuss in eclectic fashion the way the subject could be handled by different "schools" of psychology.

In order to understand the function of morality and of ethical systems in operation, we must approach the subject the way we must approach any other aspect of man's living—from the personal behavioral center of an individual who is experiencing and behaving in the concreteness of here-and-now situations.

Some tenets of transactional psychology

In order to give us a toehold on our main problem, it is necessary to sketch here very briefly some of the formulations of transactional psychology itself.[2] Most of these formulations can, we believe, be demonstrated in the psychological laboratory. They stem from our consideration of the nature of perception—a process of human behavior somewhat amenable

Prepared for presentation in a symposium on "Ethical Relativity in the Light of Recent Developments in Social Science" at the meeting of the American Philosophical Association, Eastern Division, Dec. 28, 1955. Reprinted by permission from *The Journal of Philosophy* 52, no. 23 (Nov. 10, 1955): 677-87.

to research and a problem area which, if we throw away some traditional blinders, plunges us at once into the nature of human experience in general.

Perception, according to this view, is a prognostic directive for purposeful action—not a "subjective" reaction to an "objective" given whether the "given" be an "object," a person, or a verbal symbol. The significance of any sensory impingement, of any "given" from the environment, stems from what an individual learns from his past experience in carrying out his purposeful behavior. Every perception, then, involves some degree of probability, some bet that what is "out there" corresponds to what we assume is "out there." Our perceptions of objects, people, symbols, ideologies, are all, in part, our own creations in that we view them from our own unique personal behavioral centers according to our own purposes.

From the transactional point of view, all that an individual can be aware of is his own interpretation of the importance to him of his ongoing behavioral situation in terms of the significances of prior behavioral situations. "Significance" is sensed in terms of experiencing the consequences of action intended to preserve physical well-being, to insure the repetition of previously satisfying experiences, or to enhance the value satisfaction potentially available from a situation. If our purposes are such that we might make use of any object, person, or symbol, or if any of these threaten our well-being, we take account of their possible use or their sequential significance to us. The sequential significance of some objects, people, or symbols in our field of potential experience may be of the greatest importance to us, while others may be trivial or of no importance whatever. Our awareness is like an enveloping aura protecting us and directing our purposeful action.

The significance of an object, a person, a symbol, or an ethical standard is identical from time to time—remains constant—only when it has the same sequential significance to us for carrying out the same purposes and is in the same functional position relative to our behavioral center.[3] We can carry out our purposes only because of the constancy we assign to our "objective" worlds. Constancy therefore refers to the relative continuation of conditions that enable us to carry out our purposes. It does not refer to objective characteristics themselves.

The degree of our sense of reality of our objective world is based on this constancy—not in constancy for constancy's sake but because constancy insures a higher probability for effective purposeful action. This belief is, of course, supported by the commonly shared aspects of our personal objective worlds. It is perhaps because of the high probability of the conceptually abstracted scientific world of objects that we think of this world as the ultimately real.

In order to get a greater degree of constancy and repeatability in the universe, man introduces artifacts which have definite specifications built in. A major aim of scientific endeavor is to humanize, not to conquer, an essentially neutral nature and thereby to increase the reliability with which one event of some consequence to man in carrying out his purposes will follow another event involving some specified human participation. In order to get a greater degree of constancy in his social life, man creates rules of the game, he introduces mores, rituals, customs, laws, standards. "Culture" is essentially a common pattern of learned significances.

If a person has to pay primary attention to the impingements of the here and now in trying to figure out *how* to do something by taking into account the potential significances around him, he is less able to be aware of these constancies that operate irrespective of space and time and that furnish the standards of what to do something *for* anyway. The latter—value inquiry—seems to involve very different processes than those we describe as "intellectual," "rational," or "logical" and which we put to use in common sense and in scientific method. Value inquiry—which aims to give us an understanding of the here and now in terms of more inclusive constants in our total reality—seems better described by such words as "meditation," "contemplation," "communion," or "prayer." Freedom from here-and-now pressures and demands is essential for value inquiry.

In using the word "inquiry," I am, of course, implying that a characteristic of human beings is their capacity to choose. From the transactional point of view, the process of choice involves a conscious weighing by a unique person in a unique behavioral situation in a universe where the future is undetermined. This awareness is to be differentiated from those weighing processes constantly involved on the unconscious level. These weighings are brought about by some obstacle or frustration encountered. The individual alone is responsible for his selection. Choice—as a process—further involves the initiation by action of some sequential events that will lead to the consequences desired, together with the registered effect of the occurrences that follow action. Choice is, of course, not entirely "free" but limited to certain alternatives that appear to be relevant to the situation. And the causal role a person plays in determining the choice he makes—his degree of responsibility—depends upon the extent of the various significances he takes into account or orchestrates in formulating his judgment. Individuals, then, as "causal" factors have, we say, a responsibility to behave to the best of their abilities. If they are sufficiently sensitized to their consciences, they do not need to make choices. But most of us, most of the time, seem faced by obstacles or frustrations of one kind or another that bubble into awareness and call for decision.

Since perception involves such a high degree of probability and since we must, nevertheless, act on the basis of some assumed constancies if we are to carry on at all in life, it is a characteristic of man that he develops what we call "faith." Faith appears to play a role in living when we experience a lack of surety concerning the present, when we are unable to accept the past, or when we are apprehensive about the future—all conditions where our sense of the reliabilities of some constancies is shaken. St. Paul's analysis that "faith is the substance of things hoped for; the evidence of things not seen" can perhaps be rephrased, if less eloquently, by saying that faith is a matter of hanging on to certain constancies in our own reality systems. Faith is a value sense of the worthwhileness of a reality system which transcends the boundary of time with whatever vicissitudes the present may hold.

Such, in brief, are some of the aspects of experience except for which human experience would not be what it is. Experience, then, has implicated within it: some impingements from the environment, physiological sensory processes, learned significances that have somehow become registered in us from the consequences of our past action, assumptions of constancy concerning both inorganic and organic events, choice, purposeful action, value satisfaction, some degree of faith. All of these aspects are interdependent. Hence, as any philosopher recognizes, we have borrowed the term "transaction" from Dewey and Bentley to describe experience in an attempt to rid ourselves of a universe bifurcated into "subjective" and "objective," and to avoid the oversimplification that comes from regarding different aspects of experience as discrete.

Our sense of what is real

Before we can fully proceed with the problem of ethical relativity from the transactional view, we must squarely face the question of what "reality" is, anyway. For we cannot pretend to have a workable psychology unless we account for the observable fact that values are just as "real" as mountains, chairs, or automobiles for a behaving individual.

Although "reality" is ineffable in the last analysis, from the transactional view of a nonbifurcated world, reality includes all of the phenomena involved in the ongoing process of living.

It may be useful to differentiate between different aspects of reality. First, there are those significances we are aware of and that we take into account from our personal, operational behavior centers. Such awarenesses are uniquely individual because of the uniqueness of every person and of every behavioral situation. These personal significances can be shared by others only to the extent that others have participated in the same circumstances for the same purposes. Second, we have significances we are aware of and take into account by means of conceptualized abstractions referred to by words or symbols. These may be brought to the focus of attention by certain conditions or may be recalled or referred to whenever we care to. Examples would be our scientific formulations, maps, historical events, legal, ethical, and religious systems. They are common for many people whatever their purposes. Because such abstractions refer to repeatable and nonemergent aspects of reality and because they can be communicated, can become universal, and can be experienced by everyone, they do not play the same role as the nonbifurcated significances experienced by a behaving person carrying out his purposes from his unique behavioral center. Finally, we can differentiate abstractions that can be felt, hardly conceptualized, such as aesthetic or religious experiences we may share and that are represented in various symbolic forms.

All of these aspects of reality can be negated if there is sharp and consistent lack of correspondence between them and the consequences of purposeful action with respect to them. But negation of our unique personal realities is sensed very differently than a negation of our abstracted realities. The death of a family member or close friend requires a kind of faith to sustain us that is not at all required if the laws of Newtonian physics are upset.

If we feel that other people are responsible for negating our personal reality, we may blame them, fear them, or have nothing more to do with them unless we have the infinite compassion of a saint. If our social group negates our reality, we may become antisocial, revolutionary, or try other group affiliations. Words, agreements, customs, laws, or assemblies are all viable insofar as they enable people to participate effectively in carrying out their purposes. What really matters is what people can do with these abstractions. If they cannot act usefully with them, there is only playacting, which is sooner or later recognized as such and thrown over. If impersonal forces of nature negate our reality, we may become afraid or fatalistic. If our own behavior negates our reality, we may develop inferiorities or begin to hate ourselves.

Irrespective of the causes of such negation, the effect is to disrupt our stable form-worlds and to produce a lack of surety, an apprehension, a personal doubt concerning the reality of our own reality system. And under such circumstances we may and can turn to the aspect of reality differentiated above which is not so subject to negation, is commonly shared by others, can be communicated and recalled, and seems therefore to have a greater validity for us—the abstracted aspects of reality represented by our conceptual knowledge of science, history, ethics, or religion. This reality of abstracted forms thus plays or can play an indispensable role in seeing us through breakdowns in our personal reality systems by transcending them. Yet these abstracted realities are, in the last analysis, no true substitute for our unique personal realities. For, among other things, the abstracted realities are relatively absolute and determined, cannot take account of the contingencies of specific situations in ongoing life, and do not emphasize the dignity and sacredness of the individual and permit him fully to exercise his capacity for choice and the personal responsibility concomitant with choice.

And yet all of us sometimes and some of us all the time may substitute this reality of abstracted forms for a more personal, ineffable reality in order to avoid the obstacles and uncertainties of living. They give us a sense of security. But, at the same time, they deprive us of our opportunity to develop and emerge. It is only through the experience of encountering negations of our personal realities that we can develop and emerge as individuals.

But paradoxically enough and important in our understanding of the function of ethics, it is generally only by making use of abstracted aspects of reality that we can overcome these negations of our personal realities. We do this, of course, by deliberately making ourselves aware of certain aspects of abstracted realities potentially relevant to the problem that confronts us. We accomplish this through inquiry, examination, experimentation, contemplation, or prayer. We are seeking to discover through these abstracted realities—represented by the wisdom of the ages or by contemporaries we believe in—the reasons for the inadequacies in our personal reality systems so we can alter them, encompass more significances, and emerge to more effective and profound reality systems for our own operational use.

The degree to which we crave some stable significances varies, of course, with their importance to our present well-being or its enhancement. In seeking out these relevant aspects of abstracted realities, we make them real for us only by using them as the basis for our own choice and action in specific undetermined situations. We experience what they refer to; we do not simply recall them intellectually. These abstracted realities we seek, many of which we call "values," are, then, not real for us in their own right but are real only when they are operative in concrete situations. And in the context of the concreteness of personal behavior they are indispensable realities.

If there is not continued value satisfaction derived from the constancies in our personal reality systems, then those reality systems collapse. And it seems to be the desire of human beings to continue or to enhance the value satisfaction of living that gives the urge to put order into disorder, even though, of course, the process of putting order into disorder is an abstraction which the individual who is putting the order into disorder is generally unaware of. Apparently a most basic want and responsibility of life is the urge to preserve reality and to continue this reality in an ever-changing cosmos.

Universal standards and unique experiences

Since each individual is a unique organism with his own unique form-world, since behavioral situations are unique, and since onging events are seldom completely determined, there is almost an infinity of different personal realities. At the same time, however, because of certain basic characteristics similar for nearly all human beings, certain similar significances which behavioral situations have for them, together with certain repeatable significances in their environments and certain similarities in their past experiences, there are also many universal standards or universal aspects of reality. The two are, moreover, interdependent: The more universal aspects cannot exist if the more unique aspects do not exist. And there would be little significance to any unique experience in the here and now unless there were some universal standards against which to evaluate it.

The maintenance of already-existing universal forms, or their ordered change under ever-changing conditions, is thus apparently essential for full satisfaction. Such maintenance of forms varies from taking care of our bodies to educating the young and preserving social, ethical, or religious standards. By his own choice and behavior every individual can affect—for better or for worse—the universal significances of his own form-world and the significances these may have to others. And because of the diversity of conditions, both between and within cultures, under which significant forms are maintained by individuals and groups, the perpetuation or ordered change of forms becomes a somewhat different responsibility for every individual and for every social group.

If an individual through his own responsible action is able to increase or enhance some already-existing universal form, we call him "creative"—his uniqueness has become more universal; in religious terms he has related immanence with transcendence and become one with God. From the transactional point of view, creativity and the maintenance of form are both aspects of the same process of orchestration. And even though we may not be individuals who could be called "creative," each of us in our transactions of living seems in a small way to be trying to make the immanent transcendent, trying to operate in situations so the consequences of carrying out our purposes will maintain, confirm, or enhance our reality.

The divergence and convergence of ethical behavior

We have tried here to show that the form-world which each individual develops in the course of his living is for him a reality—the only reality he knows. Unless this picutre is clear, we will fail to see (1) that our awareness of our environment, including our social environment, is only a prognosis, an assumed form which, however, we must generally adhere to; (2) that we put order into the disorder of a nonrepetitive universe by creating forms which provide for repetition and predictability and that we must generally adhere to; and (3) that in our social relations it is generally some socioethical form of behavior which makes it possible for any individual to guess how other people will behave and enable them to guess how he will behave. It is essential to understand this if we are to know to what extent conformity is desirable and when it should and should not be imposed.

If we fall into the common error of bifurcating the world into objective and subjective, then we are likely to assume falsely that both individuals and "objects" exist out there in their own right with all significances inherent in them. We will then be dealing with abstracted, mechanical individuals whom we can, to be sure, count, test, and classify as we do in the military. But we shall be denying ourselves and others any true social relationship with full-bodied individuals who are striving in the face of uncertainties and bolstered by faith as they make choices for which they are uniquely responsible in order to maintain or enhance a reality that will provide them a value satisfaction in living. All true social relationships are based on unabstracted realities. Any sense of real participation with others is based on the unabstracted togetherness of people where there is the possibility of mutual creative flow from form, of experiencing new consequences, new value satisfactions.

Furthermore, the Self, the "I," appears to be a reality only in transactional relationships in which, for human beings, other people are so crucially important. Our own significance seems to be determined in large part by the organisms and persons to whom we ourselves are significant. Hence we can never point to the "I," can never isolate it in time and space. Nor can we ever really "lose" it. The admonition of the prophets that one must "lose oneself" to "find oneself" or to experience God and reality makes sense, and eminent sense, only if we interpret it as meaning to rid oneself of those abstracted aspects which may be thwarting our personal participation in events from our own operational centers. Much of the recent criticism of fixed forms of psychoanalysis from psychiatrists themselves seems to be saying that certain intellectual abstractions concerning the Self—and the concentration of the patient's awareness on these abstractions—are inimical to recovery and self-development.

There has been an understandable tendency on the part of ethnologists and psychologists in recent years to examine the differences between cultures and between individuals within a culture. The results have been most important. But this emphasis has, I think, tended to obscure the similarities human beings have as human beings which are embedded in their chromosome structure and which must be borne very much in mind if we are to understand the function of ethical systems irrespective of their diverse forms and specifications. Some of these similarities we have already referred to: man's desire to participate in the creation of value satisfactions which will enrich the quality of his experience; man's capacity to choose; man's ability to sustain himself through obstacles and adversities with symbols and meanings of faith; man's creativity. In addition we should mention some of the more elemental similarities: the life cycle most of us go through of puberty, mating, having children, growing old, dying. Each stage of this process seems to call forth in any culture a complex of ethical standards and rituals. Further, human beings face uncertainties that are more or less similar: sickness and disease, the elements, thwarted ambitions, etc.

No matter how diverse the social and ethical standards may be that mankind has developed through the ages and in various cultural groups and subgroups, they are all ultimately attempts to increase the possibility of gaining greater satisfaction in living. And human living—as such—has, I believe, similar psychological aspects due to the similarities we have as human beings.

Established ethical principles as abstracted realities communicated from generation to generation provide the constancy and the repeatability essential for the sharing of significances. Since they are subject to recall they can become substantive aspects of faith when our personal realities are upset. In the diverse occasions of living where the determined of the past merges with the undetermined of the future, they serve as a compass that gives an unanalyzed integration to our purposes. Furthermore, ethical standards frequently provide criteria which we unconsciously use as guides of what significances to take into account.

It is little wonder, then, that we find people everywhere reaching for certain universals, certain ultimates which seem operationally so similar when their function is understood. An example might be man's age-old search for God with all the forms of deity or supernatural power this search has brought forth. Certain conditions characteristic of human living would seem not only to account for this search but to be necessary for it: man's frustrations, disappointments, and agonies; man's capacity to seek through inquiry or contemplation those future conditions that might mitigate or resolve his problems; man's capacity to act—in other ways, symbolically— to bring about the conditions he believes will alter his reality to his benefit. If "God" becomes a static abstraction, he can never be experienced; if "God" is a process he may be occasionally experienced. But the conditions for this experiencing are, to repeat, characteristically human and are necessary conditions.

Transactional psychology would, of course, be with those who urge a cultural pluralism. It would also give support to those great ethical systems which urge in different words that we do unto others as we would have others do unto us. For it would appear that the morality of any human action is to be judged in terms of the extent to which it takes account of the purposes of all others who might be affected by it. This form of neopragmatism—where action that appears to be most effective in the long run also appears to be most ethical—may be considerably speeded up by modern artifacts which are accelerating man's convergence on man. They may hasten the day when we shall all find it easier to experience in our own behavior what our ethical abstractions refer to and thus enable us to use these abstractions in our diverse and unique personal and cultural ways while still being faithful to the abstractions themselves, merging our individual realities with universal realities.

Notes

1. I wish to express again my profound indebtedness to the late Adelbert Ames, Jr., for stimulating discussion around this subject and for memoranda he wrote on many of the topics considered here. I am also indebted to my former Princeton colleague, Dr. F.P. Kilpatrick, for communion on the subject of constancy.
2. Further discussion will be found in the author's *The "Why" of Man's Experience* (New York: Macmillan, 1950) and "The Qualities of Being Human," *American Quarterly,* spring 1954, pp. 3–18. More technical papers concerning both theory and experimental research can be found in F.P. Kilpatrick (ed.), *Human Behavior from the Transactional Point of View,* 1952.
3. The word "stimulus" has meaning only in the sense of referring to some constancy experienced in the here and now, associated with some impingement which has significance only in terms of potential action relevant to experiencing intended consequences. The word can only be used as referring to something "real" and "objective" in traditional psychology because experiments are so deliberately arranged that no change in the prognostic significance of the "stimulus-datum" is permitted. A "stimulus" is only an occasion for a prognosis. Unless placed in such a behavioral context, the word can be a misleading abstraction.

10

The nature of faith

The experience of "faith" is one of the most real, yet one of the most ineffable, that characterizes human living. Without this capacity, "human nature" would be far different than it is. And so would all of man's social and political organizations.

For the process we call "faith" plays the crucial role of holding our values together and integrating our purposes. Without "faith," living would be a much more hit-and-miss affair. It would be much less directed. And it would be empty of many of the value overtones that we lump together as those that make living "worthwhile."

Faith has turned notorious sinners into saints. By means of faith, ordinary men have performed extraordinary miracles. When faith was aroused, dejected masses have been transformed into revolutionary crusaders. Faith, said the prophet, can move mountains.

Nearly all of us in our own lives can testify to the "reality" of faith: perhaps a faith we have experienced in something or someone; or a faith that kept us plugging along when the going was unusually tough. Perhaps a faith that altered our lives to some degree when we felt hopelessly bogged down. Or perhaps we have experienced the feeling of emptiness and isolation when we have "lost" our faith or had it shaken at the very roots.

In spite of the importance of faith in the process of living, contemporary psychology has rarely met the problem of "faith" head-on. In fact, psychological mention of the subject is even hard to find in the literature.

We shall examine here systematically the psychological conditions under which faith comes into being and the function it serves the individual as he goes about the process of living. Faith will be considered as a crucial aspect, as a reality, characterizing some of man's experience, except for which many of the transactions of life would not be what they are.

Reprinted by permission from the *Journal of Individual Psychology* 13, no. 1 (1957): 24-37.

What does the word "faith" refer to?

In order to answer this question, we must examine as best we can some of the conditions and circumstances without which people would not have the experience of faith or would not even know they were lacking in faith.

When do we experience the need for faith?

We are only occasionally aware of faith or of the need for faith.

Most people most of the time are not at all aware of any aspect of faith as they go about their daily life routines. Most people most of the time are too preoccupied with the present and with a "present" which they seem able to cope with in their own ways without requiring the support faith can provide.

We become aware of faith or of the need for faith only under certain conditions.

And we would have no need for faith at all if the world were static with everything neatly determined and predictable. For in such an ordered world our lives would be characterized by certainties and repeatabilities. And they would, of course, be deadly monotonous, even worse than the life of a prison inmate confined for the rest of his days.

But as everyone knows, we are not living in a static world. Change and flow are the rule. And change and flow are accompanied by the unforeseen and the unexpected.

Because the future is not entirely determined and predictable, experience for most of us frequently carries at least mild overtones of "concern" which we can label "anxiety," "excitement," "curiosity," or "doubt," depending upon the circumstances.

Living therefore inevitably creates constant frustrations. The frequency and severity of these frustrations of course depend upon the fortunes of our personal life histories, including our ability to meet frustrations. For millions of underprivileged people there may be little else than frustration.

But whoever we are, there is never complete certainty about the next moment, the next day, or the next year. We always have to do some guessing. All of us have to weigh some probabilities in a world which is an open system. In *The King and I*, the bewildered King of Siam sings: "There are times I almost think I am not sure of what I absolutely know. Very often find confusion in conclusion I concluded long ago." And the same idea was illustrated in an incident described by Carl Sandburg.

> I have always enjoyed riding up front in a smoking car, in a seat back of the 'deadheads,' the railroaders going back to the home base. Their talk about each other runs free. . . . Once I saw a young fireman in overalls take a seat

and slouch down easy and comfortable. After a while a brakeman in blue uniform came along and planted himself alongside the fireman. They didn't say anything. The train ran along. The two of them didn't even look at each other. Then the brakeman, looking straight ahead, was saying, 'Well, what do you know today?' and kept looking straight ahead till suddenly he turned and stared the fireman in the face, adding, 'For sure.' I thought it was a keen and intelligent question. 'What do you know today—*for sure*?' I remember the answer. It came slow and honest. The fireman made it plain what he knew that day for sure: 'Not a damn thing!' [Sandburg 1942: 145ff.]

Most of us are generally not as aware of our uncertainties as the lovable king or the wise fireman. For when something happens that goes counter to our assumptions, we are at least surprised: the unexpected event negates some aspect of our reality world on which we have counted for constancy.

The nature of the reaction we have to the unexpected situation will depend on the nature of the occasion. Perhaps we will experience disappointment or resentment, perhaps suspicion or mistrust, perhaps shock or grief, perhaps worry or despair. Or our experience may be one of laughter or joy, buoyancy or hope, gratitude or admiration.

Situations that provoke faith are always situations where value, worth, and importance are involved.

And situations that provoke faith are always situations where choice and responsibility come in, where there are possibilities that mistakes may be made, mistakes that may be ours. Situations that we handle with reflexes and habits involve a sense of "surety," not a sense of "faith," except in the unusual cases.

In the many varied circumstances of living, we can usefully differentiate three different conditions that give rise to faith or the need for faith.

1. *We become aware of faith or the need for faith when we lack complete self-confidence in our ability to cope satisfactorily with our present situation.* We are anxious because we are wondering if we will make it. The workman on a new job, the student in an examination, the scientist carrying out an experiment, the mother raising her child, the surgeon performing a difficult operation, the public servant assuming a more responsible office, the farmer trying a new crop are a few of the infinite variety of human conditions that may arouse in the participant an awareness of faith.

2. *We become aware of faith or the need for faith when we feel we are simply unable to accept or accede to some events or conditions that have occurred in the past.* We are unable to live at peace with ourselves in the *present* because we are haunted by the *past*. We blame ourselves, castigate ourselves. Or we resent what others appear to us to have done. Or we are upset by some condition we feel was brought about by impersonal forces.

The consequences of this situation take various forms: we may refuse to recognize either our own limitations or influences that have been part of a cause of past disappointments or failures. We may keep trying to push out of our consciousness certain memories or responsibilities we feel we flubbed. We may keep harboring a grudge against people or circumstances.

3. *We become aware of faith or the need for faith when we are apprehensive about the forseeable future,* even though we accept the past and are confident enough about the present. In this condition we are filled with doubts and misgivings when we look ahead. Since we have no clear prehension of steps we might take to bring about the experiencing of certain goals we have in mind, we are apprehensive. How are we going to earn a better living? How will we get ahead? How will we maintain or improve our health? How can we give our children the opportunities we want them to have? How can we get more security in our lives? How can we obtain or give more affection and love? How can we make sure there will be no more depressions and wars?

In any of these three conditions or a combination of them, we cannot enjoy a sense of complete well-being. We may come to doubt seriously the reliability of the reality world we have built up—the only world we know. Our experience may become tinged with a sense of disappointment, a sense of inadequacy. We may become unusually depressed. We may feel a lack of appreciation from others. We may feel a gnawing guilt, painful agony, miserable inferiority, flaming jealousy, or complete despair.

But far from being calamities, such unpleasant or painful experiences are the essential preliminary processes that catalyze faith or develop greater faith.

Faith is born of frustration; faith is kindled and nourished by difficulties. It is only through frustrations that we can achieve more workable assumptions. And it is only by experiencing obstacles to be overcome that we can develop faith. If there is a rare individual who has never felt frustration or has never faced an obstacle to overcome, then his faith, if he has any, is purely intellectual and untried. Like a bubble, it will burst when pricked.

The capacity for faith

Apparently one of the basic needs of most living organisms—certainly of human beings—is the need to preserve their sense of the worthwhileness of living.

With this need to preserve a sense of the worthwhileness of living goes a sense of responsibility to do so.

We manage to preserve the sense of the worthwhileness of living by creating a subjective reality world—a system of interpretations—that functions with passable adequacy in an ever-changing cosmos.

Since our experience is so much a matter of probability, of the bets we are constantly making in a changing world as to the characteristics of things, of people, of events, we *must* do something to put order and repeatability into the world in which we carry on our living. We are more comfortable if we think we can predict with a fair degree of accuracy the chain of events that will occur if we undertake a certain action. We crave certainty rather than doubt. We want enough form and pattern in our thoughts and feelings to give direction to flow.

So we *create constancies* concerning things, people, and events. We attribute certain *consistent* characteristics to them, so that we shall be provided with enough interpretation to guess with fair accuracy what the significances and meanings are of the variety of signals that reach our sense organs, without having to make fresh guesses at every turn.

All of these significances that we build up about objects, people, events, symbols, or ideas fuse and orchestrate together to give us our own unique reality world. Everything that has significance for us takes on its significance from our personal behavior center—in terms of *our own* purposes and *our own* actions.

These significances become more or less common depending upon the experiences and purposes we share with other people.

But in addition to these personal significances which we take into account as we participate in one occasion after another, we also utilize in our living the significances conveyed by the abstractions man has created through the ages. Man has devised these abstractions in his perpetual attempt to bring order into disorder, to explain to himself various types of phenomena, or to find universal principles and guides for more ordered living, no matter what the unique purposes or circumstances of any one individual may be.

Among such abstractions are our scientific formulations, our maps, our legal, ethical, political, and religious systems. They can be recalled or referred to at will. They can be experienced by any one at any time, since they are repeatable, fixed, spelled-out, and formulated. They can become universal.

And there are other abstractions man uses: abstractions represented by symbolic forms in art, in music, and in religion which are hard to conceptualize or put into words.

All of these abstractions are by their very nature fixed and static. Hence they can never become true substitutes for the personal meanings and significances assigned to events. For the abstraction cannot take into account the unique contingency any unique individual is likely to meet in life any more than a scientific formulation concerning the behavior of atoms can predict the behavior of a single atom.

Nevertheless, these abstracted conceptions of reality can and do play a most indispensable role in helping us through our periods of frustration and doubt if and when our personal reality systems prove strained or inadequate.

When the tangibles of our personal reality worlds break down, we can turn to the intangibles. We can recall those abstractions that have been created by others and that have proved useful to others. We can apply them to the particular problem we face. We can make ourselves aware of creeds, beliefs, parables, maxims, aesthetic representations of moods. We can recall as a symbol for ourselves the courageous or appropriate behavior of others who have faced similar crises.

If we can put the abstraction to work for us, *if* we can use it as a basis for *our* choice and action in the undetermined situation *we* face here and now, then we can transform the abstraction into a personal reality. But the abstraction becomes real *only* if it becomes functional in our *own* behavior. *For when it becomes functional, we can experience what the abstraction refers to.* Then we may get the exciting or profound sense of a fleeting identity with something more universal—a sense of identity with abstract "truth," "love," "mankind," "nature," or "God."

Men thus have the capacity to sense the experience of the immanent becoming transcendent, of the particular becoming universal, as some abstraction, not bounded by intervals of time or units of space, becomes relevant and operational in the concreteness of the here and now of a person's own behavioral center.

It is this capacity of man to *recall* and to utilize relevant abstractions that makes it possible for him to have an abiding faith, a faith which transcends time and space. It is this capacity to *create* and to utilize relevant abstractions that makes it possible for men to share their faith with people in all ages and places and to communicate their faith to others.

What faith involves

"Faith," said St. Paul "is the substance of things hoped for; the evidence of things not seen."

Less eloquently expressed is the definition of faith in Webster's dictionary as "complete confidence in something open to suspicion."

And still less eloquently we can say that, psychologically, faith is a *bet on, or a commitment to, or a value sense of the worthwhileness of a personal reality system composed of constancies that serve as guides to purposive action.*

Our understanding of what faith "is" can be more complete if we see what faith "involves;" what some of the factors are except for which faith would not be experienced. All of the aspects of faith noted here are, of course, interdependent.

1. *Faith is intensely personal.* It must be yours. Only *you* can experience your faith, only *you* can test it.

Faith must always have some referent: it must always be "about" or "in" something or someone. Just as a lover cannot be "in love with love" until he is in love with someone, so faith cannot be brought into awareness unless and until some transaction of living poses a problem that puts faith or the need for faith into operation.

This obvious point must be stressed to emphasize again the profound difference between experiencing what faith refers to and simply recalling some abstraction intellectually or giving lip service to it.

2. *Faith involves some participation in the flow of events, some action, some doing.* "Faith without works is dead." It is only in the quality of experience sensed from the consequences of action that faith is created, restored, confirmed, or expanded.

While the achievement of an intended goal is important, if the accomplishment of the goal is itself taken as the only criterion of faith, then that faith must prove temporary. For if we cannot foresee further potential value satisfactions ahead, then what faith we have will be empty.

3. *For faith to be enduring, a goal must serve as a step to other goals.* "A goal is a sign-post," said John Dewey at the age of ninety. It is in the *process* of participation and doing that one is aware of sustaining faith. And in the sequence of goals that give some direction to living, there is potentially the satisfaction of personal growth and "enrichment," as one discovers and tests new or more inclusive assumptions and value standards with the overtone that faith is being confirmed or enlarged.

4. *Faith requires a sense of assurance that means can be followed or devised to bring about the experiencing of intended goals.* Assurance, in the sense of absolute certainty, is almost never possible. But if faith is to "exist" and become functional, an individual must be able to feel that he has a workable, commonsense chance of being able to influence events that involve him. He must feel a reasonable degree of confidence in the effectiveness of the methods available to him to reach his objective.

For if we have a sense of the potential goals that may be ahead for us but at the same time have no conceivable or only the most remote prospect of realizing those goals, then faith will be difficult to sustain. This can often be seen in a person who is in virtual slavery; in the overworked, poorly paid laborer who sees no freedom from his bondage; in the industrial automaton who seeks only escape; or in the individual who finds himself in a spiritual vacuum because his faith in some creed or set of beliefs has been destroyed by events or by an education that has given him no viable substitute.

5. *Faith requires that the sense of self-constancy be maintained.* If the constancy of "self" is upset, it becomes difficult to assess change and accommodate to it. We lose the compass that keeps us going in a direction. We don't know what significances to take into account. "We" are lost.

When we say that self-constancy must be maintained, we do not imply that there can be no growth or development. On the contrary. Self-development is itself an aspect of self-constancy. But development must flow from form if it is to be recognized. Without such flow from form, there is no standard for comparison, no sure sense of continuity.

This means that our sense of "self" and our faith in that "self" must constantly be reaffirmed through our participation with others. For our feeling of "self," and our own self-constancy and self-significance are determined to a large extent by our significance to other people and the way they behave toward us.

We must, of course, rid ourselves of any notion of an abstract "Self" (or Ego) that can somehow be isolated, pointed to, analyzed, or experienced apart from any social context. The idea of an abstract self seems to be what the prophets were inveighing against when they preached that we "find ourselves" by "losing ourselves." They seem to be insisting that we not make the mistake of abstracting a nonexistent "self" out of a life setting which alone gives it meaning.

6. *Faith is made real only when hope is confirmed.* As Saint Paul observed, faith involves the hope of experiencing potentially attainable goals. Hope is confirmed through experiencing the consequences of action. And if action does not sooner or later bring about the sense that hopes are being realized, then faith will be abandoned.

Without the aspect of hope, faith could never work the miracles it does. And without the aspect of hope, faith could not involve as it often does the overtone of transcendent wonder as we experience the "full" significance of present, past, and probable future events.

Hope, like frustration, is a necessary condition for personal development and for the emergence of new value satisfactions. In a most real sense, the realization of hope through faith *is* emergence.

7. *Faith requires a sense of the worthwhileness of living and of the value of life itself.* A feeling that living is worthwhile usually involves some sense of appreciation from others. For if most human beings are to live at all, they must live among their fellow men.

This means that the satisfaction we can experience from the consequences of our own actions is in large measure a satisfaction derived from the feeling that other people appreciate our actions, or will appreciate them. This bolsters the sense of the worthwhileness of living, of the value of you yourself and of your responsibility to others.

The highest expression of this appreciation is, of course, what we call "love"—where your own well-being depends on furthering another person's well-being, and, reciprocally, where another person's satisfaction is completely dependent upon experiencing the consequences of action that provide you maximum satisfaction and well-being. The most profound love is the most universal love, the love of "all mankind," of "all living things." For a Jesus, a Saint Francis, or a Gandhi, universal love is a cornerstone of the faith they tried to demonstrate.

Keeping the faith

The great majority of people in the world are "born into" a faith represented by some codified, institutionalized religion or some political unit. They learn very early from their elders some pattern of values. It is imposed upon them. They may get more satisfaction from it than they are often willing to acknowledge. They see that it "works" in their own lives.

In order to perpetuate these formalized constancies and provide the possibility that they will acquire common and standardized significances and meanings, every institutionalized religion and every political creed has devised its own pattern of ritual and ceremony. Participation in such rituals enables the believer to associate himself through his own action with the abstraction the ritual symbolizes, whether it is telling his beads, saluting a flag, or bowing his head.

While many people, to be sure, take part in such ceremonies with tongue in cheek or without really sensing any involvement or significance in what they are doing, still for the vast majority there is a sense of being tuned in with more universal standards. In the process, the individual's faith in his own standards—the standards he lives by—is confirmed. His faith is self-validated by repeating the constancies of a ritual.

From the beginning of time man has apparently sought some ultimate, universal constancy that would serve as a repository, protector, and fountainhead of all his most personal and most cherished values and aspirations. In all ages, men have apparently searched for some sort of God and have, in their search, brought forth all manner of deities according to their needs. The concept of "God" makes it easy for people to get hold of their value constancies, hang on to them, and keep them fixed.

In accounting for this search for God and in understanding the function God serves the believer, we should recall some of the conditions that give rise to the need for faith: frustrations, disappointments, agonies, unfilled hopes.

These conditions are also necessary to bring about the search for God.

Man's amazing capacity to help create an environment within which he can carry out his purposes and mitigate some of his problems enables him to obtain reassurance that his God is working with him. Hence God *can* become part of human experience if He is sensed as a *process*. On the other hand, if God is a mere intellectual abstraction, He can never play a role in living, can never be demonstrated or experienced. "The Kingdom of God is among you," said Jesus.

Acquiring a personal faith

As man learns more and more about nature and the universe of which he is a part, he questions more and more the validity of any faith which involves supernatural explanation or forces.

But at the same time, the sense of being on his own without the aid of some outside friendly agent also increases man's feeling of helplessness and his sense of urgency for something to believe in. If man cannot create a new faith for himself from his knowledge alone, still he at least doesn't want knowledge to stand in the way of a faith. For he continues to seek a set of beliefs—a set of beliefs consistent with what he knows.

The ardent Catholic or Buddhist can identify himself with beliefs that function for him and are confirmed by his daily rituals. The Communist militant faithfully follows the discipline of the Party. But the individual who has no rigidly set institutionalized creed to adhere to must in a sense create his own faith and sustain this faith through his own transactions of living.

And at the same time man's increasing knowledge of the world around him and of himself makes his craving for certainties and absolutes harder to satisfy and to justify.

The quest seems to be that of finding a "cause" that represents value aspirations which men can share in a "scientific" age; aspirations which men can dedicate themselves to and try to experience in their own living by effective participation with others.

Circumstances seem to be forcing people to the realization that their relations with others are the crucial problem for their own well-being and for their survival. *The question of faith seems to be becoming more and more a question of how to acquire faith in other people and how to instill in other people a faith in us. It is the ancient problem of acquiring and demonstrating compassion, charity,and love.*

When we look for constancies in other people and for some correspondence between *what we think they are and how they turn out to be* when we participate with them, a variety of complications is introduced.

For other people have their own purposes, often difficult for us to understand. Their purposes will change as conditions change and as their behavior progresses from one goal to another. *Their* purposes and behavior are affected by *our* purposes and behavior, just as *ours* are affected by *theirs*.

When we deal with people, constancies and repeatabilities are not easy to find.

As noted earlier, in an attempt to increase the meanings and significances people have in common, societies have developed all manner of customs, mores, conventions, laws, and other codes of behavior. And as people sense more and more their interdependence upon each other, both as individuals and as citizens of nations, old forms are revised and new common links are devised in the attempt to keep purposes emerging and compatible with required behavior.

All of these social forms presumably serve the function of improving the degree of correspondence between what is in our awareness and what is potentially in the social environment to be aware of. And the reason for attempting to increase this correspondence is, of course, to provide purposeful action of a more predictable direction and with a greater chance to repeat itself in satisfying ways with more certain value constancies.

The process is—and always will be—a never-ending one. For correspondence where people are involved can never be perfect. Increased correspondence in our social perceptions of each other will inevitably be accompanied by increased satisfactions which themselves will point to new potential satisfactions.

In this ceaseless process, the individual searching for faith gets support for his value standards from others who seem to share them—his family, his friends, and the various groups he identifies himself with. As long as they help him carry out his purposes by their actions, help him maintain and develop his own self-constancy, he will find them fortifying his faith and deserving of it. But—to repeat—it is only in times of personal crisis and emergency when this faith in people is manifested and filters into awareness. At other times it is part of the relatively normal "neutral" world: It is *potentially* with us, and we may take it into account in our behavior even though we are not aware of it.

A person will be able to become more aware of faith, and to gain faith, when he is able to see the *potential* values in living which he has not sensed before, *and* when he feels there is a good chance that he will be able to participate effectively in bringing about these potential value satisfactions in his own experience.

But if his doubts and frustrations are continually unresolved through action, he is likely to find himself in a psychiatric condition where he either lacks surety concerning the present, where he refuses to accept the past, or where he is unduly apprehensive about the future. In each case, faith and hope are abandoned and can only be reestablished by painstaking relearning and reconditioning. Such reconditioning will require above all else a therapy which simplifies goals so that their accomplishment will be assured through the individual's own action, thereby rebuilding his confidence in himself. Once self-confidence is regained on a simple level, goals can gradually be raised.

And what holds for a single individual also holds for members of a group or culture.

The problem of gaining faith is closely related to the ancient problem of insight. The recognition of our own adequacies and inadequacies in terms of the goals we have set for accomplishment can help restore faith in those cases whose self-assessment has been inaccurate and who consequently suffer from a constant sense of inadequacy because they are aiming at the wrong thing or are looking in the wrong place for satisfaction to appear.

Frequently the counsel of a wise friend or a skilled therapist will aid in clarifying goals and simplifying means.

The process of self-examination can bring into awareness purposes we had heretofore not recognized as guiding our actions. It can also release latent abilities which we may have only vaguely sensed and insufficiently nurtured.

The inquiry we must undertake to gain faith is the sort which we can label "value inquiry" as contrasted to logical or rational inquiry. It involves "mulling things over," "meditation," "communion," or "prayer." Its purpose is to allow us to sensitize ourselves to our feelings, to reflect on the priority and weight we should assign to different value standards, and to get a sense of orchestration into the various aspirations and responsibilities we feel are right for us.

For value inquiry to occur unhampered, we must insulate ourselves from here-and-now pressures. Christ went to the top of the mountain, and Gandhi had his day of silence. The faithful Hindu sets aside a certain period each day for uninterrupted meditation. Only by getting away from immediate obligations and routines can our conscious and unconscious processes, together with our feelings, flow unhampered in surveying the widest possible range of cues to take into account in making our value judgments. It takes time. It requires leisure and is doubtless the reason why so many of the great original thoughts that have come into the world have occurred to their creator when he was relaxed while walking, sitting under an apple tree, or taking his bath.

In the West we have badly neglected to educate ourselves to the processes involved in such value inquiry. We seldom even pose the question of how to make such value inquiry more worthwhile by increasing our sensitivity to the potential value satisfaction inherent in the many occasions of living. This is essentially the true function of all religious literature, of all prayer, of all meditation.

Only through learning and practicing value inquiry can we get a sense of the full significances potentially available to us in our behavior. Only then can we guess the probable long-range consequences our actions will have on us and on the purposes of others. Only then can we see how to improve the quality of our satisfactions by improving the quality of our purposes and the quality of our actions. Only then can we begin to simplify our lives, learning that if we become sensitive to value cues we can then become aware of how even our smallest daily actions hold a possibility of transcending the immediate moment and taking on more universal value significance.

Thus, by building up our value standards, sensing their confirmation in action, and discovering revisions that will make them more encompassing, we can develop a faith of sufficient power to weather the inevitable frustrations and deprivations we will encounter.

Faith enables us to feel that come what may, life is still full of unpredictable and satisfying promises, if we will only participate selflessly in the flow of events.

And faith makes it possible for us to get at least a vague sense of awareness that death itself is the beginning of the "everlasting life" which we have as the result of the effects of our behavior on others and on the others yet to come in the long line of humanity ahead.

Reference

Sandburg, C. 1942. *Always the young stranger.* New York: Harcourt, Brace.

11

Effective democratic leadership: a psychological interpretation

Chester Barnard begins his essay "The Nature of Leadership" with the statement that "leadership has been the subject of an extraordinary amount of dogmatically stated nonsense" (1948: 80f.) Many people who have written about the subject and who are not leaders themselves often seem insensitive to the complexity of the factors involved and, because of their lack of experience, fail to take into account the variety of roles which the successful leader intuitively plays, often without being aware of the processes involved. On the other hand, leaders are not notorious as analysts of the nature of leadership. The ongoing process of leading, by its very nature, apparently precludes the perspective required for a balanced view and, if the leader does write about leadership, he more than likely has some case to defend.

There are, of course, many kinds of "leadership": political, scientific, industrial, labor, religious, artistic, etc. Each type has its own meaning and requirements. Then there are leaders who play a role only for a brief period because some situation which is itself temporary brings out in them latent and specific talents which are highly appropriate for the moment, but irrelevant when the situation that called these talents forth itself disappears.

Our concern here is with the requirements for effective leadership in democratic society. We shall try to describe what the philosopher calls the "most general specifications" for leadership of this particular variety.

To see with the eyes of the people, to feel with the hearts of the people

It is, of course, self-evident that if anyone is to become an effective leader in a democracy, he must possess an unusual ability to understand how and

Reprinted by permission from the *Journal of Individual Psychology* 14 (1958): 128-38.

why other people see things as they do. He must be able to project himself accurately into their reality worlds so that his understanding is not merely a matter of intellectual knowledge, but a feeling, a sensitivity that will guide his intuitions. Since democratic leadership is based on common consensus and mutual trust rather than on mere power, force, or cunning, the position of leadership in a democratic society depends on attaining power "with" people rather than power "over" people. The democratic leader cannot "use" people in any Machiavellian sense, exploiting them for his own interests. Neither can he "use" people merely in the sense of transacting with them the prescribed and routine duties of an administrator who is keeping the house in order. In a democracy, the leader will lead only to the extent that he "uses" people in the sense of helping to provide for them the satisfactions they feel in terms of their own cultural development are "out there" potentially available to them if opportunity is provided.

This means, then, that the democratic leader must have an accurate understanding of the assumptions, frustrations, aspirations, purposes, hopes, and fears of those he intends to lead. He must be able to create and maintain a correspondence between the unverbalized image people have of a leader and the role he himself plays as a leader. He must be able to devise courses of action which demonstrate to people that the interpretation he is giving to ongoing situations and the consequences of action based on that interpretation are providing flesh and blood to their image of what a democratic leader should be. Since common consensus and mutual trust are cornerstones for democratic leadership, the leader can never resort to means for attaining a goal which are inconsistent with the goal itself. The history of democratic societies provides ample evidence that, if the means used to obtain an end are themselves inconsistent with the end desired, people will sooner or later discern the discrepancy and lose confidence in the leader.

Because the psychological reality worlds of the overwhelming majority of people are primarily so concerned with their own personal or local problems, except when some more or less dramatic incident occurs, most people cannot be expected to become greatly concerned about or often even aware of the wide variety of basic issues that affect their lives as members of a large democratic community and as citizens of the world. Yet as people and nations become more and more dependent upon each other in a technological era, with all its complex implications for both domestic and foreign policy, new problems continually emerge and demand resolution. It is provided in the very nature of things that the status quo must constantly be upset.

If people do become aware of the specific nature of the problem, they are generally in no position to understand the intricate details of planning, financing, negotiation, administration, or instrumentation required to meet the problem. While people are increasingly recognizing that they must rely on experts to handle the manifold details required in running modern government, in the final analysis they look to their elected leaders to spell out for them in broad outline the reasons why the problem exists as a problem and the factors that must be taken into account to resolve the problem successfully in terms of their own interests. The democratic leader, then, must not only try to see things the way the people do, but must in addition assume the responsibility of trying to have people see things the way he does and the way he can with all the information available to him. He must point out to people the facts and developments that are significant for them to take into account in terms of their own interest. He must bring people along with him. This particular role of the leader was nicely expressed many years ago by Laotzu:

> A sound leader's aim
> Is to open people's hearts,
> Fill their stomachs,
> Calm their wills,
> Brace their bones
> And so to clarify their thoughts and cleanse their needs
> That no cunning meddler could touch them:
> Without being forced, without strain or constraint,
> Good government comes of itself.

In order to assist him in understanding what people are and are not concerned about, what they are and are not aware of, the democratic leader in modern times can, if he wishes, avail himself of many techniques devised by social scientists to discover just this kind of information. Among these techniques the public opinion survey is preeminent. Properly used, it can, within limits, provide an accurate reading of the public pulse and can help the leader avoid the false impression he may have of public sentiment if he relies only on such unrepresentative sources of information as his mail or editorial comment. The leader's role will, of course, be vitiated if he utilizes such devices to make himself synthetic with the mistaken notion that he must keep altering his course to conform to majority opinion. On the other hand, rather like a general in the army who has an intelligence unit to provide him information which makes his strategy and tactics more effective, the democratic leader can utilize these modern research devices to increase his political intelligence and to improve his own chances of achieving the goals he himself deeply believes in.

An example of this use of public opinion data by a democratic leader may be seen in the way in which Franklin Roosevelt kept himself in tune with the feelings of the American people between the outbreak of World War II and America's entry after Pearl Harbor. The President was aware that he could most effectively lead the people to do what he himself thought had to be done only if he did not get too far ahead or too far behind public sentiment, either in his statements or in the measures he advocated to help those who were fighting the Nazis. He was therefore particularly interested in the results of a question that was repeatedly asked during this period: "So far as you personally are concerned, do you think President Roosevelt has gone too far in his policies of helping Britain, or not far enough?" And the adroitness with which he steered his course in a constant direction is shown by the results which maintained the ratio of approximately 25% of the people saying "too far," 25% saying "not far enough," and 50% saying "about right," even though, of course, America's aid to Britain was constantly increasing throughout this time.

It is relevant to mention in this connection that the evidence from public opinion surveys indicates that when issues have become clear to people as to what they must do and what sacrifices they must make in terms of taxation, rationing, or other restrictions on their behavior, they are much more willing to make these sacrifices than would be generally supposed from the clamor raised by special groups who insist upon a "balanced budget," "higher wages," "less government interference," or some other form of self-interest inconsistent with a bold program the public as a whole would be willing and eager to set in motion.

The democratic leader is, in brief, a person who demonstrates a capacity to make value judgments which other people perceive as providing good guides for organized action which will increase the range and quality of their satisfactions. Consideration of some of the factors involved in this oversimplified description may give us a toehold for a better understanding of the function of leadership in a democracy, and of what must be taken into account in selecting leaders or in any program aimed at training leaders.

Some requirements for democratic leadership

Because of the very nature of the democratic process and the fundamental principles upon which democratic governments are founded, there are certain psychological functions a leader in a democracy is called upon to fulfill if he is to enjoy the confidence and trust of an effective majority of the population, or, in short, if a leader is to lead.

As we differentiate some of these requirements, it will become apparent that they are in a sense on different "levels" and involve quite different capacities, abilities, and skills. And we shall also see that while we are forced to describe each requirement separately, all the psychological functions are interdependent so that no one can be successfully performed unless all others are, too. Effective democratic leadership can be viewed as an orchestration of talents, capacities, and responsibilities with each theme and countermelody playing its essential role at the proper time.

The requirements for democratic leadership noted here are similar to a number of those mentioned by Barnard, but are here accented somewhat differently, since our primary concern is with the *psychological* functions they serve.

1. *The formulation of overall goals which can serve as guiding stars for proposals and actions.* In the final analysis the reality world of every individual can only be held together if his specific purposes and actions are integrated around some value standards that make sense to him, with which he can identify himself, and in terms of which he can judge the worthwhileness of his behavior. People can take value standards with them wherever they go, and can recall them in all the diverse occasions of living. Value standards are the top-level directives. They therefore hold out the possibility of being the most lasting and the most universal standards human beings can have, since they are not bound by time and space.

In deciding what to do in any situation, we turn consciously or unconsciously to value standards to give us the answer to the question of what our action is *for* anyway. If we don't sooner or later find an answer that satisfies us, we become deeply disturbed and bewildered because of an inability to sense the direction in which we *should* go and *why*. If this situation is prolonged, we may become apathetic or fatalistic. Or we may become so haunted by our lack of basic guidelines that we feel lost, and become highly susceptible to the appeals and blandishments of potential demagogues or anyone else whom we think can give meaning and significance to our lives.

What we are talking about here is what is often referred to as "spiritual" or "moral" leadership, an aspect of democratic leadership that is unfortunately often only vaguely understood even by those who talk most about it and who, therefore, often fail to see just when it is needed and why, and just how it can be provided. It is essentially what Gandhi described as "soul-force," a term that sounds quite mystical to most Western ears, but a force that Gandhi demonstrated was exceedingly powerful and that served as the cornerstone of his practical politics.

The formulation of goals on the level of the highest human values and in terms that take account of the exigencies of the times will invariably appear as idealistic. There seems to have been a tendency in the West in recent times to shy away from any such emphasis, possibly because the need for such formulations has not been recognized, or possibly because of a fear of being regarded as naive and impractical. Yet, on analysis, it often turns out that whenever people are anxious and bewildered by a sense of lack of direction concerning where they or their society are going or should go, the highest idealism proves to be the greatest realism, and is, in fact, the necessary keystone for any program of action that is to prove itself realistic, workable, and durable. This is immediately apparent if we review the names of a few historical figures we call great leaders—for example, Jesus, Caesar, Napoleon, Jefferson, Lincoln, Lenin, Wilson, Gandhi, or Churchill. Each in his own way and in his own time was a rank idealist.

In order to formulate such overall goals at the value level, to sustain them with surety, or to revise them in favor of more embracing goals, the democratic leader must have the capacity to indulge in the kind of self-inquiry at the value level that involves very different psychological processes and conditions from the kind of effort involved in figuring out *how* to get something accomplished once goals have been formulated. Value inquiry involves the kind of soul searching that takes place in meditation, in contemplation, in brooding, in prayer, in mulling things over. It is a process which requires leisure and an atmosphere unhampered by the urgent demands of the here and now. It is a process in which the mind must be able to range freely as it tries to sensitize itself to feelings that refer to such factors as rightness and wrongness, goodness and badness, charity and love, duty and responsibility, loyalty and conscience. It is the process Jesus engaged in when he went to the top of the mountain, that Gandhi engaged in during his rigidly enforced days of silence, that Lincoln engaged in as he paced the halls of the White House during early morning hours. It is the process symbolized in the hymn which says, "Lead, kindly Light, amid the encircling gloom."

It is only if and when a leader is himself clear on the pattern of values he believes in that he can judge immediate and short-term events and problems with any perspective, weighing alternative courses of action open to him in terms of long-range objectives and often exhibiting in the process an exasperating patience, casualness, or humor in the midst of frustrations, trying times, or temporary failures or reversals. Only if a leader has formulated overall goals that he deeply believes in can he weather storms of abuse and unpopularity, keep faith in himself, instill faith in others, and solidify their faith in him.

2. *Effectively communicating the nature of goals.* Unless a democratic leader makes a systematic attempt to give people a basic understanding of the goals he believes they should pursue and a feeling of the value standards upon which these goals are based, then the goals themselves will remain as inert abstractions, lifeless concepts, or high-sounding phrases. The art of effective political communication is the art of showing people in terms of their own experience just what words, ideas, and proposals *refer to*, what

their *significance* is to the citizen, how they impinge on and fit into his own reality world, and why they are important and useful to him. The leader must use the language of the people, with all the overtones of feeling and value which make language meaningful and alive.

Such effective communication can perhaps best be achieved if the leader conveys the meaning of his concepts in terms of action which people understand. Ideals, goals, or proposals come alive and their import is recognized if people can understand what symbols mean in terms of some action, some "doing" that puts them into operation and makes them relevant and useful. It is most unlikely that Jesus would have had the influence he had without his skillful use of parables which quickly and simply brought home to people what he was referring to by the most abstract ethical concepts; it is most unlikely that Gandhi would have had the influence he had, if he had not undertaken such symbolic acts as his march to the sea and his prolonged fasts. Roosevelt quickly conveyed the meaning of his "Good Neighbor" policy when he used the analogy of lending a neighbor your hose if his house is on fire. Lenin was constantly reminding his revolutionary colleagues of the necessity of showing people what Communism meant in terms of their own daily living. For example, writing in 1920 during the early days of the Russian Revolution, Lenin pointed out:

> Without labor, and without struggle, book knowledge about Communism obtained from Communist brochures and other writing is absolutely worthless where it would continue the old gap between theory and practice. . . . The generation which is now fifteen years old and which in ten to twenty years will live in a Communist society must so conceive the aims of learning that every day in every village, in every city, the young should actually perform some task of social labor, be it ever so small, be it ever so simple.

It should also be noted in passing that people in a democracy are quick to discern insincerity, dissemblance, or anything that smacks of playacting. For this reason democratic leaders must be wary of relying too much on ghostwritten speeches, no matter how eloquent they may sound. For such rather formal communications invariably place a screen between the people and the leaders which is likely to distort the consistent image people want to have of their leader, even if the screen is not recognized as such.

3. *The creation and guidance of means to attain goals.* Here the leader's problem is to determine *how* to accomplish the goals he has decided upon. But we should hasten to point out once more that the problem is not quite as simple as it sounds, since goals and the means to attain the goals are so completely interdependent. In the determination of the goals themselves the successful leader must invariably keep taking into account what are the potential or forseeable methods of attaining those goals. Yet when the

leader asks himself the question, "What shall I do?" the differentiation between the two aspects usually involved in such a question—"*Why* should I do this?" and "*How* should I do this?"—is essential for clarifying the psychological requirements of democratic leadership. For in answering the question of "How," quite different capacities are involved than those described earlier as the leader tries to clarify for himself the overall nature of the goals he wants to pursue anyway.

In answering the question of "How," the processes involved include reasoning, the gathering of information, the analysis of facts, the understanding of the details of specific situations which must be acted upon in the immediate future, the conferring with others on possibilities, the consultation with experts. All of these processes are concerned with the achievement of some particular overall and long-range goal already decided upon.

This process involves an ability to come out on top in the invariable political give-and-take and compromise that characterizes the democratic process; it involves maintaining an effective relationship with parliamentary bodies and with the various agencies of government; it involves planning and budgeting; it involves maintaining and guiding a political organization.

It is unnecessary here to spell out in detail the diverse activities in which the modern democratic leader must engage if he is to put his program across. This has been done many times by able students of government. Psychologically, the important point to remember is that the process of revising and implementing means is another requirement of democratic leadership, and that the means devised and maintained must themselves be consistent with the goals toward which they are directed and the value standards that have guided the formulation of the goals themselves.

4. *The ability to demonstrate resourcefulness in meeting new, emerging situations.* This requirement of successful democratic leadership was implied in Lincoln's statement in his Second Inaugural Address, when he said: "The dogmas of the quiet past are inadequate to the stormy present. The occasion is piled high with difficulty and we must rise to the occasion. As our case is new—so we must think anew and act anew." The psychological process involved here is the demonstration of an ability to make swift evaluations that turn out to be accurate appraisals of the significance or potential significance of new occurrences in terms of the most general value standards, together with the capacity to devise, adapt, or revise the practical measures necessary to accommodate the situation. It means the capacity to discern cues and signs of the times which seem to be pointing to serious crisis in order to avoid the crisis itself, or to mitigate its effects if it

proves to be unavoidable because of circumstances beyond the leader's control.

The problem of demonstrating resourcefulness involves the important capacity of timing, of knowing when objectives need a clear statement or restatement, when programs need formulations and revisions, when the times are ripe to put some new program into effect, and just how and when to convey to people the sense of urgency that something new and different must be done. A characteristic of many great leaders is their uncanny sense of timing as, for example, Churchill's speech to a vacillating world the day after the Nazi attack on the Soviet Union during World War II, which indicated in clear and uncompromising terms what he felt must be done.

An important aspect of resourcefulness is the capacity of a leader to recognize the tentativeness of his assumptions, no matter how much he may have believed in them. It involves the ability to know when he has made a mistake, when his assumptions have proved false, combined with the courage to admit his mistakes. For, like anyone else, only to the extent that the leader can recognize his errors and admit them can he make better, more accurate, more adequate judgments. Confucius said, "He who makes a mistake and refuses to admit it, makes another mistake." In his auto-biography, Gandhi talks of his "Himalayan errors." Mayor La Guardia used to say, "When I make a mistake, it is a beaut." Horace Greeley illustrated the point in describing Lincoln. "He was open to all impressions and influences, and gladly profited by the teachings of events and circumstances, no matter how adverse or unwelcome. There was probably no year of his life when he was not a wiser, cooler and better man than he had been the year preceding."

Without availing himself of the opportunity for learning which is provided when assumptions prove wrong, the leader is constantly apt to be confronted with things that just "couldn't happen" and, in the process, bring about a crisis in leadership which people will be quick to recognize. The shock of the consequences of mistakes and misjudgments can be tempered if the leader has the intuitive sense to use understatement rather than overstatement. In so doing he sets up the possibility of giving an impression of overperformance if things do happen to turn out as he had privately predicted.

5. *Providing a sense of participation through close identification with the people.* It is becoming increasingly recognized in all areas of social, indus-trial, and political life that when people are required to work together to accomplish a purpose, their morale, their satisfaction, their output, and their willingness to sacrifice will be greatest only if they have a sense that they themselves are somehow involved in decisions, if their action is in part

their own responsibility because they feel they have exercised some choice in the matter.

The wise democratic leader will therefore make every effort to avoid signs of dictation. Even when decisions must be made quickly, he will try to execute them or state them in a way to avoid an impression of imperiousness. He will continually bear in mind that his power derives from the people, and is a power "with" the people, not "over" them.

While it is obvious that any democratic leader must make innumerable decisions on which the public at large cannot be expected to have a seasoned judgment, and about which they may show very little interest, it is essential that when people *are* concerned about a problem and *do* feel strongly, an effort be made to give them a sense of involvement. Insofar as this can be done, the democratic leader will live up to the ideal leader described by Laotzu:

A leader is best
When people barely know that he exists,
Not so good when people obey and acclaim him,
Worst when they despise him.
"Fail to honor people,
They fail to honor you";
But of a good leader, who talks little,
When his work is done, his aim fulfilled,
They will all say, "We did this ourselves."

The problem

The combination of characteristics and capacities required to fill successfully the role of a democratic leader, particularly at the national level, are of course to be found in few people indeed. Most who try are apt to lack one or more of the essential ingredients. With the increasingly exacting demands on democratic leaders created by domestic and international problems of mounting complexity, ways and means must be constantly sought to give the leader every chance for success by freeing him from all unnecessary tasks which drain his energies, eat into his time, and divert his attention from major responsibilities which he himself must in large part define within the context of his times and situation.

As democracy competes with authoritarianism and despotism in its various modern forms, the problems of discovering, training, and utilizing leadership obviously become of the utmost importance. For it is now more than ever to democratic leadership that people are looking for expressions of their hopes, and for dynamic programs of action that will confirm these hopes in the concreteness of living and will thereby sustain and kindle their faith in democratic government.

Reference

Barnard, C. 1948. *Organization and management.* Cambridge, Mass.: Harvard University Press.

IV

"Transaction" in psychology and neurology

12

A transactional inquiry concerning mind

Man as a struggler amid illusions, each man fated to answer for himself: Which of the faiths and illusions of mankind must I choose for my own sustaining light to bring me beyond the present wilderness?
—Carl Sandburg (1938: 134)

Whatever approach we take for the theory of mind can at best be only a slice of our own life history and our own concern. "No one is a privileged observer," said Poincaré. Mind, like matter, can show itself in a variety of forms, each different from the rest but within limits each as "real," as "true," as the next. As a psychologist and more particularly as a social psychologist, my own primary concern in trying to decide what the abstractions of "mind" refer to is to bracket those aspects or preconditions except for which "mind" would not be what it "is" and would not reflect as it seems to the psychological and social consequences of being human. In view of the wonders and intricacies that come to mind whenever I think of what the word refers to, together with the realization that through the centuries some minds have become famous for contributing to an understanding of what "mind" is, I should like to register here at the outset my own sense of humility as I begin my probing.

I take it for granted, of course, that we are dealing with an organism equipped with particular qualities and ranges of physiological sensitivities and with a particular pattern of neurophysiological organization. I begin with the assumption that the "reality" of mind is to be accounted for as a process in its own appropriate terms. What we describe phenomenologically must obviously be congruent with neurophysiological description.

Reprinted by permission from Jordan Scher, ed. 1962. *Theories of the Mind.* New York: Free Press, 330–53. Some of this chapter is based on previously published material, particularly Cantril 1958, ch. 1; Cantril and Ittelson 1954; and Cantril 1955.

And the reverse is equally true: The awesome and baffling characteristics of "mind" must not be lost sight of or oversimplified because of limitations in our present understanding of the potentialities of matter. The revolution in the physical and biological sciences during the past century has even further dispelled the inadequacy of accounting for mind with "materialist" laws or Cartesian mechanisms. The exciting new developments in neurophysiology can, for example, enormously aid us in translating organic necessity and organic consequence into psychological necessity and psychological consequence—and vice versa.

While there is every expectation as time goes on that our understanding of the relationships between mind as we experience it and the naturalistic processes collateral with this experience will continually increase, the gap between what Sir Russell Brain (1951, 1959) distinguishes as the representative "perceptual world" and the "physical world" will always be there. While such a differentiation is obvious and generally accepted by psychologists, it is worth mentioning here to avoid confusion and to make clear that our discussion is entirely concerned with the "perceptual world" aspect of mind. Discussion of the "physical world" aspect of mind and the apparent relationships betwen the two worlds must be left to competent neurophysiologists (Brazier 1958; Solomon, Cobb, and Penfield 1958).

Most psychologists today steer clear of the word "mind." If it appears at all in their textbooks, it is generally in discussions of the history of psychology. The word has an old-fashioned sound to most Western psychologists who pride themselves on being "scientific" and tend to be impatient with philosophical discourse.

There is, of course, some justification for this view since this man-made abstraction has all too often been treated as an explanatory concept in a way that has little meaning in terms of its operation. But in avoiding the term and a concern with it, many psychologists have also lost sight of inclusive dimensions the word can refer to and have therefore ended up with explanatory concepts that are just as man-made but that leave a wide gap between scientific accounting, on the one hand, and the nature of human experience, on the other. (Psychiatrists, I feel, have sinned far less on this score.) Yet if the abstraction of "mind" *is* to be useful to psychologists, it must be viewed in such a way that its validity can be checked and tested in terms of what it refers to in concrete, real-life situations involving as they do a variety of overtones such as anxiety and satisfaction, frustration and accomplishment, joy and sorrow, exhilaration and apathy, loneliness and love.

When I try to get a toehold on what the word "mind" refers to by starting from my own naive experience (which is, I believe, all anyone can do as a start), I immediately run into two difficulties familiar to nearly all who have pondered the process that enables each separate individual to come in contact with the world, make more or less sense out of what goes on around him, and contribute his bit to the fashioning of an environment within which he can carry out his purposes, some of which he is aware of while others propel him on his way without his knowing exactly how, why, or whither.

The first difficulty is that when we try to capture the meaning of "mind" as a noun, it immediately seems to turn into an active verb. It becomes at once a process, a process in continuous motion, sometimes flowing smoothly like a great river, sometimes unevenly and with the whirlpools, rapids, and falls of a mountain stream. The process somehow changes speed, changes direction, changes focus. There is nothing fixed or static about it. "Mind" seems to lose its "reality" when isolated from the matrix of some ongoing situation, some content.

Yet if the psychologist is to get a grasp on this complicated subject matter so he can take a good look at it and communicate whatever understanding he gathers, he is forced to break up into distinguishable parts what is really an indivisible and functional aggregate; he is forced to consider separately the many variables that together make up "mind" and which are all interdependent and interrelated in such a way that no one of them would function as it does except for all the others. The process of "mind" is, then, an orchestration of many ongoing processes, each of which can be understood and has the meaning it does only when it serves at the appropriate time and in the appropriate phase of the total orchestration.

The second source of difficulty in thinking about "mind" stems from the fact that this conceptual abstraction, like all others, is several steps removed from our primary data, namely, naive experience. In order to bridge the gap between naive experience and conceptual abstractions, the psychologist must consider areas of complexity and abstraction that become progressively further removed from his first-order data. We can differentiate at least four different ways in which the process of mind may be viewed.

1. *Mind as reflected in ongoing, naive experience.* This is the level of immediate, "pure" experience as experience—unanalyzed, unconceptualized, unmediated, almost ineffable, and with no concern on the part of the experiencing individual to describe, analyze, conceptualize, or communicate what is going on in his mind. This ongoing, naive experience is what Korzybski called "first order" or "unspeakable" experience.

As has frequently been pointed out, any attempt to describe or analyze experience immediately alters that experience. When we are trying to describe or analyze mind or any aspect of it, we are functionally organized quite differently than when we are participating in the process of living and not describing or analyzing it.

2. *Mind when described.* Verbalization and communication, either retrospectively or simultaneously with the occurrence of some activity of the mind, may be distinguished methodologically from the naive experience mind provides us because of a special form of awareness required to select aspects of the variety of mental processes involved. Some focusing, categorization, and coding are operating in the process of dealing consciously or verbally with any selected phase of the mind's activity. It is as if with any such focusing, awareness is shifted from the full orchestration of the whole to the role of a particular instrument in the orchestra.

It is important for a psychologist using descriptive material of any kind never to lose sight of the fact that reports of mental activity are not to be equated with the mental activity itself. Yet such protocol data still provide the psychologist with some of his most valuable raw material while some of the most penetrating descriptions of experience have been given us by poets, novelists, composers, and religious prophets.

3. *Mind when analyzed and conceptualized.* Instead of focusing on a selected phenomenon "going on in our minds" as we must if we are trying to describe, we may in the midst of some occasion of living try to "figure out" analytically and conceptually what is going on. We of course do so for some purpose: Perhaps we are trying to work through some personal problem, perhaps we are delving into our mental processes in the hope of discovering hunches or clues that will provide us with some hypothesis. Whatever the reason, analysis of any occurrence is a very different operational state of affairs than ongoing purposive behavior itself or than a focus on some aspect of it. It is perhaps what the poet Wordsworth had in mind when he said, "We murder to dissect."

4. *Mind as an abstraction for specification.* Any attempt to understand the nature of mind is ultimately an attempt to distinguish components, to choose those by means of which we may be able to interpret the significance of any functional aspect of mind, and to describe the variables on which the singularity of any of mind's processes depend. If the abstracting we make can be effectively related to our presuppositions, then we will have an instrument to render communication more accurate and to enable others to understand the abstractions without reference to any particular item of behavior that might illustrate it.

Such abstractions are not affected by individual behavior and are not altered when conceptualized from the point of view of different persons. If they were so affected or altered, they would prove useless; it is their static quality that gives them the utility they have in understanding the significance of concrete behavioral situations. This does not mean, of course, that such abstractions never change. They are, on the other hand, constantly evolving and being modified by scientists and philosophers themselves to increase their usefulness. Any creative individual must test his abstractions by their performance and not by their consistency, realizing that any abstraction is highly tentative. All that we mean by the "static quality" of an abstraction is that an abstraction would be operationally useless if its significance were not somehow "fixed."

It should be emphasized again that when we are dealing with this fourth level of complexity which makes scientific and philosophical communication possible, we are necessarily violating phenomenal data. A full awareness of this fact and of some of the omissions involved in operating in this area may give us some perspective to increase the usefulness of our abstractions.

Mind as transaction

Much as we might like to do so, we can never somehow isolate mind or reduce it to a "pure" state for investigation. It strikes us as nonsensical even to think of such a thing for the simple reason that the processes of mentation can only be studied as part of the situation in which they operate and except for which they would not be what they are. There seems to be an increasing agreement among psychologists that perceiving—a central aspect of mind's activity—can no longer be thought of in any sense as "mind reacting to" or being "acted on." Mounting evidence from a wide variety of experiments, demonstrations, and field investigations supports the view that mind may be appropriately described as a "transactional" process. The concept "transaction" was used over a decade ago by Dewey and Bentley to differentiate the processes involved in "knowing" from views based on interaction or self-action which have affected so much of psychological theory. While the word "transaction" is hardly inclusive and dynamic enough to encompass the novel and creative aspects that emerge in so many "transactions" of living, it serves as a useful concept in helping us avoid misleading bifurcations that all too easily inject themselves not only into everyday commonsense accounting but also into psychological explanation. Such a term keeps us more aware of the fact that there can be no "knowing" without "doing," just as there can be no "person" except for an "environment," nothing "personal" except for what is "social."

The concept of transaction, implying as it does the process of interdependent variables, may also eventually discourage thinking about mind and its operation in terms of "cognition," "cognitive structure," "conation," and so forth, which are viewed as being "influenced by" other factors such as "set," "intention," "motive," or a host of other forces denoted by psychologists who are often seduced by their own abstractions and discuss mental activity and behavior as though such factors were rather discrete ingredients that we can know about separately, that already exist, and that simply get mixed together without transforming and losing their own identities as useful abstractions in the activity that is the stuff of mind. It is the very process of "interaction" that constitutes the event for fruitful inquiry. We must repeat again the danger to psychologists of being caught in the net of their own abstractions without coming to grips with what the abstraction refers to in real-life situations.

We can illustrate the problem with reference to Ittelson's analogy of a batter in a baseball game:

> It is immediately apparent that the baseball batter does not exist independent of the pitcher. We cannot have a batter without a pitcher. It is true that someone can throw a ball up in the air and hit it with a bat, but his relationship to the batter in a baseball game is very slight. Similarly, there is no pitcher without a batter. The pitcher in the bull-pen is by no means the same as the pitcher in the game. But providing a pitcher for a batter is by no means enough to enable us to define and study our batter. The batter we are interested in does not exist outside of a baseball game so that in order to study him completely we need not only pitcher, but catcher, fielders, infielders, teammates, officials, fans, and the rules of the game. Our batter, as we see him in this complex transaction, simply does not exist anywhere else independent of the transaction. The batter is what he is because of the baseball game in which he participates and, in turn, the baseball game itself is what it is because of the batter. Each one owes its existence to the fact of active participation with and through the other. If we change either one, we change the other. [Ittelson and Cantril 1954: 3f.]

Mind and externality

An essential feature of the operation of mind is the external orientation, the "objectivization," of some aspects of experience. We attribute parts of our own experience to events external to ourselves and in whose independent existence we firmly believe. We experience the things we see, hear, taste, and touch as existing apart from our minds, outside of ourselves, and as possessing in themselves the characteristics we find in them.

The view that something in some sense goes "into" the organism has persisted from the time of the Greeks who spoke of the objects emitting small replicas of themselves which were received by the perceiver, right up to much present-day psychology, with its interest in "stimulus determination" of perception. This belief is strong in all of us, and, as we shall point out later, it *must* be strong if we are to be able to act at all effectively. But the great danger of such a belief when inquiring into the nature of mind lies in the fact that it gives us the answer to our problem in advance of our inquiry. For if the objects of perception exist in their own right as perceived, then all we have to do is to fit the perception to an already existing object. The error of this naive view is nicely expressed by Whitehead, whose comment referring to the physical sciences applies even more forcibly to the world as perceived: "We must not slip into the fallacy of assuming that we are comparing a given world with given perceptions of it. The physical world is in some sense of the term, a deduced concept" (1949: 166).

More recently, the same point has been made by two other distinguished British scientist-philosophers. J.Z. Young, the biologist, writes: "The form we give to this world is a construct of our brains, using such observations as they have been able to make. Only in that sense does it exist" (1951: 107). And Sir Russell Brain, the neurologist, says, "The scientific account of perception, however, teaches us that the objects which we perceive outside our brains are not as independent of us as they appear to be: they have qualities which are generated by our brains and which have no other existence" (1959: 35).

When we perceive, we externalize certain aspects of our experience and thereby create for ourselves our own world of things and people, of sights and sounds, of tastes and touches. "The act of perceiving itself so implies the act of considering-it-real that the latter can be called an attribute of the act of perceiving" (Shilder 1953: 40). The problem then, as rephrased, is the problem of what is done *by* the organism, *by* the mind. To say that the mind externalizes certain aspects of its experience is by no means to answer this question but merely to point out one characteristic of the process. Bridgman writes that

> in seeking the precision demanded by scientific use we have thus been led to discard the common sense method of handling our environment in terms of objects with properties, and have substituted for it a point of view that regards a reduction to activities or operations as a safer and better method of analysis. ... What we are in effect doing in thus preferring the operational attack is to say what we *do* in meeting new physical situations has a greater stability than the situations themselves and that we can go further without revising our operations than we can without revising our picture of the properties of objects. Or, expressed somewhat differently, our methods of handling the external world have greater stability than the external world itself. [1950–1: 255–7]

Without taking any metaphysical position regarding the existence of a real world, independent of experience, we can nevertheless assert that the world—as experienced—has no meaning and cannot be defined independent of the experience. The world *as we experience it* is the product of perception, not the cause of it. The study of perception just as the study of mind must take the active perceiving individual as its proper point of departure.

Learning significance

The business of making sense out of what goes on around us involves the fashioning of an environment for ourselves within which we can carry out the process of living. A "happening" thus becomes an "event" for us only when *we* assign it some importance or consequence. And the meanings taken on by the impingements constantly bombarding us through our sense organs have significance and the particular significance they do because of the potential purposive behavior they serve. "Naked sense impressions simply do not occur, and the traditional analysis of our conscious experience into naked sensations as building blocks is palpably bad description" (Bridgman 1954: 98).

Just what the significance of any impingement will become, if any significance is attached at all, depends on the way we learn to utilize it in the course of our experience from infancy onward. It is only through experience that the "environment" or the "thereness" around us becomes differentiated into parts as we learn some of the potential significances of the infinite variety of aspects the environment around us has for us. G.H. Lewes observed in 1879 that "the new object presented to sense, or the new idea presented to thought, must also be *soluble in old experiences*, be recognized as like these, otherwise it will be unperceived, uncomprehended."

A major function of "mind," then, is to process and sort the consequences of its own activity and its own participation so that patterns of interpretations or assumptions are created and organized to serve as reliable guides for action, bringing the satisfactions an individual seeks.

These assumptions begin to bring some order into disorder by enabling us to predict what will happen in a given situation if we act in a particular way or possibly if we do not act at all. In this process we are trying to improve both the range and the degree of *correspondence* between the meanings and significances we *attribute* to situations and the meanings and significances these situations *turn out to have* for us as we experience the consequences of our action in striving to accomplish our particular purposes. Our actions, of course, will be effective only insofar as the predictions derived from our perceptions correspond to what we actually experience when we do act.

It should be emphasized that the degree of correspondence is inevitably to be judged from the point of view of the participant, from his own unique behavioral center in any occasion of living, and not from the point of view of an outside observer. The word "center" is used here in the dictionary sense of "the point toward which any force, or influence takes its origin; as a storm center." A major contribution a psychologist can make to an understanding of mind is to increase his knowledge of the process by means of which the degree of correspondence between the significances which we *externalize* and those which we *encounter* is achieved. We should perhaps note in passing that the word "correspondence" is not used here in the sense of identity between experience and some outside "reality" but as correspondence between two kinds of experience. Once some aspect of the environment acquires a potential significance of a high order of reliability, then a person can and does think of it as existing apart from himself just as he can and does think of the purposes and values of other people as existing apart from himself. According to our view, all aspects of the environment, whether they are physical or social, exist for us only insofar as they are related to our purposes. If you leave out human significance, you leave out all constancy, all repeatability, all form.

Purposive activity

As we try to bracket some of the variables except for which "mind" would not be what it is, it becomes increasingly clear that we must include in our consideration the purposive behavior of the organism of which mind is an aspect. Otherwise we isolate mind as a complicated machine engaged in coding, sorting, predicting, generating. For all these processes cannot go on and cannot be evaluated outside the context of what all this elaborate activity is *for* anyway. When we do something, we nearly always do it because of some intent, aim, or purpose of which we may be more or less aware. Generally we are aware of a single purpose or aim; we have a vague sense that "we" are involved in directing the doing because of "our" decision or hunch or bet as to what will be the best thing for us to do under the particular circumstances.

But how, operationally, do we define "best"? What is it, fundamentally, that impels us to action at all and that requires the complex organization we call mind as a guiding and protecting force embedded in the total organism?

For a number of years it has seemed to me that the most general specification we could make concerning the central and overriding motivation permeating all of man's behavior is the desire on the part of human beings to experience greater value satisfactions, on the one hand, or, on the other, to insure for themselves the repetition of those situations or circumstances which have already demonstrated the satisfaction to be derived if one participates in them. And if we are to account for the higher-order processes that distinguish the mind of man, which has such characteristics as creative imagination, we must emphasize that the quality of experience human beings seek is far different than that sought by any other type of organism.[1] It is important here to point out the use of the word "value" as a description of the satisfactions characteristic of human beings. For it is man's capacity to experience values and his apparent desire to exercise this capacity that helps us account for the range and novelty, the subtlety and the uniqueness, of human experience; that makes it possible for us to appreciate a poem, a symphony, a mathematical formulation, a sunset, an act of heroism or of sacrifice. There seems to be no word more appropriate than "value" to differentiate those affective components of human experience so very different from the more primitive emotional states involved in the reflexive activities that accommodate the urges for food, sex, shelter, and protection from bodily harm.

The varieties of situations in which people implicate themselves in their search for value satisfactions are, of course, infinite. The nature of the situations that hold out some possibility for the experiencing of value satisfactions varies, of course, with the life histories, the capacities, and the circumstances of every individual. But however diverse the occasions or the strivings apparently may be, all human activity and all human undertakings seem to me to be geared to the search for participation in situations that would either insure the repetition of the valueful experiences we have had or enable us to obtain new or "richer" value satisfactions from what we have learned to expect may be potentially available to us.

In emphasizing man's apparently ceaseless search for new value satisfactions, we must by no means underemphasize the concern of man to protect and preserve what he has. The bewildering variety of both informal and formal organizations and institutions man has created all appear to be more or less organized social devices to insure greater value satisfactions through the role they play as protectors of form or providers of the insurance of flow and development, or both. This would include all of those social devices studied by the modern cultural anthropologist which, somewhat like the unseen forces that hold the nucleus of the atom together, keep individuals from being split off from each other so that together each can play more of a role on his own: family systems, our customs and mores, our use of language and the subtle communications devices provided by many of our manners and codes of behavior, our commerce and industry, our social, political, military, and religious institutions together with the ideologies behind them.

It is in terms of our attempts to insure or increase the value satisfactions of living that our minds perceive and fashion the world around us. We see things, people, social occurrences, and old or new ideas in terms of their use or their potential use to us. The whole process of perceiving the world around us is the process of trying to make accurate guesses of the stance, the orientation, or the action we should take in order to carry out our purposes.

From the vast array of happenings going on around us, we select for *at*tention those related to our *in*tention. We become aware of what we sense is probably important for us to be aware of. In his consideration of "attention" the psychologist must not neglect what Harry Stack Sullivan referred to as the mind's "selective inattention." In our concern with the creations of mind, we must not forget mind's creative forgetfulness. For both inattention and forgetting often serve a most valuable function, allowing us to focus on what we feel is important to us without cluttering up our minds with the irrelevant. It is an individual's "sensed values," that is, his own feeling of what is "important," "worthwhile," or "satisfying," that are ultimately the impelling aspects of living and that lead him one way or another to any mentation or behavior at all.

So the psychologist's inquiry of "why" mind plays the role it does as this is reflected in what people think and what they do emphasizes again the requirement that the psychologist must always begin his inquiry from the point of view of the individual whose "mind" is operating, is having the experiences, doing the behaving, working out the correspondences. For if we try to record and observe the experience of a person from the point of view of an outside party, we may become insensitive to many aspects of experience *as it is going on:* We may miss completely, for example, the fact that the individual is, probably without being aware of it himself, constantly making choices, weighing probabilities for effective action, wondering about the alternative responsibilities that will be his if he does make a certain decision. The point has been nicely stated by the physicist Arthur H. Compton:

> When one exercises freedom, by his act of choice he is himself adding a factor not supplied by the physical conditions and is thus himself determining what will occur. That he does so is known only to the person himself. From the outside one can see in his act only the working of physical law. It is the inner knowledge that he is in fact doing what he intends to do that tells the actor himself that he is free. [1957: 73]

Or the experimental psychologist may forget that for purposes of experimental procedure it is frequently necessary for him to deduce from some kind of knowledge gained from outside observation the nature of experience the observer would have if he were able to act with its implication that this deduction is only a substitute for potential experience on the part of the perceiving individual.

When we stop to analyze our everyday activities from this point of view, we will find that nearly all of our behavior is characterized by a whole orchestration of purposes going on simultaneously and at different levels. Whatever mind is, it has the amazing capacity to juggle a number of different balls of different colors and sizes.

For example, in nearly every transaction of living one might differentiate the purposeful aspect of the transaction into, first, that involving and insuring the preservation of physiological and psychological processes; second, that directing action and sensing experience in terms of the accent of purpose; third, that involving the sense of the consequences action will have once it is initiated or completed.

It becomes apparent, then, that the mind of man more than the mind of any other living organism enables man to take an active part in determining what his experience will be, to contribute to the quality and range of the continual flow of diverse events that constitute living.

Varieties of significance learned

As we try to accommodate our needs and resolve our urges, we learn through our experience what significances are related to each other and to characteristics of the situation of which we are a part. As experience accumulates, we learn which relationships have high probabilities of occurrence and which only low probabilities of repeating themselves. The mind weights these probabilities in terms of their relevance to the purposes of the experiencing individual as these are involved in the unique situation encountered. Just how a person experiences new occasions will, then, in the long run be determined by the assumptive complex he brings to that occasion.

The process of acquiring assumptions to increase the effectiveness of behavior is guided and channeled by cultural norms. Our perceptions, as we externalize them, are fashioned much more than most of us ever realize by the diverse forms of our particular cultural and subcultural groups. We might almost define culture as the common pattern of learned significances. Modern cultural anthropologists describe experience as "something man projects upon the outside world as he gains it in his culturally determined form (Hall 1959: 144). Rapid developments in the field of linguistics demonstrate, as Whorf pointed out, how.

> we dissect nature along lines laid down by our native languages. The catego-
> ries and types that we isolate from the world of phenomena we do not find

there because they stare every observer in the face; on the contrary, the world is presented in a kaleidoscopic flux of impression which has to be organized by our minds—and this means largely by the linguistic systems in our minds. We cut nature up, organize it into concepts, and ascribe significances as we do, largely because we are parties to an agreement to organize it in this way—an agreement that holds throughout our speech community and is codified in the patterns of our language. [1940: 42]

Our own awareness of what goes on in our minds as our assumptions are triggered into operation by the relevance a situation potentially has to our purposes may be a very limited awareness. At other times, awareness may be both extensive and profound. There are obviously great variations according to the nature of the situation, just as there are great variations within and between individuals. But regardless of how restricted or how wide-ranging awareness may be, what we are aware of in our minds comes about through a process in which we take account of many more and many different aspects than we are probably aware of. All complex relationships between externality and impingement, between impingement and excitation, and between excitation and assumption, are taken account of in the perceptual process of the mind insofar as they are available to mind through its experience or physiology.

It may be useful to differentiate at least some of the varieties of assumptions if for no other reason than to show the intricacy of what apparently goes on in the mind as it makes its transition from one situation to another. By comparison, the operations of the most modern electronic computer seem very simple indeed.

1. *Assumptions concerning the significance of objects.* The objects in the world around us have the meaning they do for us because we attribute to them certain characteristics, sizes, shapes, or properties. We have built up these significances in the course of our dealings with these objects. For example, even though the pattern a piece of writing paper forms on our retina may not be rectangular as we look at it on our desk, we assume that the sheet of paper *is* rectangular; even though the top of a drinking glass may be seen as elliptical when we stop to "look at" it, we still "know" that it is circular. Even though we see only the head of a horse projecting from behind the barn, we will report that we are seeing a horse because we have learned to take for granted that the rest of the horse is there. We assume that things are "wholes." We learn to regard objects as "large" or "small," as "far" or "near," as moving "fast" or "slowly" because of the experiences we have become used to relative to these objects. All of this may be seen most dramatically when we read reports of individuals who have been blind from birth but who in certain rather rare instances can gain their sight after surgery. In summarizing some of these reports, J.Z. Young writes:

The patient on opening his eyes for the first time gets little or no enjoyment; indeed, he finds the experience painful. He reports only a spinning mass of lights and colours. He proves to be quite unable to pick out objects by sight, to recognize what they are, to name them. He has no conception of a space with objects in it, although he knows all about objects and their names by touch. [1951: 61]

2. *Assumptions concerning the significance of people.* When a situation in which we are participating or intend to participate involves other people, the assumptions by means of which our action is guided include new and different aspects. For other people have their own purposes which it is up to us to guess and to understand. In the process we must realize that the purposes of other people are just as "real" as any of the physical characteristics of objects. We must predict upon the basis of our assumptions what effect our intended behavior will have on others' purposes, how others will see us, and how their reaction to us in turn will affect our own subsequent action in the endless chain of events in which we are involved. We attribute certain significances to certain individuals because of assumptions we have learned concerning the meaning of the roles they play, their vocations, their place in the status hierarchy, the neighborhood, the nation, the race they represent. All of these personal attributes are often thought of as "fixed" characteristics of people according to the particular purpose any such grouping may serve us. The gestures of a people, their manners, their customs, the way in which they regard and utilize time and space are often cues which are either not understood or misunderstood until a person from another culture learns the standards upon which significance is based.

3. *Assumptions concerning the significance of sequential happenings.* Obviously the world of objects and people does not remain passive and static. Things keep changing. There is a ceaseless flow of happenings around us. Day follows night; our life follows certain rhythms; our hunger stops when we eat; the motor of our automobile comes to life when we turn on the starter; the traffic policeman stops us if we disobey his signal. In the course of living, a whole host of sequential significances are built up in us as we carry on in a world that is in continual flux.

In order to make more certain that we can "count on" a particular event to follow another event, man has devised a whole host of artifacts with built-in specifications. Many of the tools, instruments, machines, buildings, power systems, communications devices, and bewildering variety of man-made equipment that characterize modern life have been devised to insure that certain events or satisfactions will follow each other in directions that are predictable and reliable. Often this standardization is at considerable cost to the richness of experience if one looks at other aspects than efficiency. For example, symbolism with all the aesthetic, intellectual, and spiritual overtones it provides is almost entirely ruled out as man's artifacts become more streamlined and functional. When we look at the combinations of our assumptions concerning people and our assumptions concerning sequential significance, we begin to get some insight into the complexities of understanding each other in a social world which, like the physical world, is constantly changing. For example, the quality of the relationship we have with other people depends in part on our capacity to comprehend simultaneously the sequential significances other people are experiencing in a chain of events, together with the sequential significances we ourselves are experiencing in the same phase of this chain of events. The experiences each of us has in the same phase of the sequence of events may either show how closely we are linked together or how diff -ent and far apart we are. For we are able to share the same experience of what is significant in our participation with other people only insofar as we and they experience the same significances simultaneously in a chain of events in which we are all involved. Anyone who has watched an American football game with a foreigner who is seeing the game for the first time has sensed the disparity. Unless the significance of sequential events can be shared by people, then the event as the same "event" simply does not exist. Our allegiances and loyalties to others come about because of the way in which we have learned to share these sequential events and have experienced a particular quality of value satisfaction from joint participation in what we are therefore able to call the "same event."

4. *Assumptions concerning the significance of actions.* Each of us eventually learns, sometimes gradually, sometimes suddenly, what the probable significance of certain of our actions will be. We learn what experience we are likely to have if we initiate a certain chain of behavior. The child learns that a rubber ball will bounce if he throws it on the floor, that the cat will scratch him if he pulls its tail, that he has a better chance of getting the cooperation he desires if he says the right thing in the right way at the right time to his parents or friends. Each individual, according to his purposes, learns through the repeated testing of his own action to become more effective in bringing about the consequences he wants. The rituals, customs, ceremonies, and laws of a culture all insure a greater repeatability in social affairs by providing more predictable directions, enabling more people to chart their courses of action, and thereby obtain greater satisfaction for each participant.

5. *Assumptions concerning temporal significances.*[2] Permeating the learning of all varieties of assumptions is its temporal aspect. This is such an integral part of all the processes of mind that we are seldom aware of the variety of assumptions concerning time that we are taking into account. Social psychologists and cultural anthropologists have often pointed out

the different meanings and significances of time-measures, the different values placed on units of time, and the effects of technology on the time standards of different groups and their operational definition of "promptness," and so forth. But the assumptions we build up concerning subjective time become much more complex and subtle when considered from the first-person view. For example, the subjective "present," as so often pointed out, is likely to be a span of time more or less unique to every individual and gauged by him in the context of his own life, his age, his circumstances, and so forth. Similarly with the "past" and the "future."

The subjective time a person may associate with the realization of some value will vary by the "level" or "universality" of the value symbol serving as a standard for personal experience, for example, the differing standards of a Hindu mystic and an American businessman. Different purposes will be implicitly embedded in different temporal dimensions as will assumptions concerning different sequential events and the use and manipulation of different objects. The "timing" of political action by Soviet leaders in terms of their long-range purposes will likely have quite a different baseline than the timing of political action by Western leaders who tend, for example, to give weight to such a factor as the next forthcoming election.

Most of the time for most of us, a variety of these temporal significances are being taken into account simultaneously, being given different priorities in awareness as the pattern of purposes propels the stream of behavior through what we conceptualize as periodic time.

6. *Assumptions concerning the significance of value standards.* In almost any concrete situation in which we participate, we are faced with alternative choices of action. Whether we are aware of the process or not, we weigh alternative courses of action in terms of the value significances they are likely to have for us, the relative value satisfactions we will obtain if we do this or that or if we do nothing at all. Evaluation among various alternatives is made on the basis of the relative probability that each possible course of action will lead to the desired consequences, will produce the desired results. The process of guessing at the possible value satisfaction our behavior will bring is enormously complicated since an almost infinite number of subprobabilities relating to each of the above classes of significances must be taken into account. The process involves feelings or overtones that we sometimes sense only vaguely, that are often not bounded by space or time, and that only become real and meaningful as they operate in determining what we will do in the here and now. In this process we may consciously or unconsciously refer to certain abstractions that are embodied in some code of ethics, some political ideology, some religion, and which we have learned to accept as possible guides that we may put to use as possible tests on appropriate occasions. While not real in their own right,

these abstractions can become real for us if they operate effectively in concrete situations. And in this context, they are often indispensable "realities."

This is only a brief list of some of the significances, of some of the varieties of assumptions, constituting part of the active storage facilities the mind apparently provides. Assumptions move in and out in various complicated combinations in fractions of a second. Some of the assumptions endure for a lifetime, others are fleeting. Our differentiation of assumptions into various headings is, of course, quite arbitrary. There is no clearcut line dividing them. Furthermore, we must emphasize again that these assumptions are by and large interdependent in terms of their operation in a specific occasion of living.

Constancies

The effectiveness of our behavior in terms of carrying out our purposes is dependent upon our ability to act so we can experience the consequences we want to and intend to. This requires some way of knowing what can be "counted on" in the environment to bring about the desired consequences when we do act. For obviously we would not get far in the human venture if we carried on our lives with the continuous and conscious realization that we were acting on the basis of probabilities by assigning significances to the hieroglyphic stimulus patterns around us. If this were the unhappy state of affairs, we would be forever stopping to figure out what objects were, what people were going to do next and what they were really up to, what validity there was anyway to the many abstractions customarily used to guide our own activity. We would be frustrated to the point of near paralysis.

When we do discover from experience what can be "counted on," we can say that our mind has built up "constancies" or, more accurately expressed, "continuities." We begin to attribute certain continued characteristics to an object, a person, a situation, a government, a nation, and so forth. These provide a sense of surety, the feeling that the same significances will repeat themselves, will prove reliable as we act to carry out our purposeful behavior. The mind transforms the probabilities of assumptions into the certainties of constancies. Every act is based on the assumption that probable events are relatively certain events,

In spite of the long and venerable history the subject of "constancy" has had in the history of experimental psychology, there has been comparatively little consideration of the *function* of constancy, of what constancy *does* for us. What constancy does is, essentially, to enable us to "size up" the relationship of our own unique position to some object, person, or situation so that we can make a prediction with a fair degree of certainty of what will be the most effective action for us to take at some particular point in time.

And so we create and maintain a whole variety of constancies that provide us the anchoring points for evaluation and the springboards for action. The constancies we attribute to objects in terms of their size, shape, distance from us, and various other "properties" are familiar to every reader of an elementary text in psychology. And we can well add to this list what we might call the "social constancies" we build up and maintain. Psychologically, their function is the same as the function of "object constancy." Here we can refer again to words and symbols with all the intricate relationships between naming and the named that have received so much attention from semanticists; we can refer again to the artifacts man creates in order to increase the range and predictability of his behavior; we can refer again to the mores, customs, loyalties, and laws of a society devised to give greater regularity to social life.

A most important by-product of the constancies we build up is our sense of the constancy of our own self. It is only as we participate in the world around us that we discover our selves. And our own self-significance and self-constancy become increasingly real for us as we participate in the physical and social environment around us and experience the consequences of bringing our assumptions and our constancies to bear on the concrete situations of living.

The mind of the creative individual is a mind that generates new standards: Sometimes these are new standards for value inquiry, sometimes new aesthetic forms or models, sometimes new variables for scientific specification, sometimes new social or political organizations, sometimes the creation of new artifacts. The great leaps and developments that constitute so much of the story of man's history have been generated in the minds of comparatively few representatives of the human species. Just what accounts for the creative imagination of these gifted individuals is yet only dimly understood.

Flux and change

Apparently one of the most basic wants and responsibilities of the human being is the urge to preserve his sense of what is real in a constantly changing world. By acquiring a reliable set of constancies we help ourselves preserve this "reality world" to which we have ourselves contributed so much in its creation. But since the environment around us is in a continual state of change and flux, our problem is not one of merely preserving our "reality world" unchanged but of continuing our reality in an ever-changing, undetermined cosmos. Situations are never exactly alike, and many of the situations we face have elements of novelty and diversity for which we sometimes find ourselves ill-prepared and therefore face with a particular sense of insecurity, doubt, apprehension, or uncertainty. Obstacles are encountered which demonstrate to us in our own experience that our reality system is somehow inadequate. For the consequences of our action turn out not to be what we had predicted they would be: Sometimes we are disappointed, shocked, frustrated, surprised, or embittered. And the transition from what we are used to, to something new and different has, of course, been enormously accelerated by technological developments with their unpredictable social and psychological effects.

The process of living, then, involves participation in situations which we do not by any means sail through without experiencing obstructions or problems. Sometimes these are big problems, sometimes they are small; sometimes they are relatively enduring, sometimes they evaporate quickly. Our frustration may come from not knowing *how* to act effectively in order to arrive at some predetermined goal. Or, on the other hand, our frustration may result from a lack of surety as to *what* goal is the proper one for us to pursue anyway.

We can, of course, become aware of the fact that no matter how annoying or upsetting the hitches or problems may be, they are almost inevitable aspects of living in a world where the future is undisclosed and where we, as participants, can play a role in determining that future. Successful actions can only confirm our assumptions, reinforce our constancies. Furthermore, we can become intellectually aware that it is only insofar as we encounter these frustrations, obstacles, surprises, and disappointments that we ourselves "learn" something and that we ourselves have an opportunity to test out new choices, new hunches, new formulations, by experiencing the consequences they lead to in action. If the "now" or the "present" drags on more or less indefinitely and involves no anticipation, no potential foreseeable emergence, we grow despondent, we say "the future is empty" or "there is no future."

Except for activity based on reflexes or habits, nearly all of the transactions of living involve in more or less degree a set of conditions that present a problem for choice or action. Our ability to meet the problem depends upon the adequacy and appropriateness of the patterns of assumption our minds enable us to call forth for the occasion.

We sense sometimes vaguely, sometimes intensely, that what we do involves the choice we make of alternatives and possibilities; the hunch we have that our intended actions will result in the intended consequences with their intended value satisfactions. We have a sense of greater or less surety concerning the probable effectiveness of our choice; a sense of more or less conflict between alternatives involved in making our choice. And in the process of choosing and carrying out selected behavior resulting from our choice, we have a sense of more or less personal responsibility. We can be intellectually aware that we have no absolute control over future occurrences and that chance is likely to play a greater or lesser role in our behavior. We can become intellectually aware of many of the factors we are taking into account in the process of choosing. We can observe that many of our choices concerned with long-range goals involve the selection of alternatives and possibilities which we feel will in turn lead to further alternatives and possibilities that will make future choices more effective. We sense that our minds, by enabling us to choose, connect the "now" of our experience with the past and future.

We can become intellectually aware that insofar as our behavior is completely reliable, certain, and effective, we will go on to further behavior which will lead us to further desired consequences, but that when we run up against some obstacle, some difficulty, some sense of inadequacy, we become aware of this and must undertake some inquiry. If the difficulty encountered is one of *how* to achieve a predetermined goal, we make use of rational, logical inquiry involving conceptual abstractions. In its most highly developed form we label this "scientific inquiry." On the other hand, if a difficulty involves a choice of goals, a lack of surety with respect to *what* our goals "should" be, then we undertake a different kind of inquiry: Instead of indulging in rational and intellectual processes alone, we undertake what we refer to as "mulling things over," "reflecting," "meditating," in which we try to weigh the reliability of different value standards. We can sense that associated with inquiry of the former type is the collection of facts, the accumulation of knowledge, the attainment of skills, the use and development of artifacts, the development of "know-how," the proper use of scientific method, and so forth. Associated with the latter type of inquiry are the less tangible but equally "real" experiences concerned with the development of faith, the acceptance of things past, the cultivation of charity, the broadening of love, and so forth.

In any transaction of living there is a multiplicity of alternative possibilities with respect to *what* goals an individual may pursue just as there is a multiplicity of possibilities with respect to *how* he may best realize any intended goal. If we are to maintain our faith in achieving a goal and continue to sense it as "real," then we must be able to foresee or bet on the possibility of some time foreseeing some means to achieve that goal, some sequential steps leading to the desired end. If we cannot sooner or later find means to achieve the goal, then we may abandon it or considerably alter it.

Since psychologists have by and large neglected the form of inquiry involved when we must decide *why* we should do one thing rather than another (or possibly why we should do anything at all), I should like to emphasize here the important function of the mind involved in what I call "value inquiry," the type of inquiry which provides us with a value standard that can serve as a compass, a directive for action. In "value inquiry" we are seeking standards of rightness, wrongness, more right than, goodness, badness, beauty, ugliness, and so forth, which will serve as signs or cues and indicate to us the nature of the probable consequences we will experience by following a particular course of action. The standards we use and question in "value inquiry" concern our duties, loyalties, and responsibilities. Hence, the value judgments we reach through "value inquiry" involve "conscience," "humility," "ambition," and so forth.

Since the standards we "mull over" and "contemplate" in value inquiry are not bounded by time and space, we often like to insulate ourselves from the pressures of the here and now as we pursue this inquiry. We do not want to be disturbed. If we seek the companionship and advice of others, it is for the purpose of communion, or in the hope of gaining from them some wisdom. By insulating ourselves from space-and-time considerations we are able to allow our conscious and subconscious processes of mentation and feeling their widest possible range. Furthermore, some such insulation also allows us to make a more accurate distinction between those feelings and emotions related to our physiological bodily activity and the conditions at the moment of which we are a part and, on the other hand, those overtones of feeling which derive from the standards for value that have become a part of our own reality world and are not dependent on a specific set of conditions or actions in the here and now. It is these value standards that sustain us between one doing and the next. It is these value standards that enable us to weather frustration and deprivation. If we lose such standards or cannot find any, then we say "we are lost."

The value standards each of us uses are the consequences of our action in the past that have been registered and have become a part of our reality world insofar as they have proved to be good bets for further judgment and action. It is important to emphasize that this registration is not of an intellectual nature. It is a chance, a confirmation, or a denial of the weight to be given different assumptions concerning the "worthwhileness," the "goodness," the "rightness," the "decency" of any action. Our value standards thus serve both as our criterion of satisfaction and as our best guide for effective action.

The process involved in "value inquiry" is one of trying to expand the range of the cues we can include. We attempt to increase our value specifications. Hence, if a person accepts as absolute and inviolable any variety of ideology, the cues he uses in his value inquiry will be restricted and the directive for action indicated by his inquiry will lack the reliability it otherwise might have. Similarly, if he is bounded by any particular cultural complex, there is restriction. The reliabiltiy of the directives reached through value inquiry is directly related to the adequacy of the cues taken into account.

While rational inquiry is not excluded in the resolution of difficulties on the *why* level, it is of only secondary importance. This extension cannot go on freely, as we have indicated, if an individual is disturbed by impingements from his senses. Apparently the function of our senses is to give us a standpoint in time and space so that we *can* act *after* we have decided *why* we should act. These decisions involving purpose are peculiarly our own, since the value standards that compose so crucial a part of our reality world constitute a complex of value assumptions unique to each of us. These decisions, therefore, involve both responsibility and opportunity. And these interdependent responsibilities and opportunities are highly personal: they are products of our unique biological equipment participating in the culture unique to our own life history. Clarification of purposes in terms of creating value standards that serve as effective and satisfying guides for action can be one of the mind's never-ending processes. And it is such for individuals who themselves surmount the continuing obstacles of frustrations brought about by changing conditions.

Such are some of the aspects of mind that must be taken into consideration as I see them from the vantage point of a psychologist. But as I read over what I have written so far, I am sadly aware of my own inability to capture even remotely the wonder that mind is, especially when I think of such products of mind as the Fifth Symphony, the Sermon on the Mount, the *Brothers Karamazov*, or the calculus. Whatever it is that enables mind to create and to appreciate such marvels seems to elude almost completely the crude nets of any psychological jargon. Perhaps in the distant future minds will have discovered how to reveal themselves in a way that will communicate both what the scientist will then know and what the poet will continue to feel.

Notes

1. This point of view concerning the nature of human motivation has been elaborated at greater length in Cantril 1950: chaps. 2, 3.
2. I am indebted to Dr. F. P. Kilpatrick for discussion of this aspect of our assumptions.

References

Brain, W.R. 1951. *Mind, perception and science.* London: Oxford University Press.
———. 1959. *The nature of experience.* London: Oxford University Press.
Bridgman, P.W. 1950–1. The Operational aspect of meaning. *Synthese* 8: 255–7.

_____. 1954. The task before us. *Proc. Amer. Acad. Arts & Sci.* 83: 98.

Brazier, M.A.B. ed. 1958. *The central nervous system and behavior.* New York: Josiah Macy, Jr. Foundation.

Cantril, H. 1950. *"The why of man's experience.* New York: Macmillan.

_____. 1955. Toward a humanistic psychology. *ETC.: A Review of General Semantics* 12: 278–98.

_____. 1958. *The politics of despair.* New York: Basic Books.

Compton, A.H. 1957. Science and man's freedom. *Atlantic Monthly* 200 (Oct.): 73.

Hall, E.T. 1959. *The silent language.* New York: Doubleday.

Ittelson, W.H., and Cantril, H. 1954. *Perception: a transactional approach.* New York: Doubleday.

Sandburg, C. 1938. *The people, yes.* New York: Harcourt, Brace & World.

Shilder, P. 1953. *Medical psychology.* New York: International Universities Press.

Solomon, H.C., Cobb, S., and Penfield, W. eds. 1958. *Brain and human behavior.* Baltimore: Williams and Wilkins.

Whitehead, A.N. 1949. *The aims of education.* New York: Mentor Books.

Whorf, B.J. 1940. Science and linguistics. *Tech. Rev.* 42.

Young, J.Z. 1951. *Doubt and certainty in science.* London: Oxford University Press.

13

The concept of transaction in psychology and neurology

with William K. Livingston

No single word in the English language satisfactorily carries the meaning embodied in what the ancient Greeks expressed by *genesis,* "the process of becoming." They used the concept to characterize the ongoing changes exhibited by all forms of life in their progress from birth, through growth and maturation, to old age and death. Like the movement of the hour hand on a clock, these changes in the living organism may take place so slowly as to be imperceptible to the casual observer, although with the lapse of time it becomes apparent that the organism has been constantly changing into something different than it was before. A comparable "process of becoming" can be observed in certain inorganic materials, such as the radioactive elements, radium, for example, being involved in a complex chain reaction which, on completion, is transformed into lead leaving no trace of its original elemental identity.

This ongoing change in life is not a haphazard process but proceeds in a discernible direction, conforming to a progressive outline determined by the pattern of elements, of genetic structure, of built-in rhythms, or of motives as these all play their role in the orchestration of living.

The concept of transaction

The philosophers Dewey and Bentley have suggested that the word "trans-action" be used to designate any "process of becoming" in which

Reprinted by permission from *Journal of Individual Psychology* 19 (May 1963): 3–16.

the individual or "thing" is itself undergoing alterations by action through time when involved as a participant in any ongoing situation. They reserve the word "inter-action" to refer to those simpler forms of action taking place "between" elements, or "things," in which the outward aspect of the "thing" may be altered although its own elemental nature is not changed. Dewey and Bentley (1949) maintain that scientific thought during the nineteenth century primarily emphasized interactions or reactions *to*, while interpretive thinking of the twentieth century is more characterized by the concept of transaction, or action *within, through, of,* and *by* an environment in which the participating individual is himself an integral part.

One objection to this use of the word "transaction" is that few dictionaries and few individuals make any fundamental distinction between transaction and interaction. Most of us think of transaction as it is used in commerce to designate some relatively simple act of exchange, such as buying or selling, which neither implies any profound affect on the participants nor emphasizes the factor of time. To give the word the meaning Dewey and Bentley ascribe to it may seem an arbitrary notion, recently concocted. Yet this meaning for the word transaction goes back more than a century before the birth of Christ when the Greek historian Polybius of Megalopolis wrote that if anyone really wanted to understand history, he must study its "transactional" branch. Arnold Toynbee (1952: 44), an admirer of Polybius, believes Polybius coined the word to characterize his own descriptions of the Roman conquest, which was his principle topic of interest.

Polybius was frankly critical of contemporary historians who gave discrepant versions of identical events or who "failed to refer to the starting point showing how and why that point led up to the transactions of the moment." Polybius wrote:

> The monographs of the historical specialists give no inkling of the whole picture, and if any reader supposes that a survey of the leading countries in isolation from one another, or rather, the contemplation of their respective chronicles, can give intuition into the scheme of the world in its general setting, I must hasten to expose his fallacy. To my mind, persuasion that an acquaintance with local history will give a fair perspective of the whole phenomenon is as erroneous as the notion that the contemplation of the *disjecta membra* of a once living and beautiful organism is equivalent to the direct observation of the organism itself in all the energy and beauty of life. I fancy that anyone who maintains such a position would speedily admit the ludicrous enormity of his error if the organism could be revealed to him by some magician, who reconstituted it at a stroke in its original perfection of form and grace of vitality. While a part may conceivably offer a hint of the whole, it cannot possibly yield an exact and certain knowledge of it. [Toynbee 1952: 46].

We find the concept of transaction as used by Polybius a particularly apt one to give us a somewhat better toehold in our understanding of the broad implications of many recent investigations both in psychology and neurophysiology that have a bearing on the ancient problem of mind–brain relationships. If we start from the premise that behavior and neural activity can be correlated without invoking any Cartesian dichotomy, we need a term to describe the processes—and the significance of the increasing evidence for them—characterized by the change and alteration of the participants in those processes and the directional development they show.

Perception as transaction

The basic problem of "how" an individual perceives the external world around him has preoccupied many psychologists for many years since even the simplest perception is an enormously complex activity involving a wide variety of factors (Cantril et al. 1949). Among the factors except for which perception would not serve as the meaningful signal it is, we would list the following: 1. Some sort of *"externality"*—some object, person, symbol, and so forth, in the world outside the individual. 2. Some *physical energy* related to this "externality," which has the capacity to initiate a physiological process in the sense organs, as, for example, the light rays reflected from an automobile we see coming down the street. 3. Some *physiological excitation,* including the stimulation of peripheral nerve endings and the entire path of neural transmission both leading to and coming from the higher neural centers. 4. Some *assumptions,* or weighted averages derived from past experience, that have been somehow registered in the nervous system and are activated by the particular situation we are confronting, and that indicate the probability that what *is* "out there" is what we *assume* is "out there." 5. Some *purpose* or some *intention* that catalyzes the individual to pay attention in order to experience or to avoid a particular consequence.

We can focus our discussion by mentioning only three broad and divergent interpretations of the various theories formulated in the effort to answer the question of how we perceive the environment around us.

First, there are the theories that emphasize the native capacity of the sense organs to transmit to the brain the elementary attributes of the external object, such as its size, shape, color, brightness, and so forth, with the brain somehow compounding these into a "perception" of that particular object. Second, other psychologists do not believe a perception represents a summation of separate attributes but, rather, that the external object and its field constitute a single pattern, form, or Gestalt which dictates what the perception must be. According to this hypothesis, the sensory systems transmit this intact stimulus pattern to the brain where it creates a perception that is a replica of reality. Third, there are psychologists who feel that these two interpretations greatly underemphasize the contribution the perceiving individual makes in shaping his own perceptions and who doubt that either the physical attributes of the external object itself or intact stimulus patterns are the dominating factors in perception. They stress, on the other hand, the crucial role played by assumptions, derived from past experience, which an individual brings to every situation concerning the probable significance of the stimuli the sense organs receive.

Each of these three general approaches to perception is in a sense correct as far as it goes: Our senses are adapted to transmit some of the elementary attributes of external objects; certain stimulus patterns may be registered in the brain as reasonably accurate replicas of the external object and its field; and the assumptions we make about the significance of a stimulus certainly do often play a crucial role in the final meaning we assign to what we perceive.

While the proponents of any one of these approaches might have a wider conception of their theory than the emphasis epitomized here, each approach could become more adequate and more valid if it were more inclusive. For example, the Gestalt approach could readily subsume the approach of those who stress subjective factors in perception, if it included the notion of an "internal" or "longitudinal" Gestalt built up in the individual in the course of his past experiences, while the subjectivists would be more convincing if they did not at times appear to neglect the fact that one cannot perceive a square as a circle and that many perceptions do seem to become organized into a figure–ground Gestalt.

The functioning of the central nervous system as a transactional process

The most crucial test of any of these or other interpretations of the process of perception would be to know how they fit our knowledge of what the brain is doing. The cybernetic theory with its concept of "feedback" has provided useful models of what may be going on in the brain. Yet the evidence so far of the activities of the brain seems to indicate that there is far too much plasticity and flexibility to conform to any strictly mechanistic operation. In the past decade, teams of investigators composed of psychologists, neurophysiologists, pharmacologists, anesthesiologists, and computer specialists have developed increasingly sophisticated techniques for studying the activity of the brain by the use of freely implanted electrodes. The result is that brain activity itself is now being described as transactional in nature. In his book *The Waking Brain,* H.W. Magoun states that

> within the brain, a central transactional core has been identified between the strictly sensory and motor systems of classical neurology. This central reticular mechanism has been found capable of grading the activity of most other parts of the brain. It does this as a reflexion of its own internal excitability, in turn a consequence of both afferent and corticofugal neural influences, as well as of the titer of circulating humors and hormones which affect and modify reticular activity. [1958: 115]

Role of the reticular formation

The "central transactional core" consists of many different kinds of nerve cells centrally situated throughout the length of the spinal cord, forming great masses in the core of the brainstem, and extending into the thalamus to surround many of its nuclear masses (Figure 13.1) The fact that this "reticular formation" was found in the nervous systems of all vertebrates, its axial location, and its many types of nerve cells would suggest that it must perform important functions. Yet what these functions might be is only recently becoming apparent.

One reason for the delay in demonstrating its functions is that in an anesthetized animal few signs of electrical activity can be demonstrated in this part of the brain. Another reason is that the reticular formation as a whole shows little evidence of a functional organization into definite tracts and nuclei that characterize the arrangement of the sensory and motor systems of classical neurology. Furthermore, the absence of definite and long tracts made it difficult to identify the source and destination of any impulses the reticular formation might transmit along its short synaptic relays. These factors combined to give rise to the impression that the nerve cells in the reticular formation had no more function than anatomists ascribed to glia cells, and they were thought to act in supporting and padding the tracts and nuclei of the known sensory and motor systems like excelsior packed around dishes in a barrel to keep them from rattling about and breaking. In fact, the great mass of reticular formation in the midbrain was sometimes jocularly referred to as the "manure pile of the brain."

Until some thirty years ago about all that was known about the reticular formation functions was that it contained a vaguely located "center" in the medulla that controlled respiration and heart beat, while other portions served as relay stations in the "extrapyramidal" system that modulated the output to muscles from the pyramidal tracts. Then, in 1932, William F. Allen (1932) read a paper before the Washington Academy of Science

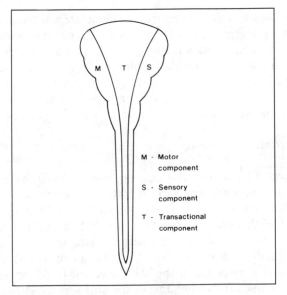

M - Motor
    component

S - Sensory
    component

T - Transactional
    component

Schematic diagram of central nervous system. "The functional attributes of the central nervous system may be better explained and investigated by admitting the possibility that they consist of "trans-actions" occurring in many portions of the brain and spinal cord. Such trans-actions may be initiated by sensory input and always find their expression in motor activity, but have an identity of their own which is greater than the sum of these two component parts" (Livingston, Haugen, and Brookhard 1954).

entitled "Formatio reticularis and reticulo-spinal tracts." His investigations had shown this formation to be a very old structure phylogenetically, and he said of it, "It apparently serves as an effective mechanism which enables these animals to adapt themselves properly to their various inside and outside conditions."

Allen's paper attracted little attention until about 1945 when Moruzzi and Magoun discovered that, in addition to contribution to the extra-pyramidal outflow, the reticular formation was also transmitting sensory impulses. They demonstrated that sensory impulses were ascending to higher centers through the reticular formation by way of short relays, along paths quite apart from the sensory tracts of classical neurology. They showed that the anterior portion of the formation represented an "arousal" center, which has since been demonstrated to have much to do with maintaining animals in states of alertness and attention, as well as waking them from sleep. Still more recently, investigations have indicated that "downstream" influences from the cortex can modulate activity in the reticular formation. Furthermore, this downstream influence can be transmitted by way of the reticular formation throughout the nervous system to modulate all sensory input at any relay station along the route it must follow to reach the cortex. Indeed, there is now evidence that this regulating effect on sensory input may extend all the way out to peripheral receptors in sensory organs outside the central nervous system.

Some experimental evidence

By the use of implanted electrodes neurophysiologists have been able to record what is happening in various parts of an animal's brain when it is unrestrained and fully alert. Using this technique, Sharpless and Jasper (1956) showed that when a cat had become "habituated" to a tone signal of given pitch and intensity, the response reaching the auditory cortex was markedly suppressed or abolished. Later, Galambos (1961) demonstrated that the cortical response in the habituated cat could be restored to its original amplitude if the sounding of the tone was accompanied by some added stimulus which gave the tone a new "significance" to the cat. In other series of experiments, Hernandez-Peon, Scherrer, and Jouvet (1956) found that anything which diverted the "attention" of the cat produced a suppression of the cortical response in much the same way as did "habituation." For example if, while the tone is producing a cortical response of good amplitude, the cat is shown a bottle with mice in it, or has the odor of fish oil blown into its cage, as long as its attention is thus diverted, the cortical response at the auditory cortex is seen to be suppressed.

From these and many other experimental observations a new picture of function in the central nervous system is emerging. Instead of its having only the classical sensory and motor systems to control adjustments to the outside world, it has two control mechanisms. The second one is centered in the reticular formation, and it is now known to exert a constant modulating influence on sensory input as well as on motor output. This less discrete and more generalized control of sensory input is of particular interest to psychologists because the evidence indicates that the ability of the brain to "police" its own sensory input is conditioned by past experience together with the "innate drives" that serve to direct behavior and determine for the animal at that particular time the "significance" of all it may be seeing, hearing, or feeling.

It may not be justifiable to assume that a cat "hears" the tone each time its cortical response is being recorded or that it no longer hears the sound when its attention is diverted or it has become habituated to the tone. Yet, we know from common experience that we, ourselves, no longer hear the ticking of a clock, the noise of city traffic, or other familiar sounds unless we give them our attention. We know, too, that the significance we ascribe to a particular sound may let us hear it while other sounds of less significance but much greater intensity are no longer heard. The classical example of this is the Chicago housewife living in an apartment beside the elevated railroad who is instantly wakened from sleep by the faint cry of her baby yet fails to awaken in response to the roar of the passing trains. Such a highly selective "tuning" of a person's auditory system is a phenomenon of great interest, and it is only now that we begin to understand how a brain is able to "police" its own sensory input so effectively that it lets go by only the traffic it wants to reach perceptual levels, while blocking out all traffic lacking in significance.

Implications

Observations of this kind have a direct bearing on perceptual theory. For if the brain can selectively block out sensory impulse patterns long before they can reach perceptual levels, "nip them in the bud" as it were, it becomes apparent that neither the "elementary attributes" of the external object nor the Gestalt can be the *sole* determinants of a perception. Instead, it seems that an animal's perceptions are constantly subject to modulation from higher centers in the brain, based on all the animal has learned from past experience, including its "purposes" as determined by hormonal and other internal drives, and its entire physiological status at that particular time.

Neurophysiology and motivational systems

Many psychologists working in many different areas are increasingly concerned with what is loosely called "motivation." In their effort to conceptualize this important subject, various theories of needs, purposes, and motives have been proposed. A particular concern of modern psychology is to understand the role of motivation as it is brought to bear on perception, determining in part the range, the intensity, the quality, and the meaning of what a person becomes aware of. Since "motives" cannot be directly observed, all the psychologist can do is to infer what such motives might be and to create abstractions which seem to him best to conform to behavioral evidence. Some psychologists have invoked the concept of homeostasis as helpful in understanding the stability an individual maintains and the continual process of readjustment he makes to situations. But this appeal to homeostasis does not encompass the type of change in which the individual or the various factors involved in the ongoing process of living are themselves modified and altered by experience.

Again, a test of what the concept of motivation might best refer to is a search for some physiological equivalents without sacrificing the subtlety, complexity, and development of purposive behavior as it is observed. While the neurophysiologists still cannot give us clear-cut answers, they are now finding basic systems in the nervous system which do apparently propel the organism toward or away from certain situations and further help to account for the interdependence of perception and motivation.

Two systems differentiated

Olds and Milner (1954) found that a rat with an electrode in its posterior hypothalamus apparently derived some kind of satisfaction from electrical stimuli to this area. If the experiment was arranged so that by pressing on a lever, the rat could deliver an electrical shock to its brain, it would "self-stimulate" up to several thousand times each hour, apparently preferring to experience the effects of the stimulation to eating or resting. That the rat "liked" the effect could be readily demonstrated by disconnecting the electric circuit. When pressing the lever no longer produced its previous "affect," the rat soon stopped pressing it and turned to food or lay down to rest, coming back once in a while to give the lever a tentative push. If the circuit was again closed, the rat promptly resumed its persistent self-stimulation performance.

At first, Olds and Milner thought they had demonstrated a "pleasure center" in the rat brain. However, further studies showed that an animal will self-stimulate in a similar fashion, though perhaps at a lesser rate, when the needle is situated in many other parts of its basic brain. Other investigators have confirmed this fact and have assisted in proving that all of the higher vertebrates have, within the most primitive parts of their brains, a "system" rather than a true "center," which when activated produces *approach behavior.*

There has been no agreement as to what this system should be called. John Lilly (1960) has referred to it as the "I Like" system since its activation evidently produces some sort of "affective state" that is interpreted by the animal as rewarding and desirable. In fact, the rewarding effect produced by its activation seems to supersede the rewarding effect of food, so that in the study of animal behavior in running mazes and other tests, the direct stimulation of some part of this system has largely replaced the use of food as a reward. Since no one knows just what sort of sensation an animal experiences during such stimulation or can tell how the animal interprets the effect, most observers simply prefer to say that the system produced "approach behavior" rather than giving a label to the affective state.

There is also evidence now of the existence of another system extending throughout the basic part of the animal brain, sometimes found only a few millimeters away from the system just described. The activation of this second system has been called by Lilly the "I Dislike" system. The behavior of the animal when this second system is activated certainly suggests that it dislikes the effect because it may vocalize exactly as it would if subjected to great pain and will struggle frantically to escape. This is particularly true when the more caudal portions of the system are stimulated. In fact, the first intimation that such a system existed came in 1954 when Jose Delgado (1955, 1956) demonstrated what he then thought were three "pain centers" in the brain of a monkey. However, it soon became apparent that he was not dealing with a true center for pain but was stimulating the lower portions of an extensive system influencing "aversive behavior." It was found that when more cephalad portions of this system were stimulated, the behavior of the animal was less suggestive of "pain" than of such emotions as "horror" and "fear."

The problem of finding an appropriate name for these two systems is complicated by the fact that behavior may change while a single area is being activated, and also by the fact that the two systems are not invariably in opposition to one another in any simple "yes" and "no" relationship. For instance, a rat will cross an electrically charged grid for the privilege of initiating a series of electrical shocks to part of its brain and then will run back over the same grid to turn off the series of shocks after it has experienced a short train of stimuli.

As another example of the complexity of a single system, there are two areas, not far apart, in the hypothalamus, both producing approach behavior and both related to food intake. Stimulation of the laterally situated area increases the rat's appetite for food, while the activation of the medially located area seems to produce a feeling of satiety and leads to the avoidance of food. Opposite effects are produced by destructive lesions in the two areas—so that a laterally placed lesion can lead to the animal's death from starvation in the presence of food, while a medially placed lesion can induce overeating to an extent that can immobilize a rat from excessive obesity. There is also evidence to show that the stopping of a train of stimuli to an "I Dislike" area may have a "rewarding" effect, an observation that reminds one of the man who said he liked to have someone kick him in the shins because "it feels so good when he quits."

Although the exact anatomical limits of these two systems have not yet been established and the study of their functions is yet in its early stages, the mere fact of their existence is of wide significance. One gets the impression that in them may arise those vague sources of motivation that have been called "instincts" and "drives" and are related to food intake and sexual activities. It is possible that some day these terms may lose much of their vagueness when their source can be definitely ascribed to a particular part of one or the other of the two systems. It is also conceivable that when we know more about how these systems function in a human brain we might be able to name the sensations and emotions that are associated with each kind of "drive."

The concept of appetite

No one who observes the facial expression of a monkey or watches his frenzied efforts to escape when some part of his "I Dislike" system is being stimulated can doubt the intensity of his emotional state. To call this system "one which produces aversive behavior" seems to give only a superficial description of what is happening. We prefer, for want of a better designation, to think of the two systems as "appetitive" in the way that Aristotle used this term.

In clarifying what he meant by sense, Aristotle (Hicks 1907: 59, 105) wrote: "In regard to all sense generally we must understand that sense is that which is reception to sensible forms apart from their matter, as wax receives the imprint of the signet ring apart from the iron or gold of which it is made: it takes the imprint which is of gold or bronze but not *qua* gold or bronze." And he goes on to say, "Where sensation is found, there is pleasure and pain and that which causes pleasure and pain; and where these are, there also is desire, desire being appetite for what is pleasurable."

Webster's International Dictionary defines appetite as "an inherent or habitual desire or propensity for some personal gratification, either of body or mind." We like this inclusion of mind in the definition because we believe that perceptual events as well as behavior are modified by purpose and that purpose may have its origin in influences derived from past experience and learned values as well as from bodily appetites.

However, the designation given the two systems is of less importance than the fact that the brain is now known to possess "built-in" mechanisms in control of behavior. When we combine this fact with the knowledge we are gaining about how the brain can "police" its own sensory input, we begin to get a new picture of the *transactional* nature of all perceptual processes.

With this new picture we no longer see a "perception" as *solely* dependent upon the elementary attributes of the external object nor upon its object–field relationships, nor on past experience and purpose. Instead, we get a glimpse of how all of these factors work together to create a perception that may or may not be an exact replica of what is "out there," depending on what parts of the incoming stimulus pattern have significance for the individual at that particular time.

Some implications for developmental psychology

These findings also give us a glimpse of how an infant actually "creates" its own "mind" and its own "self." From the time Dietrich Tiedemann in 1787 published his meticulous observations of the behavior of his infant son, followed nearly a century later by Charles Darwin's *Biographical Sketch of an Infant*, up to the ingenious studies of today, such as those of Piaget and Gesell, child psychologists have demonstrated that the infant begins at birth learning what things are and what he himself is. Tiedemann (Murchison and Langer 1927), for example, records that when his son was a month old, "the boy did not beat or scratch himself with his hands as frequently as before; so it seemed that painful, oft repeated experience had taught him to draw some distinction between himself and foreign bodies." Most of us have observed that infant development involves a gradual selectiveness in favor of objects and people associated with its nourishment and well-being, at first, for example, reflexively sucking on everything it can get into its mouth regardless of what the object may be or what effect it may have and gradually discriminating so that it sucks longer and harder and with more signs of satisfaction when it is experiencing some reward.

We can assume that at birth, aside from a few preformed reflex circuits, the association areas of an infant's brain and the reticular formation from which these areas are fed represent little more than an unorganized diffusion system. The great areas of interposed "neuropil" are still trackless, not yet organized into the complex patterns necessary to control skilled motor performance or to "police" sensory input. But into this vast reticulum come impressions of the outside world from the sense organs, leaving faint imprints in the neural substance. At the same time, the scanty information from the sensory input is activating parts of the appetitive system so that certain inputs are beginning to acquire significance because of their emotional coloration.

Without intent or anything that might be called "thought," the child is impelled toward objects and people that give it comfort and satisfaction and away from objects or people that cause it distress. The traces left by these early experiences lead to an association between certain objects and persons and the feelings they elicit. These associations, in turn, lead to "intelligent" recognition of objects and persons and to selective behavior in relation to them as information is transformed into useful knowledge through the processes of intake, digestion, assimilation, and utilization, to borrow the terms Paul Weiss (1960) has used in describing growth.

It is at this point, we think, that "mind" is born, establishing its own identity as definitely as did the first mass of living protoplasm originating from the chemicals in the sea.

And just as a person participates in the creation of his own mind, so too he inevitably participates in the creation of what he believes is "reality," drawing upon many sources as he weighs innumerable cues transmitted in terms of their potential significance to him. The continual refinement and discrimination of ways and means to satisfy the appetitive system becomes essentially a search for a concept of reality that will provide a greater degree of correspondence between what is "out there" to be adjusted to and experienced, and what actually is experienced after purposive action is undertaken.

Simultaneously, the individual gradually builds up a concept of Self in which the nervous system provides the unity, supplying the individual with built-in purposes that become refined and directed in the course of its particular development and according to its individual capacities, regulating output toward greater efficiency in accomplishing these purposes, and policing input so that what is most significant in achieving purposes can be appropriately attended to and evaluated.

While such an interpretation is, to be sure, still based on somewhat sketchy evidence, it does seem to indicate that a transactional view of human behavior and of its development may be worth thinking about as an aid to rid us of any conception that leads to mind–body dualism.

References

Allen, W.F. 1932. Formatio reticularis and the reticulo-spinal tracts. *J. Washington Acad. Sci.* 22: 490–5.

Aristotle. 1907. *De anima.* Book 2. Trans. R.D. Hicks. Cambridge: Cambridge University Press.

Cantril, H., Ames, A., Jr. Hastorf, A.H., and Ittelson, W.H. 1949. Psychology and scientific research. *Science* 110: 461–4, 491–7, 517–22.

Delgado, J.M.R. 1955. Cerebral structures involved in transmission and elaboration of noxious stimulation. *J. Neurophysiol.* 18: 261–75.

Delgado, J.M.R. Rosvold, H.E., and Looney, E. 1956. Evoking conditioned fear by electrical stimulation of subcortical structure in the monkey brain. *J. Comp. Physiol. Psychol.* 49: 373–80.

Dewey, J., and Bentley, A.F. 1949. *Knowing and the Known.* Boston: Beacon Press.

Galambos, R. 1961. Processing of auditory information. In *Brain and behavior,* ed. M.A.B. Brazier, 171–204. Washington: American Institute of Biological Sciences.

Hernandez-Peon, R., Scherrer, H., and Jouvet, M. 1956. Modification of electrical activity in cochlear nucleus during "attention" in unanesthetized cats. *Science* 123: 331–2.

Lilly, J.C. 1960. The psychophysiological basis for two kinds of instincts. *J. Amer. Psychoanal. Assoc.* 8: 659–70.

Livingston, W.K., Haugen, F.P., and Brookhart, J.M. 1954. Functional organization of the central nervous system. *Neurology* 4: 495.

Magoun, H.W. 1958. *The waking brain.* Springfield, Ill: Thomas.

Murchison, C., and Langer, S. 1927. Tiedemann's observations on the development of the mental faculties of children. *J. Genet. Psychol.* 34: 210.

Olds, J., and Milner, P. 1954. Positive reinforcement produced by elecrtrical stimulation of septal area and other regions of rat brain. *J. Comp. Physiol. Psychol.* 47: 419–27.

Sharpless, S., and Jasper, H. 1956. Habituation of the arousal reaction. *Brain* 79: 655–80.

Toynbee, A.J., trans. 1952. *Greek historical thought.* New York: Mentor books.

Weiss, P. 1960. Knowledge: A growth process. *Science* 131: 1716–19.

14

Sentio, ergo sum: "motivation" reconsidered

Introduction

The term *motivation* as such seems to be somewhat unpopular in general psychology.[1] It is not difficult to see why. For one thing, psychologists have fashioned diverse terminologies to suit their predilections and to provide descriptions of thought and behavior that satisfy their own perceptions of problems. As a result the literature in the field is rife with concepts, such as "drives," "motives," "needs," "goal-seeking behavior," "ego-involvements," "need-gratification," "self-realization," and "self-actualization." Some of the more sophisticated descriptions utilizing such concepts provide valuable insights indeed concerning the intricacies of behavior and the phenomenology of experience, and keep us from becoming too myopic. But in less cautious hands, they often become oversimplified with a single "need" picked out as an "explanatory" concept, or a hierarchy of needs or motives used to pigeonhole the whole gamut of human behavior and striving. Often, too, the particular words used not only have different meanings for different investigators but change their meanings with the single investigator as he modifies his concepts to fit his new thinking. Some time ago, P.W. Bridgman noted that "the meaning of a word at any epoch is to a certain extent fortuitous, significant of the special features in past usage of the word which happens to have stuck in the memory of the users" (1950–1: 251).

Another reason for the apparent demise of the concept "motivation" is certainly that more "hard-nosed" investigators turn their backs on the

Reprinted by permission from, *Journal of Psychology* 65 (1967): 91-107. Copyright 1967 The Journal Press.

term and the vagaries of words substituted for it, as they seek specific mechanisms for specific "drives" and insist that there be some demonstrable referent within the organism that can be pointed to and, if possible, measured as explanation for a particular segment of behavior. Historically, this emphasis can perhaps be traced back to Descartes, who saddled Western thought with his mind–body dichotomy and his mechanistic, atomistic emphasis wherein the interdependency of all aspects of body, mind, and Self and the realities of process and becoming had no place, an approach from which psychology has only within the past few decades partially emancipated itself as more pockets of holistic approaches appear.

We see, then, a wide gulf between behavioristically inclined psychologists, on the one hand, and those psychologists concerned with the full gamut of human behavior, including the apparent self-generation of motives, on the other hand. The former often convey the impression that man is a robot, made up of various neurological centers, glandular activities, and moving parts, but without any overall motive power. The latter are impatient with any traditional mechanistic stimulus–response formulations, seem rather unaware of the revolution in neurophysiology, and continue to use a variety of abstractions as "explanations" without much concern as to what their naturalistic bases might be, getting around the problem with speculative qualities or attributes assigned to the intangible "mind" or "person" and creating systems, subsystems, and taxonomies of all sorts, fitting human experience and behavior into them.

Some people who seek the sources of man's motivation have turned to existentialism, perhaps in despair. But this can only prove to be a cul de sac, ending up as it does with a nihilism, an artificial bifurcation between the individual and society, and a complete lack of concern for any accounting based on known facts concerning the human organism. Others turn to modern philosophers of science or epistemologists for answers and solace to the complexities of human behavior which, they insist, is not mechanistic but reveals conscious choice and other characteristic qualities unique to human behavior, which can never be accounted for solely in terms of chemistry, physics, cybernetics, and so forth. But this, even in the best of hands, seems to lead us into some form of vitalism to explain man's consciousness and human qualities and emphasizes all over again Descartes' old dichotomy, ignoring common sense and common observations as well as modern neurophysiological discoveries.

The resulting situation is that psychology seems rather to be straddling the problem of "motivation": either dealing in many cases with partial problems in precise ways, thus sidestepping main issues; or, on the other hand, fashioning concepts as "explanations," making extrapolations, and not bothering about the possibility of any naturalistic bases for speculation. Because of this state of affairs, other investigators, particularly social scientists, are at a loss to know how to give any valid and adequate account of the complex problems they face when they turn to the psychologist's microcosm for help, whether these problems deal with the family, the community, group or national loyalties and tensions, or international affairs. Often they have to create their own interpretations or fall back on textbook teachings of some simple need theory or unrefined Freudian account.

What the writer is trying to do here is merely to bracket the problem as he sees it, to put his thoughts into the simple language of the empiricist, avoiding technical jargon as much as possible. For the concept of "motivation" dies hard and he feels it can still serve a most useful function for any investigator dealing with the ramifications, the range, and subtleties of individual and social behavior, whether he be a neurophysiologist, a psychologist, or a student of international affairs, if we try to track down what the concept can refer to. The writer is assuming that it is much more important to analyze crucial questions with whatever methods are available, even if they are sometimes fuzzy, than it is to study trivial problems with precise methods and to search for nice quantification. He is particularly interested here in formulating a view of motivation that will at least be consistent with the exciting new developments in neurophysiology reported in the avalanche of information pouring out of the laboratories, in part so that humanistic psychology itself may eventually find some scientifically established underpinning which will clarify definitional problems. It is not the purpose of this article to consider the implications of neurophysiological findings in any detail.[2] The aim here, rather, is to sketch the broad picture now becoming visible.

Feeling and the appetitive systems

The normal newborn infant can be thought of as a bundle of feelings. When he gets hungry or uncomfortable, he wiggles, tightens up, and makes certain sounds. The baby who has just been fed or relieved of discomfort gives every impression of being relaxed and produces gurgles of contentment. The feelings of a newborn infant and the undirected behavior accompanying them are built-in activities. They are universal, the same behavior and sounds made by infants in every country the world over. Such early expressions are not expressions of a "mind" or "Self" but of an undifferentiated totality. In expressing these early feelings, the infant, of course, has no conception that anyone will notice them or do anything about them. He seems only to be revealing the fact that "I am uncomfortable" or "I feel great," depending on his bodily state. Descartes would have been more accurate if he had written *Sentio, ergo sum,* since being is more reliably indicated by an awareness of feeling than by any rational thought.

The same point was made by the philosopher John Macmurray in his Gifford Lectures of 1954:

> The infant's original consciousness, even as regards its sensory elements, must be feeling, and feeling at its most primitive and undiscriminated level. What it cannot be is a set of discriminated "animal impulses," each with its implicit reference to a mode of behaviour, in relation to the environment, which would satisfy them. We have no ground for thinking that the newborn child can distinguish between a feeling of pain, a feeling of sickness and a feeling of hunger. This discrimination, too, we must assume has to be learned. The most we have a right to assert, on the empirical evidence, is an original capacity to distinguish, in feeling, between comfort and discomfort. We postulate, therefore, an original feeling consciousness, with a discrimination between positive and negative phases. [Macmurray 1961: 57]

When the infant grows up, no matter where he lives he is likely to use as a common greeting the expression "How are you?" *"Comment ça va?" "Wie geht's?"* according to the language he has learned. Both he and the person to whom he is speaking will understand what is meant by the question and it will not be hard to respond. It will refer to "well-being" in the broadest possible sense. It is feeling that makes the world go 'round. Goethe said *Gefühl ist alles.*[3] It is feeling of some sort reflected by the behavior of any organism that differentiates it from a plant, a machine, or a robot.

While concepts such as "needs," "purposes," "motives," and the like are certainly in no sense "wrong" and good descriptions of them have great heuristic value in helping us understand the phenomenology of experience and behavior, they are not "there" in the organism as entities that have a naturalistic foundation. Hopefully, they themselves, as abstracted ways of starting at the top to slice experience, can be better understood or take on more precise meaning when seen in the light of systems that seem rooted in the organism and are becoming discernible.

Thus in stressing the role of feeling, the writer hopes he is not merely introducing another word to describe "motivation" but is following the implications for psychology of the neurophysiological discoveries of what he thinks may best be termed two great appetitive systems built into the chassis of all living organisms and that act as tuning mechanisms responding to all the transactions with the internal and external environments. The writer will not describe them in any detail here, since this has often been done before (Delgado 1955; Delgado and Hamlin 1960; Lilly 1960; MacLean 1959; Olds 1956, 1960; Sem-Jacobsen and Thorkildsen 1960; Wooldridge, 1963). His concern here is with the function of these systems in providing a coloration to experience as a base against which significances are judged.

Suffice it to say that both of what William Livingston and the writer termed "appetitive systems" (1963) were discovered in 1954: the first by two young psychologists, J. Olds and P. Milner, then at McGill University, who found that electrical stimulation of certain parts of a rat's brain apparently produced clear-cut feelings of satisfaction, or of experiencing something desirable, of wanting more of the same. Later research has shown that there are many parts of the active brain in all higher vertebrates that produce this approach behavior when stimulated. When stimulation occurs in human subjects, they describe their experiences in terms of elation, deep satisfaction, complete relaxation, and the like. The other great system, first noted by J.M.R. Delgado of Yale, was one which, when the brain was stimulated electrically, produced just the opposite effect with every evidence that the animal was suffering extreme pain, anger, and rage. In human subjects, later research has shown that stimulation of various parts of the brain has been described by them as horror, fright, terror, anxiety, extreme depression, and the like.

Livingston and the present writer used the phrase "appetitive systems" to describe these processes rather than any concept of "centers" corresponding to particular "drives." For the experiential and behavioral effects noted by the electrical stimulation of the brain may well be due to large field effects rather than to the activation of particular nerve cells, or may be due to some pattern of impulses transmitted somewhere else in the brain as well as to a whole array of various "mechanisms." The word "appetite" was used following Aristotle's use of the term and because it can avoid the overtones and loadings of a simple hedonistic pleasure–pain principle. The appetitive systems are much more complicated, varied, and subtle than any pleasure–pain dichotomy, including as they do both raw emotions and such complex affective states as love, sympathy, and wonder—all of which, too, are subsumed by the concept of "feeling." These appetitive systems can be conceived of as an orchestration of neural mechanisms or a tuned ensemble of many instruments concerned with all the activities of an ongoing organism which have an affective coloration that influences the organism to approach or move away from situations it learns to perceive may affect it for good or ill. They are, of course, subject to the influence of hormones, glandular activity, satiation, and aging, to mention only a few other components of the orchestration.

The main point to stress here is that it is these primitive, built-in appetitive systems of feeling against which specific purposes are formed and develop even though the relationship is only infrequently and vaguely in conceptual awareness. All sensory data coming into the central nervous system seem to be constantly processed en route by an organism tuned like a fine violin before such data can give rise to conscious perceptions. It is to satisfy feeling favorable to the well-being of the organism that intention develops and without which there is no attention.

Feeling, then, appears to be the great activating force, the motivator against which all else that happens to the human being is measured and judged. It is this coloration of experience, of feeling, provided by the built-in tuning appetitive systems that not only gives the push and motive power to behavior but that is used by the organism as the guide and the *raison d'être* for assigning significances to all the impingements encountered in life and give the occasions of living their quality, coloration, and intensity.

In the many excellent reports of the activity of the reticular activating system (RAS), various descriptive phrases are used by investigators to describe the amazing capacities it has and the functions it serves. It is, for example, called an "awakening" and "arousal" system; it is involved in "focusing attention;" it is used in "selectivity" and "discrimination of what is important or suitable," "selecting out what is useful to the organism." We know that the RAS is involved in "habituation," disregarding what is not important or helpful or necessary to the welfare of the organism; it "registers impressions" and somehow signals, as a computer, its NOW PRINT order of command for recording experiences that may sooner or later be valuable. What is registered is described as becoming "stored" as "weighted averages" for future use as the RAS serves in "regulating," "controlling," and "policing" the impacts of environmental stimuli. Briefly restated, the reticular activating system apparently has the capacity to assign significances both to what comes in as stimuli from the external and internal environments and signalling what behavior, if any, is most appropriate in handling the constant input. William K. Livingston pointed out in 1954 that because of the activity of the RAS it was appropriate and useful to think of a great vertical or transactional component of the nervous system which regulated both input and output (Livingston, Haugen, and Brookhart 1964).

A description of the general situation is given in Ralph Gerard's broadly gauged article "Neurophysiology: An integration:"

> One last note is due on subjective experience and objective behavior. The latter depends on efferent nerve impulses to appropriate effectors. These neurons are fired by impinging impulses from other neurons, and so by regression to the afferent messages from receptors. But it is clear that not all entering messages or information bits find their way out in prompt action; some, probably most, end by altering the material nervous system and become stored memories or information. With reverberation and feedback and synchrony, much can happen within the brain—and presumably accom-

panied by some kind and intensity of consciousness, including the unconscious—with no immediately correlated behavior. Conversely, from this rich
central store overt behavior can flow which is not immediately related to any
input. Such separation in time and type (and locus) of stimulus and response
gives the richness and spontaneity of behavior experienced as volition and
rationalized as free will. Behaviorism is thus too narrow a straight jacket
comfortably to contain the mind; but the alternative is not the "uncaused
cause" of a choice by the psyche. Whatever the degree of contingency at each
level or organization, there is no place for a directed random event, and a
general chain exists—of causality down levels and of purpose up them.
[Magoun 1960]

Again, to repeat, it would appear that what Gerard describes as
"causality down levels and of purpose up them" is basically due to the
organism's ceaseless attempt to achieve a feeling of satisfaction and well-
being and avoid antithetical feelings. It is this attempt, beginning with
birth, that provides the push and pull of living and gives the matrix for the
elaborate extensions acquired throughout life to implement feeling, as the
recording apparatus begins to function, to bring in information that is
registered, "printed," and stored, all of which is colored either by a sense of
pleasure and satisfaction or of unpleasantness or pain.

Extension of feeling and appetitive systems

These primitive, built-in, appetitive systems become quickly extended
and conditioned, especially in the human being, as the infant, then the
child and the adult transact with their internal and external environments.
Simple colorations of feeling, such as warmth, satisfaction of hunger, and
the like, with which the infant starts out are soon extended through his
trial-and-error random movements, signaling to him which ones bring
satisfaction and which do not. The infant, as well as the adult, is probably
relatively unaware that it is feeling that serves as the guide and director of
his activities, impelling him to do what he is doing to make him feel better
or not feel worse. Soon, even the young infant begins to learn to direct his
behavior and make sounds or movements that will bring his situation to
someone's attention for gratification or relief. When the infant begins to
develop the capacity to anticipate and make choices, then we can properly
say that mind is born.

Concurrently, the infant learns that there is something "out there," independent of his own being, that has apparent characteristics and attributes
of its own. As he discovers his own body, so he also discovers the externality
of the things and people around him, and we can say that at this point Self
is born.

Both "mind" and "self" develop, of course, largely according to the particular cultural situation an infant is in as he discovers new and reliable ways of activating his appetitive systems and experiencing the consequences that satisfy or relieve him. He experiences the sensations he does in the way he does as a result of weighing indications in terms of his feelings and of learning more specific purposes within the matrix of feelings as he finds out what is "important" to him and what he can and should be "concerned about." Learning, then, proceeds as a function of the appetitive systems and the accompanying feeling that serves as the compass or selector against which significances are generated and judged and by means of which awareness is extended to new potential satisfactions which can be sought out.

Perceptions are conceived and born in purposeful action. Perceptions instrument feeling. Perceptions are not so much responses to any discrete external "stimuli" as they are to assessed differences. These differences occur and are assessed as constancies develop. When the boundary lines of constancies are crossed in awareness by some situation that appears important or potentially important, then a signal is transmitted that the organism should do something about that situation. So perception involves the continual asessement and reassessment as ceaseless change goes on, both in the external and internal environments.

Generally, we are in complete ignorance of the significance of a situation unless and until some future action on our part discloses its nature and what its significance is to us. We are then in a position to register the assumption on the basis of which we have acted, to store this in our developing "mind," and gradually to build up a more and more reliable pattern of assumptions or weighted averages by means of which we can more appropriately direct our choice and behavior to bring about the state of feeling we desire. Gradually, we learn to orient ourselves in relation to what is both possible and potential.

What we attend to in the external or the internal environment are those assessed differences that begin to assume some significance in terms of our feelings. William James, among others, long ago pointed out that "attention" is an intervening variable that itself explains nothing. "Attention" refers to some significance we become aware of because we have learned to sense that it will affect our feeling states in one way or another. A useful phrase to describe this instrumentation of feeling via perception is the colloquial expression "to size up." We are constantly "sizing up" situations, people, sets of symbols, alternative courses of action, and so forth. As we learn to weigh events and alternatives more successfully, we might say that we develop greater "free will." Obviously where one and only one type of action will aid us, then the role of awareness and consciousness is minimal and action becomes reflexive or habitual.

In this continuous process of "sizing up," of making prognoses concerning what something "is," what its characteristics are, what the probable behavior or probable purposes of other people are, and the like, we judge all new encounters and situations in terms of the up-to-the-now pattern of assumptions which we have found have some pragmatic basis in past experience. Back in 1879, G.H. Lewes noted that "the new object presented to sense, or the new idea presented to thought, must also be soluble in old experiences, be re-cognized as like these, otherwise it will be unperceived, uncomprehended." We continually compare the prognoses of the changing new external and internal events with the pattern of assumptions derived from the past. If we find they conform—that is, if they "work"—then we may either no longer be concerned or have minimal concern. But insofar as they do not work, we must take stock of the situation, reassess it, and make a choice which has some degree of probability concerning its final outcome.

Both the reticular activating system and the cortex make it possible for us to register and store the quality of feeling we have experienced in our continuous transactions. They enable us to build up all manner of constancies—about the characteristics of things, of people, of symbols, of groups and ideologies—that make our appraisals easier and more reliable. We become frustrated when we sense a conflict between the significances we bring to a situation and which have worked in the past but seem to have no correspondence or clear relevance to the emerging situation we face and which requires some decision and action on our part if we are to relieve or enhance our feelings.

All perceiving thus has an anticipatory aspect, and the registration or storing of a perception has an anticipatory quality that we extrapolate in the immediate or more long-term future. Thus, Grey Walter finds that the "expectancy wave" develops in response to a warning stimulus only when a person knows the warning will be followed by a second stimulus requiring an action or decision (1964). The detailed work of Soviet physiologists and psychologists on the orienting reflex points to the same conclusion. All expectation is relative to the assumptions we bring to an occasion. It is an obvious fact in everyday life that if we "expect" the dentist's drill or the doctor's probing to hurt us, if we "expect" some person to act in a particular manner, our subsequent reaction is thereby altered. On the other hand, there are numerous instances of men who have been seriously wounded in battle who, in the excitement and urgency of combat, have felt no pain whatsoever. Every perception that is registered seems to involve an extrapolation of some sort of the potential significances of an event or transaction of a certain matrix of experience with significance always referring back basically to its significance for our feelings.

Just as "memories" are registered and stored, so also are other varieties of psychological states imprinted and stored. Complex psychological qualities and patterns described by words like assumptions, purposes, opinions, and values are similarly learned and registered. They become a crucial part of the internal environment, providing human experience with its varied nuances, its ranges, its capacity to judge what is significant. Without the registration of such processes of mentation and feeling, it would be impossible to account for the reality of much of human experience: of intentions, curiosity, ingenuity and devising; of persistence, ego-involvements, a sense of morality; of the human being as a unique chooser of possibilities.

Such a conception is completely consistent with modern neurophysiology. A prominent neurologist, for example, has written:

> A central nervous control is exerted even out to the peripheral sense organs, and acts throughout the entire trajectory of the ascending sensory pathways. This control, which was unknown until a few years ago, appears to be exercised in accordance with internal value systems which themselves are affected by previous as well as concurrent appetites and purposes. Thus the modulation of incoming sensory impulses seems to be based upon expectation, relative significance to self, and so forth. Value systems are incorporated in central nervous mechanisms of reward and punishment, emotional experience and expression, and are accessible to the presumably more objective and depersonalized systems of the neocortex. This complex set of value systems is built into the chassis, so to speak, and cannot be divorced from either the ascending signals coming in from the outside world, or from the outgoing sensory-control impulses which can modulate these incoming messages. Evidently the nervous system is continually exercising and refining its control over sensory pathways, just as it has long been known to do in relation to motor performance. Presumably the brain can shape our perceptions more or less as it shapes our comportment. [Livingston, 1962: 91]

Obviously it is because of the registration of such qualities that human experience is so different from that of any other organism in its subtlety, its moods, its appreciations, and its anxieties. Marcel Proust, a particularly keen observer of the well-springs of his own experience, reported that "I write nothing of what I see, nothing at which I arrive by a process of reasoning, or of what I have remembered in the ordinary sense of remembering, but only of what the past brings suddenly to life in the smell, in a sight, in what has, as it were, exploded within me and set the imagination quivering, so that the accompanying joy stirs me to inspiration" (1955: 410). In a similar vein, Albert Einstein said to his biographer:

> The most beautiful emotion we can experience is the mystical. It is the source of all true art and science. He to whom the emotion is strange, who can no

longer wonder and stand rapt in awe is as good as dead. To know that what is impenetrable to us really exists, manifesting itself as the highest wisdom and most radiant beauty which our dull faculties can comprehend only in their most primitive forms—this knowledge, this feeling is the center of true religiousness. In this sense and only in this sense I belong to the ranks of devoutly religious men. [Frank 1947: 284]

As mind and Self develop, behavior becomes infinitely diverse and complex in its quality and range. It is because value systems can become "incorporated in central nervous mechanisms" that any simple pleasure–pain dichotomy or hedonistic theory becomes inadequate to account for a wide range of human behavior. One observes this in the case of mothers who forego many personal gratifications for the welfare of their children, among doctors and priests who give up their rest and comfort for the ill, among soldiers who suffer the hardships of warfare, among martyrs or Buddhist priests and nuns who practice self-immolation, among revolutionary leaders who give up security and worldly pleasure for the sake of their cause. All such behavior seems guided by a desire to achieve the fulfillment of some value system that has become registered.

The "purposes" we learn and intellectualize to ourselves as we act in various situations assume enormous variety both in kind and in degree. But basically the purposes which constitute the intentions we try to fulfill by our actions all seem to derive from the primitive appetitive systems which have become conditioned and refined and which are, furthermore, generally beyond our intellectual control This is confirmed over and over in everyday life occurrences and in psychological experiments which show so clearly that a person with a special interest does not and cannot "size things up" intellectually with any impartiality, that he "sees" things as they are colored by his feelings and not simply as they are rationalized by his intellect.

Social participation

It is abundantly clear to anyone concerned with an understanding of human behavior that, as Macmurray expressed it, "the Self exists only in dynamic relation with the Other" (1961: 17); that "we are not organisms, but persons. The nexus of relations which unites us in a human society is not organic but personal. Human behavior cannot be understood, but only caricatured, if it is represented as an adaptation to environment" (1961: 46). Nearly all human experience is in one way or another experience that involves other people. And unless we are among the tiny minority of persons who for some misanthropic reason choose complete isolation as a way of life, we all have a yearning to communicate with others in one form or another, to experience a sense of participation which will give us a sense of mutuality, an opportunity to express our feelings and have them responded to in some manner, and, in the process, have our feelings satisfied and our sense of isolation and insulation reduced.

Frequently we feel rewarded simply by being with others, hearing their voices on the telephone no matter what the content of conversation, joining with them in almost any kind of shared activity that provides the participation we yearn for. We know that even infant monkeys cannot develop into normal adults without participation of some variety with their peers. The phrase "interpersonal relatedness," so common in the literature of social science, often tends to pass over in its implications the warmth, the overtones of feeling, the love that binds so many people together and that can become a cold, antiseptic phrase when applied to family, community, and other human relatonships that we regard as the most valuable and cherished we have. Even psychologists have seemed to shy away from underlining the desire to love and to be loved that shines through so much of their own data and that provides, perhaps, the most satisfying feeling a human being can experience. When feeling is left out of any social equation, including the equation of the social engineer or the responsible official planning national policy, it is ignored at great peril and the equation will sooner or later be found "wrong," in the sense that it will not work. Any ideology will eventually wither away if it does not operationally at least adjust itself to accommodate human feelings.

In the normal course of development, the Self is expanded as we become "ego-involved" with more and more situations, individuals, groups, or ideologies which both broaden and solidify our sense of Self and Self-constancy and thereby enhance our basic feeling of satisfaction. The manner in which the Self becomes extended throughout the course of living by learning the norms of some reference groups—with the standards of the group becoming the standards of the individual—has been convincingly demonstrated many times experimentally and is, of course, a familiar enough occurrence in everyday life. Similarly, the many studies of conformity, appeals, and propaganda point to the same conclusion: A person is influenced or becomes ego-involved when he perceives that the standards of a social grouping, a belief, or an ideology can provide him with criteria of judgment and action that will enable him to enrich his sense of worthwhileness, whether the group whose standards and norms he accepts be that of a gang engaged in violence, a monastic order, or some variety of political, national, or social movement. From the point of view of "motivation," all such learned identifications serve as vehicles for the extension and expression of feelings, and the particular vehicles utilized are matters of circumstance and temperament to be understood in terms of an individual life history. All of them provide the social constancies except for which there could be no sense of Self.

Some years ago when the writer was investigating the reasons for the large Communist protest vote in France and Italy, he visited a predominantly Communist *borgata* (slum area) on the outskirts of Rome. The chief police officer for the district was an exceptionally fine, compassionate man much beloved by those in the *borgata* who brought their troubles to him so that he served informally as judge, priest, and general counsellor. The writer complimented him on the decor of the waiting room outside his office with its new and clean furniture, its framed pictures, its newspapers and magazines, its bouquets of flowers in lovely vases. Then the officer explained why he had fixed the room up as he had. Apparently couples who were at odds with each other or men who were accusing each other of some sort of petty crime used to come in to see him and while they were waiting would frequently get into violent arguments that led to beatings or fisticuffs. In trying to cut down on this sort of behavior outside his own office, he said he thought it might work if he had the whole place decorated as nicely as he could afford to make it, thus reminding all his visitors symbolically of the norms of a good and decent society. Since the redecoration there had not been a single instance of undesirable behavior. The writer mentions this illustration for it shows in a nutshell the power of social norms that one knows are appropriate as guides to action in a particular situation and the violation of which would cause a feeling of distress within the individual who has transgressed.

Apparently ever since the human race began its career on this planet, it has devised ways and means of insuring or enhancing the possibility that the individual could, if not in slavery or prison, experience the value qualities of feeling that human beings cherish and that make living worthwhile. All manner of organizations and institutions with their rules and regulations have been devised to help guarantee or give expression to the feeling of personal mutuality and the sharing of significances. Rituals, such as those created for baptism, puberty, marriage, or burial, enable a number of people to share the same experience simultaneously, help to bind one person to another, and enrich feeling by deliberately making an event out of what would otherwise be an isolated happening. Such occasions provide people a symbol that allows them to express both their awareness of a situation and their joy or grief, as the case may be, of his awareness. Symbols are created and perpetuated which make wider communication and identification possible; myths develop to give a coherent vision which satisfies until accumulating knowledge corrodes them. All of these social creations—institutions, symbols, and myths—implement the search for commitment and the satisfaction it can bring.

The concept of *"culture"* itself, from a psychological point of view, can be defined as a relatively stable pattern of common significances which people have learned and which they accept. The term *"political culture"* which has become part of the vocabulary of the political scientist would, then, refer to a common pattern of significances people have learned and accept that deal with the power and influence structure of a community, nation, or region. The deep and pervading influence of the "cultural patterns" that have been learned with all their norms of behavior is occasionally forgotten, even by the psychologist and social scientist, whose account of modern man sometimes can become naive in its sophistication and its disregard of how much our feelings have become channeled. Thus, for example, Lewis Mumford has pointed out that

> if we could recapture the mentality of early peoples, we should probably find that they were, to themselves, simply men who fished or chipped flint or dug as the moment or place might demand. That they should hunt every day or dig every day, confined to a single spot, performing a single job or a single part of a job, could hardly have occurred to them as an imaginable or tolerable mode of life. Even in our times primitive people so despise this form of work that their European exploiters have been forced to use every kind of legal chicane to secure their services. [1961: 102]

Investigations of social discontent, such as riots, uprisings, or revolutions, together with any measures taken to avoid them or calm them, will fall wide of the mark if the feelings of the participants are neglected, if their sense of inferiority and frustration are not recognized, if their pride is violated, or if they feel that they or their aspirations are not understood. For no amount of data collected about the "objective conditions," the poor standards of living, the lack of educational or job opportunities will have real meaning until translated into the human dimension.

The matrix of our reality worlds

Throughout the course of his life, then, an individual is an active participant in the creation of his own mind, the development of his own Self, and, more generally speaking, his own reality world. As the writer has often emphasized, this reality world, composed of the whole complex of learned assumptions brought to an occasion of living when it takes on significance because of them, is the only world a person knows, the world within which he has his being. All we can ever know and be aware of about the activities that envelop us is their significance to us in terms of our reality world.

A person tries from infancy onward to build up for himself a pattern of assumptions that will increase the correspondence between what he perceives in the environment around him and what this environment turns out to be when he acts within it to experience some intended consequence. And the intended consequence derives from the built-in tuning mechanisms of feeling. Generally we try to maintain the continuity and constancy of this reality world at the same time we try to enlarge and expand it, as we must, when we meet frustrations and find our previous assumptions do not work. By means of foresight, curiosity, imagination, and devising we try to improve the range of inclusiveness and the validity of our assumptions as we seek what appear to be new potential satisfactions.

This general accounting of what Whitehead called form and flow seems supported by neurophysiology. Ralph Gerard has stated that

> the physiological zero for activity, alertness, vigilance and behavior in general is not at the absolute zero level of somnolence, sleep, inactivity and inattention. It is somewhere between this equilibrium level and the other pole of continued change, adjustment, tension and vigilance. In the adult, too little environmental challenge leads to fatigue, anxiety and finally sleep. Presumably the adult mammal, at least, tends to regulate the physiological neuron reserve at an optimal level of partial activation of neurons, which makes them easily accessible, and with little over-reverberation or over-synchronization, which tends to withdraw them from the pool. [Magoun 1960: 1952]

The concept of homeostasis, when applied to human motivation, is clearly an inadequate model to account for the essential restlessness characteristic of human behavior.

Throughout this whole process, a person acts as a functional unit because of the vertical functioning of the reticular formation broadly defined which stores the significances of inputs and outputs, filters and regulates them, guides its own organization and reorganization using as its North Star for direction the increasing range and richness of feeling which impels, generates, and sustains more specific purposes over whatever time is required to accomplish them, perhaps a few seconds, perhaps decades. What we call "values" provide the most generally useful compass and standards of worthwhileness and satisfaction, integrating as they do far more cues and significances than can be intergrated conceptually. This accounting likewise seems consistent with the interpretations being given by modern neurology. Gerard has also pointed out that

> attention is directed to a considerable extent in terms of goals or "purposes"; so values—perhaps just "significance"—must be "givens" at any time. They have been established by experience, racial or individual, and are related to survival. Outcomes of action, rated "good" or "bad" on such criteria, can reinforce or attenuate future acts—by reasonably understood mechanisms—

and so establish a hierarchy of choices embedded in the nervous system. [Magoun 1960: 1952]

Hence the apparent push from behind and the pull toward the future as we attempt to experience something we have learned to want. John Dewey held that "'Reasonableness' or intelligence, as 'the perception of the continuities that take action out of its immediateness and isolation into connection with past and future,' acquires more and more an autonomous power of motivation"(Visalberghi 1953: 752).

The apparent self-generated drives, motives, and needs psychologists have delineated and the apparent self-realization and self-actualization of the human being are, as the writer stated at the beginning, accounts that start at "the top" and have been fashioned to describe the full gamut of behavior, often with the implicit premise that they also explain it. What the writer has tried to do here is to indicate that no matter how subtle human feelings are, they are all playing on the same basic built-in neurophysiological appetitive systems the baby uses, instrumented by the vertical organization of the nervous system, in the human endeavor of becoming; a Self striving to maintain its identity by changing itself in the ceaseless effort to enhance the quality, the adequacy, the range, and the validity of its own reality world.

Notes

1. This discussion is in a sense a sequel to a paper published with Dr. William K. Livingston under the title "The concept of transaction in psychology and neurology" (1963). It represents in condensed form a small part of a book Dr. Livingston and the present writer had planned to write after working for nearly 10 years trying to bring out the implications for psychology of modern neurophysiological research. The writer had to abandon the plan for the book with Dr. Livingston's death in March 1966, just after we had spent a month together in Oaxaca, Mexico, outlining the various chapters. The whole discussion here owes much to him.

2. A lucid account of recent research in neurophysiology will be found in Wooldridge's book *The Machinery of the Brain* (1963); also in R. B. Livingston's article "How man looks at his own brain: An adventure shared by psychology and neurophysiology" in Koch (1962). Those interested in more technical aspects of the research will find excellent summaries in the volumes on neurophysiology (edited by H. W. Magoun) in the series *Handbook of Physiology* (1960). See especially the following articles in this volume: Galambos and Morgan, "The neural basis of learning"; Lindsley, "Attention, consciousness, sleep and wakefulness"; MacLean, "Psychosomatics"; and Gerard, "Neurophysiology: An integration." Also see French (1957).

3. Immortality of the soul without a body to give it feelings would be a dull and dreary prospect indeed!

References

Bridgman, P.W. 1950-1. The operational aspect of meaning. *Synthese* 8: 251-8.
Cantril, H., and Livingston, W.K. 1963. The concept of transaction in psychology and neurology. *J. Indiv. Psychol.* 19: 3-16.
Delgado, J.M.R. 1955. Cerebral structures involved in transmission and elaboration of noxious stimulation. *J. Neurophysiol.* 18: 261-75.
Delgado, J.M.R., and Hamlin, H. 1960. Spontaneous and evoked electrical seizures in animals and in humans. In *Electrical studies on the unanesthetized brain,* ed. E.R. Ramey and D.S. O'Doherty, pp. 133-58. New York-Hober.
Frank, P. 1947. *Einstein: His life and times.* New York: Knopf.
French, J.D. 1957. The reticular formation. *Sci. Amer.,* May: 54-60.
Lilly, J.C. 1960. Learning motivated by subcortical stimulation: The "Start" and the "stop" patterns of behavior. In *Electrical studies on the unanesthetized brain,* ed. E..R. Ramey and D.S. O' Doherty, pp. 78-102. New York: Hober.
Livingston, R.B. 1962. How man looks at his own brain: An adventure shared by psychology and neurophysiology. In *Psychology: A Study of a science,* ed. S. Koch, pp. 51-99.
Livingston, W.K., Haugen, F.P., and Brookhart, J.M. 1964. Functional organization in the central nervous system. *Neurology* 4: 485-95.
MacLean, P.D. 1959. The limbic system with respect to two basic life principles. In *The central nervous system and behavior.* ed. M.A. Brazier, pp. 31-118. New York: Macy Foundation.
Macmurray, J. 1961. *Persons in relation.* London: Faber & Faber.
Magoun, H.W., ed. 1960. *Handbook of physiology.* Section 1: Neurophysiology (vol. 3). Washington: American Physiological Association.
Mumford, L. 1961. *The city in history.* New York: Harcourt, Brace & World.
Olds, J. 1956. Pleasure centers in brain. *Sci. Am.,* Oct: 105-16.
————. 1960. Differentiation of reward systems in the brain by self-stimulation technics. In *Electrical studies on the unanesthetized brain,* ed. E.R. Ramey and D.S. O'Doherty, pp. 17-51. New York: Hober.
Proust, M. 1955. *Jean Santeuil.* Trans. G. Hopkins. London: Weidenfeld & Nicolson.
Sem-Jacobsen, C.W., and Thorkildsen, A. 1960. Depth recording and electrical stimulation in the human brain. In *Electrical studies on the unanesthetized brain,* ed. E.R. Ramey and D.S. O'Doherty, pp. 275-90. New York: Hober.
Visalberghi, A. 1953. Remarks on Dewey's conception of ends and means. *J. Philos.* 50: 737-54.
Walter, G. 1964. Discovery rings Pavlovian bell. *Med. World News,* Nov. 20: 75.
Wooldridge, D.E. 1963. *The machinery of brain.* New York: McGraw-Hill.

15

Brain, mind, and self

with William K. Livingston

From the beginning of reflective thinking, men have tried to provide an adequate account of human experience and behavior. For more than two thousand years, this effort of imagination has involved attempts to explain how *brain* can function as *mind* and how this conjoined affair constitutes an individual *self.* The idea of "mind" as a separate entity first appeared in the writings of Heraclitus (533–475 B.C.), who conceived of the soul as an essence emanating from a universal spirit or world pneuma and temporarily inhabiting the body. The world pneuma was thought to account for different degrees of complexity in living things—vegetal, animal, and rational. At death, this spirit flies away, *ex-spiritus,* hence expiration.

According to Snell, Homer and earlier authors made no distinctions between spirit and material things, and they had no words to characterize what we understand by the terms *mind* and *matter.* These notions have been inherited essentially intact from Plato to our day. Evidently there was no equivalent concept throughout Asia and the Mediterranean in antiquity. With compelling conviction, Plato established the notion that spirit and matter are disparate and incommensurable. Plato's idea of the separateness of soul and body was strenuously reinforced by Christianity. Throughout Western civilization, dualism became a deeply ingrained feature of "common sense."

Mind–brain duality, thoroughly infused into our thinking, language, and literature, has been with us for so many centuries that we take the idea entirely for granted. This dichotomy directly affects the training of physi-

William K. Livingston, former Chairman, Department of Surgery, University of Oregon Medical School, died March 22, 1966, after developing with Dr. Cantril the central thesis of this essay.

cians and allied health professions; it affects the location, architecture, and operation of mental hospitals; it dramatically isolates the therapeutic regimen for mental patients from the rest of medicine; it influences the relationship of the mentally ill to the society around them and affects their attitude toward themselves.

Descartes added to dualism the impetus and authority of science. He assumed that the nervous system operates as an automaton which relates intimately to a "rational soul" he located in the pineal gland. Descartes was aware of the difficulties involved in automaton–soul interactions and inquired, without answering, how is it that some things affecting the nervous system are received by the soul as pleasant, and others as unpleasant or painful? (see Figure 15.1)

Contemporary evidence puts doubt on the disparateness and incommensurability of mind–brain processes, although the consequences of such doubt have only begun to modify medical and, to a lesser extent, general cultural assumptions. Certain drugs alter specific brain mechanisms and mind functions *pari passu*; many physiological and pathological processes affecting the nervous system, such as sleep deprivation, dehydration, fever, bodily fatigue, starvation, and old age, interfere with thinking; locally applied electrical and chemical interventions permit specific correlations between brain activities and mental states. These commonplace observations may be persuasive but not compelling for abandonment of the dualistic theory. Nevertheless, they imply that instead of trying to imagine how two disparate aspects of reality can influence each other, we might progress more rapidly if we abandoned the idea that these two aspects of reality are really disparate and conceive instead of one indivisible system.

What considerations would encourage our displacement of the dualistic view sufficiently to permit us freely to conceive of bodily and mental functions in such a way that the logical discontinuities of dualism would no longer interfere with progress? Dualism does actually interfere with present ways of thinking and doing. Dualism is so institutionalized that separate, isolated career-training experiences are undertaken for acquisition of professional standing in the neurological and psychological sciences. Students ordinarily seek training in either one distinct line of professional endeavor or the other. Rarely does anyone seek coequal training experiences, and he is likely to be looked upon askance by both groups of preceptors. Individuals trained according to one tradition end up with conceptions and methods of practical application which *are* disparate and *are* largely incommensurable one with the other. Observing the approaches and contents of these two educationally and professionally isolated traditions, one can scarcely imagine that individuals on these separate tracks are actually engaged in studying interdependent processes.

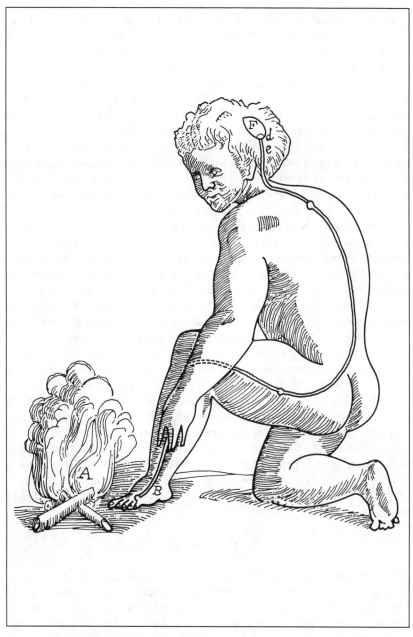

Descartes (1596–1650) added to dualism the impact and authority of science. By placing body functions in a mechanistic-scientific framework, he further reinforced the conceptual separation of mind and body.

Dualism radically affects the way knowledge is applied in the care of the sick. Major features of the patient's history and physical examination are deliberately designed to eliminate one potentiality or the other, as being wholly or even partially responsible for a given illness, to "rule out" brain disease, *or* mental disorder, as the cause of the illness. We proceed in such a way that even without there being an intrinsic barrier, the two aspects of brain and mind are forced to be independent of each other by means of both social and scientific operations. Dualism drastically modifies the points of view whereby scientists define their experiments. The philosophical limits we inherit become imposed on what we conceive, and this in turn places categorical limits on what we can discover. They similarly restrict what we aspire to transmit to our students, and hence, they confine the range of conceptual departure for coming generations.

Brain processes have abundant complexity, sufficient to account for the dynamic and subtle phenomena involved in mental processes such as perception, feeling, motivation, emotion, judgment, and volition. Mental phenomena are sufficiently orderly and recurrent to be accountable by scientific methods. Lack of time, of labor power, and of support for more intensive and extended research continues to keep us from adequately comprehending the full scope of human nature and human potentialities. Because there is an urgent need to achieve this goal, we must apply the most effective strategies for rapid, economical, and insightful progress. Occasionally we must stand aside from our daily work and committed schemes of thought in order to identify possible conceptual shortcuts.

In this essay, we shall not attempt to review principles and observations known to those familiar with contemporary brain and behavioral sciences. Our aim is to escape from the assumption of mind–brain dualism and to seek concepts that will bypass traditional interpretations and bridge the gap between the neurological and psychological disciplines. We believe that it is more important to try to develop alternative ways of thinking than it is to try to beat the old mind–brain dichotomy into some kind of combined form.

Emerging insights

Contemporary neurological and psychological disciplines are converging toward simpler, more holistic views which perceive brain and mind phenomena arising from a common stem of processes that can be explained, in principle, without recourse to parallelism, virtualism, interactionism, or other systems by which the two parts of the traditional dualistic frame of reference have been articulated in the past. Participants in this disciplinary convergence can point to three developments which originated a few generations ago and which are rapidly accelerating as the result of recent experimental observations. Attention to these three developments provides a more holistic view of the natural history of brain, mind, and self. Self is a construct we use to include all the significances an individual attaches to his own experiences, all he believes, and all he feels when initiating his behavior, witnessing his surroundings, and viewing the consequences of his own actions. The self is a system of perceptual and behavioral continuities that begins to emerge when an infant differentiates his own parts from his surroundings. It persists and flourishes variously throughout his life, and it attaches values to all his experiences. Consciousness of self focuses and guides behavior into channels that maintain and enhance his individuality (his moderately modifiable constancies in the midst of changes occurring in both internal and external environments). Consciousness of self provides a conceptual and experimental point of union for investigations of mind–brain problems. We perceive that this convergent, interdisciplinary insight is more of an emerging consensus than a radical conceptual departure.

The three conceptually germinative developments involve: (1) improved comprehension of integrative processes subserved by longitudinal control systems; (2) improved understanding of diffusely projecting systems and distributed functions; (3) gain of knowledge concerning mechanisms involved in subjective feeling states and mechanisms which control learning and memory.

These three conceptual developments have made communications between neurophysiologists and psychologists increasingly meaningful, and they provide a better integrated interpretation of how mind, brain, and self appear from an indissoluble unity.

Longitudinal integration

As in slicing a sausage or a loaf of bread, the simplest way to slice the nervous system is to cut across its longitudinal axis. Long ascending and descending tracts thus cut across were early recognized as "sensory" or "motor" because they begin and end in the vicinity of peripheral nerve inputs and outputs. Strictly speaking, however, all central neurons are internuncial rather than either "sensory" or "motor." All incoming sensory fibers branch downward and upward and contribute to reflexes below and above as well as at the level of input. All such circuits involving local and longitudinal reflex arcs, the dorsal columns, medial and lateral lemnisci, spino-thalamic paths, thalamo-cortical projections, and pyramidal and extrapyramidal pathways begin and end in complex feltworks of nerve cells, glia, and associated processes known as the neuropil. The neuropil provides far more abundant interconnections than can be detailed experimentally at present, infinitely more than are depicted in the simple, directional relays of textbook diagrams (see Figure 15.2).

Longitudinal conduction systems have been shown to provide several additional ascending "sensory" conduction systems which parallel the classical ascending lemniscal and spino-thalamic pathways. These are called extralemniscal sensory pathways to suggest an analogy with extrapyramidal motor pathways. They are found to be important as measured by analysis of both electrical and behavioral consequences of sensory stimulation. They are thought to provide a background to sensory perception analogous to the background provided by extrapyramidal systems to musculature and to postural coordinations underlying smooth motor performance.

More recently, longitudinal centrifugal projections have been found capable of controlling sensory input. Projections, directly and indirectly involving the brainstem reticular formation, cascade downward, paralleling the classical (ascending) sensory pathways. These centrifugal projections influence individual sense receptors, and each of the classical and extraclassical sensory relays conveying ascending impulses from body wall and special sense receptors to sensory receiving cortex. This system of down-

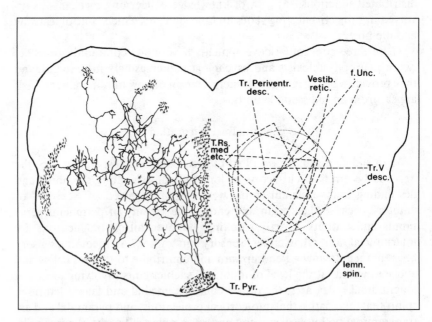

A schematic "suggestion" of the complexity of connections within the neuropil and its potential for modifying central activity. (A cross section of the lower brainstem.)

ward projections possesses the capacity to alter the amplitude and distribution of impulses upon which perception depends, by enhancing and inhibiting sensory impulses throughout all sensory systems.

These lines of evidence radically compromise any simple mechanistic conception of stimulus–response, the familiar S→R paradigm. A "sensation" can no longer be assumed to relate necessarily, directly, or even primarily to stimulus quality and intensity, even though, with directed focus of attention and stereotyped conditions, such relations can be experimentally established. Since modulation of incoming signals can take place at the level of the receptor and at every subsequent relay all along the central trajectory of sensory impulses, the influence of the stimulus is only partly responsible for the quality and distribution of signals finally reaching higher centers. Significant alterations may take place prior to the arrival of incoming signals to perceptual levels. Moreover, these centrifugal systems for central control of sensory transmission can be conditioned according to past experiences. They appear to be influenced in respect to processes of expectation, purpose, attention, and habituation.

Distributed functions

Attempts to determine the operational organization of the nervous system concentrated initially on the discovery of point-to-point connections which were conceptually anchored to "centers" responsible for particular functions. It is now recognized that point-to-point and diffuse connections are companion mechanisms which are complementarily important within both small-scale and large-scale dimensions of the nervous system. Initially, investigation of central nervous system mechanisms was aimed at defining connections among specialized centers and fields of representation. Point-to-point connections were discovered anatomically and were demonstrated to be physiologically competent in animals examined while under the influence of anesthesia. Connections have been found to be more specific, localized, and reproducible in anesthetized than in unanesthetized preparations. Three decades of work by many anatomists and physiologists in a number of laboratories around the world provided maps of point-to-point connections which formed a basic, skeletal plan of the neuraxis. But anatomists persisted in identifying structural complexities that could provide far greater potentialities for transactions among neurons than was implied by the relatively simple maps established using physiological exploration of anesthetized animals. Opportunities for widespread influence of cells upon one another seem to multiply with increasing magnification from low power to electron microscopic examination of all networks, including the retina, thalamic and hypothalamic, brainstem and spinal nuclei, sensory and motor relays, and layered grey matter, such as the tectum, hippocampus, and cerebral and cerebellar cortices (see Figure 15.3).

Diffusely projecting connections are characteristic of the phylogenetically oldest components of the nervous system, the grey matter spread throughout the central core of the neuraxis. It is through this central grey substance, during embryonic life, that all the more differentiated cells migrate on their way to establishing the classical sensory and motor nuclei and tracts. This central grey reticular formation and the neighboring white reticular formation extend the whole length of the neuraxis but are maximal in development at midbrain level. Throughout, they are predominantly diffusely projecting, with only occasional semicircumscribed bundles of nerve fibers and clusters of cell bodies. This central core region retains cells exhibiting primitive and undifferentiated cellular characteristics. A majority possesses small cell bodies and short, diffusely projecting processes. Many cells, however, possess long, tortuous, branching processes that reach out in all directions to form long-distance connections with other cells and with fibers of passage. The spinal and brainstem reticular formation provides multimodality sensory, motor, and vegetative regulatory systems which are re-represented and redistributed throughout the nervous system. It forms a system for neuronal convergence by which

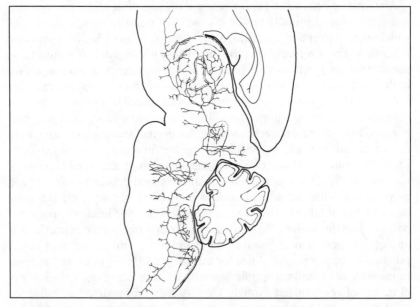

A schematic "suggestion" of the complexity of the longitudinal connections provided by the reticular network of the brainstem, and its potential for modifying central activity. (A longitudinal section of the brainstem.)

incoming and outgoing messages are integrated to form a unified system of perceptual experience and behavioral performance. It appears to provide for the coherence of idiosyncratic individuality in experience and expression.

The reticular formation provides fibers for generalized projection throughout the neuraxis as well as for diffuse projections within the central core areas of the spinal cord and brainstem. Fibers arising in the brainstem, for example, may extend axonal processes the whole distance to the frontal lobes, and other branches to other parts, including the lower end of the spinal cord. Long, diffusely projecting systems also arise, for example, from the intralaminar and reticularis nuclei of the thalamus and from the subthalamus as well as from the tegmentum of the midbrain and the remainder of the brainstem and spinal reticular formation. All these regions originate as outgrowths of the brainstem reticular formation.

Since neither the local nor the widespread diffusely projecting reticular systems show organization into compact bundles of fibers and well-circumscribed nuclei, such as characterize the arrangement of the classical sensory and motor systems, it has been difficult to appreciate their functions and to identify the sources and destinies of impulses, convergent and divergent, which they transmit. Diffuseness of anatomical organization led to conceptual and experimental neglect: the reticular formation was jokingly referred to as the "manure pile of the nervous system." Some anatomists persisted in recognizing the importance of diffuse as well as point-to-point relationships and maintained that there might be unique potentialities for widely distributed communications. But they could not be confident from pure morphology whether the connections would be facilitatory or inhibitory, or even whether any given connection would be competent to excite or to block excitation.

The functions of the "formatio reticularis" were anticipated in a remarkably prescient paper based on anatomical observations by William F. Allen in 1932:

> It is known from embryology that most of the leftover cells of the brain stem and spinal cord which are not concerned in the formation of motor root nuclei and purely sensory relay nuclei are utilized in the production of the formatio reticularis. This is a very old structure phylogenetically. It is but little differentiated in the lower vertebrates, where it apparently serves as an effective mechanism which enables these animals to adapt themselves properly to their various inside and outside conditions. In the higher vertebrates there is little reticular formation in the spinal cord but considerable formation in both the median and lateral portions of the medulla, pons and midbrain, where for the most part it exists anatomically in its original undifferentiated state. Reticular formation surrounds or partially surrounds the sensory nuclei of the thalamus; and, when considered phylogenetically, the

nucleus ruber, substantia nigra and other differentiated hypothalamic and midbrain nuclei should probably be considered as specialized derivatives. . . .

Presumably all of the sensory cranial nerve fibers communicate in one way or another with the reticular formation. The many vestibular connections to the undifferentiated and differentiated formatio reticularis . . . should be of considerable significance. . . .

Some of these fibers (efferent fibers from the formatio reticularis) obviously synapse with the various motor root nuclei of the brain stem. . . . Van Gehuchten, Probst and Papez have described ventral and lateral reticulospinal tracts in the spinal cord. The former run in the ventral column and the latter approximate the gray in the lateral column. The reticulospinal tracts have received some attention as extrapyramidal tracts on account of their cerebral connections. The course of the rubrospinal tract in the brain stem and lateral column of the spinal cord is well known. . . .

All physiologists agree that the medulla contains centers for altering the rate of the pulse and the level of blood pressure. . . . Many investigators . . . have placed the medullary respiratory center within the limits of the formatio reticularis. . . .

Many investigators . . . have emphasized the importance of certain hypothalamic nuclei as centers for visceral and humoral impulses. Beattie thinks this area has both sympathetic and parasympathetic centers. . . . The writer's work indicates that the respiratory and vascular changes elicited from stimulation of the cerebral motor cortex and the superior colliculus are not conducted within the spinal cord by the pyramidal and rubrospinal tracts or by a "tectospinal tract" from the colliculus, but by relays to the reticulospinal tract. It was further demonstrated that the well-known rigidity and clonic contractions elicited from stimulations of the superior colliculus were dependent on the integrity of the median portion of the lateral columns of the spinal cord as well as the ventral columns, a region traversed by the reticulospinal fibers. . . .

Concerning the two efferent pathways from the cerebellum to the formatio reticularis of the brain stem, the brachium conjunctivum and its main ascending division to the nucleus ruber and thalamus have generally been associated with muscle tone, but its descending division and its many endings in the formatio reticularis of the pons and medulla have apparently been ignored in this connection. . . .

To the writer the afferent connections to the formatio reticularis from the cerebrum, colliculi, corpora striata, and especially the diverse and extensive connections from the cerebellum suggest that considerable portions of the formatio reticularis function as efferent centers for tonic impulses. It may be that there are separate areas for inhibition as well as for augmentation. The usual explanation of the experiment of Magnus, where the decerebrate rigidity which resulted from transection of the brain stem below the nucleus ruber did not disappear with successive transecting of the medulla caudally until a level was reached directly below Deiter's nucleus, is that this section excluded all of Deiter's nucleus. On the other hand, it might be explained that the section below Deiter's nucleus eliminated all or practically all of the connections of the formatio reticularis of the brain stem.

The extensive distribution of the reticular formation through the brain stem and spinal cord may be used to good advantage in the "summation" and "recruitment" phenomena. . . .

Considerable evidence has accumulated in support of the formatio reticularis containing the chief visceral effective centers of the brain stem, which if true, would make the reticulospinal tracts the main pathways for effective visceral impulses in the spinal cord. There are also indications that this system may be associated with tonic impulses and clonic contractions.

Interpretations based on anatomical evidence were largely overlooked, however, until Magoun and his associates began to explore in unanesthetized preparations what they later referred to as "Allen's Alley," in honor of William F. Allen, just quoted. Magoun, Moruzzi in 1949, and others following in their footsteps, discovered that stimulation of the reticular formation in the midbrain tegmentum can elicit generalized cerebral and spinal activation: Behavioral arousal and wakefulness of the forebrain and generalized readiness for action of spinal mechanisms. A medial zone in the bulbar reticular formation had been earlier found by Magoun and Rhines to yield generalized inhibition of motor performances. Jouvet has recently described zones thinly distributed along the midline pontine and mesencephalic and diencephalic brainstem, and Clemente has identified functionally similar forebrain loci from which sleep can be induced. Portions of these widely ranging, diffusely projecting systems are involved in modulation of sensory input, thereby contributing to the central control of perceptual processes. It is becoming increasingly evident that small-scale, locally diffusely projecting systems provide somewhat analogous functions by locally distributing backgrounds for facilitatory and inhibitory influences within the retina, motor and sensory-relay nuclei, tectum, hippocampus, cerebral and cerebellar cortex, and so forth. There is evidence supporting this interpretation, although, because of the scale of such locally distributed influence, their effects are not yet well defined.

Functions of longitudinal components of the neuraxis that provide extralemniscal (sensory) and extrapyramidal (motor) pathways contribute to sleep, wakefulness, and other generalized states and participate in the central control of sensory and motor transactions. This led W.K. Livingston and his associates in 1954 to identify these systems as a "transactional component" interposed between the classical lemniscal sensory and classical pyramidal motor systems. The interdependence of many simultaneously active parts of the nervous system provides that the relationship between stimulus and response is not rigid and imperious and that both input and output relations of the nervous system depart from simplistic patterns of interaction. This transactional component provides for considerable modulability in the nervous system. This is probably attributable in part to (1) the pleurisynaptic pathways and (2) the multimodality pathways characteristic of the reticular formation. The idea of transactions among multiple systems in simultaneous interdependent activity is obviously more in keeping with dynamic psychological phenomena than are concepts previously available from the neurological disciplines.

Interpretations dealing with the functions of the vertical and diffusely projecting components of the nervous system invited employment of descriptive terms and phrases from the lexicon of psychologists. These systems are known to be importantly implicated in induction of "arousal", "wakefulness", "focus of attention", "recognition of novelty", "selection", and "reaction" to signals that are "meaningful for this organism at this time". Longitudinal and diffusely projecting systems are implicated in interpretations of goal-seeking behavior. Figure 15.4 depicts this transactional component of the nervous system, illustrating its functional intimacy with extralemniscal (sensory) pathways and extrapyramidal (motor) pathways, and indicating how the ongoing activity of this transactional component can modulate forebrain arousal, incoming sensory signals, and motor outflow.

These systems have been implicated in what is called a *Now print!* order, a generalized neuronal mechanism that is postulated for inscription of recent experiences into memory. The Now print! order is conceived as a command distributed to all areas of the brain whenever feeling, appetite, and satiety systems, which are parts of the transactional component, are involved in abrupt shifts in their level of activity. The Now print! order is thought to release a growth factor or synaptic facilitator, which increases the likelihood that subsequent neuronal firing will be influenced in accordance with the just previously occurring neuronal firing patterns. The result will insure repetition of those behaviors which are successful in procuring biological satisfaction. Neuronal activities aroused by any given event, self- or externally induced, which are followed by shifts in feeling, appetite, or satiety, will yield the Now print! order and consequently tend to promote synaptic facilitation and growth in accordance with those same neuronal patterns (see Figure 15.5).

The postulated Now print! order is conceived to be diffusely projected and thereby capable of capturing in memory any combination of neuronal patterns ongoing anywhere in the nervous system. When any arbitrary pattern is reiteratively associated with biologically meaningful consequences, it will tend to be *printed, reprinted,* and *re-printed* throughout

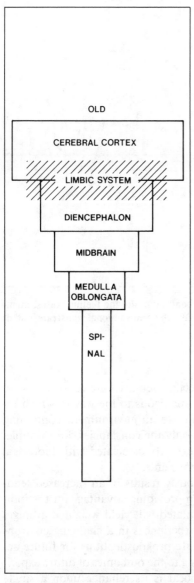

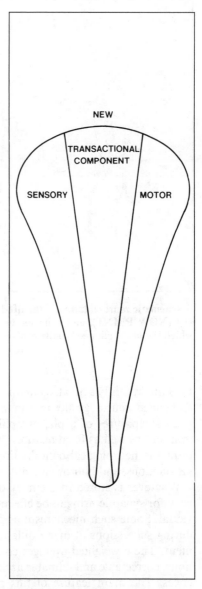

Left: The "old" schema based on the segmental reflex pattern of organization of the nervous system with successively higher levels representing increasing complexity of function.

Right: The "new" schema representing a concentric pattern of organization with its transactional core providing a continuum of "horizontal" and "vertical" integration of the system as a whole.

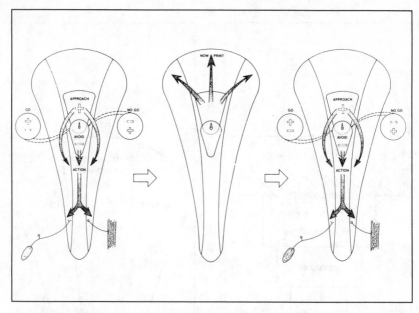

A schematic representation of the life-long continuum linking feeling states, memory (NOW PRINT), and behavior to provide the transactional substrate out of which the brain-mind-self unity evolves.

the same recently activated circuits. Specific memories are conceived to be embedded neurologically in a manner analogous to the way in which repeated exposures of a photographic film to an environment containing transient as well as fixed features print only the constancies, for example, print the neurological combinations regularly associated with biological satisfactions, and blur or fade out the transients.

Whatever is stored in memory obviously results in an increased tendency for synaptic firing to be effective in providing advantage for the individual. Some such mechanism as postulated will yield weighted averages during successions of many different experiences in a changing environment. These weighted averages constitute prognostications for future actions, correctable and refinable according to the outcomes of future experiences. The main feature of this proposal is its reliance upon a single generalized message which can assign mnemonic significances to any combination of sensory, central, and motor signals resulting from external and internal biologically meaningful events. The entire transaction, from recognition of novelty (by the reticular formation) to the assignment of biological significances (by systems of feeling, appetite, and satiety) to discharge of the postulated Now print! orders commanding memory, is probably involved in inducing what Karl Lashley called the engram. No wonder, in light of these interpretations, that Lashley found memory storage to be such a ubiquitous, distributed function!

Mechanisms of feeling states

Feeling is the inmost, primary sensation. It constitutes our first and probably our last perception. Throughout life, feeling provides the gauge of our well-being. Feeling results from neuronal activity, partly spontaneous and partly responsive to inputs from sensors located elsewhere in the brain, visceral organs, body wall, and distance receptors. Feeling seems to be generated by neuronal activity occurring in a continuous column of cells near the midline of the neuraxis from cells which formed the neural tube in embryonic life, and which, in adult life, line the ventricles, border the central aqueductal grey, occupy the floor of the fourth ventricle, and continue along the central canal of the spinal cord. Feeling is expressed by approach (adient) and avoidance (abient) behavior and by mechanisms of emotional expression. Feeling is evoked in man by stimulating the homologous midline and limbic regions which were discovered by Olds and Milner to lead to approach behavior in animals and those discovered by Delgado, Roberts, and Miller to lead to withdrawal behavior in animals.

We are continuously subjectively aware of the setting on the gauge of this feeling system. We are ordinarily not aware, however, of how this system generates any given feeling state. Feeling is undoubtedly made up of a vast flux of competing appetites and satisfactions, and it is composed from many neuronal activities relating to wakefulness and sleep and activities accompanying visceral well-being and dis-ease. We are even less aware of how this system, which is engaged in governing, experiencing, and expressing feelings, provides a "go/no go" switch for all our behavior. Grastyán has evidence that the hypothalamus and immediately associated limbic and brainstem mechanisms are involved in the final restraint or release of behavior. Altogether, this system provides an impetus and focus of direction for behavior which is propelling an individual toward what both his evolutionary and his individual experiences have determined according to weighted averages will be advantageous for him and which (generally) make him "feel good."

We consider that the word *feeling* is more fundamental and inclusive than *pleasure, pain, hunger, fear, love, anguish, discomfort,* and other terms used to describe more specific subjective states. Expressions such as *pleasure* and *pain* have assumed stereotypical meanings which limit their usefulness. *Feeling* we employ to include (1) spontaneous, intimate, pervasive states of subjective experience that are identified as "moods" when specially focused, (2) deep reverberations of past meaningful experiences as these invoke and modify feelings, and (3) the subjective experiences associated with the outward expression of our feelings, the outward expression of our internal state, the e-motion, or ex-motion of Yakovlev.

All conscious experiences and all behaviors are accompanied by feelings. We can recognize the consequences of a good or a bad night's sleep, the fatigue of drudgery, the "happy tiredness" resulting from strenuous play, the deep and abiding satisfactions of affectional activity, the outcomes of various forms of consummatory behavior, and the more or less specific satisfactions of visceral harmony.

Feeling constitutes the most fundamental aspect of subjective awareness of self. Any feeling state is available for introspective evaluation, and prominent feeling states intrude themselves actively on consciousness. Existent feeling states can be subjectively evaluated in comparison with past feelings. Past feelings yield prognostications for future experiences, for example, anticipatory delights and dreads. Feelings constitute a spectrum, with the torture of excruciating and inexpressible pain at one end and the thrill of sublime and inexpressible ecstasy at the other. Feelings encompass a multitude of profiles of qualities, patterns, and intensities within an extended range. Feelings at any given moment manifest the weighted average of the entire flux of internal and external neural events. The momentarily obtaining feeling state varies according to physiological conditions, age, level of appetites, satieties, past experiences, expectations, purposes, and the immediate context of both environmental and bodily conditions. Feelings are capable of relatively rapid transition and displacement in infancy and youth, and they exhibit increasing "hysteresis" with age.

Genesis of brain–mind–self

The nervous system is the most continuously prominent organ of embryonic development. Although at the time of birth the nervous system is already highly developed in external appearance, Conel and others have shown that a vast amount of further microscopic structural elaborations take place during the first few weeks, months, and years following birth. During the first six months after birth, the brain doubles in weight. It doubles again by the fourth year. Thereafter, the brain increases in size only about 10 percent by about the age of twenty. It shrinks more or less slowly from that time on.

We suppose that even the unborn fetus can experience subjective feelings of well-being and distress, accompanied by "spontaneous" fetal activities and restlessness. At birth, the infant must be aware of a great storm of changes in neuronal activity involving visceral sensory and body-wall signals, even though he has had no previous comparable experience. The newborn can have no basis for comparing, sorting out, or reflectively evaluating such signals except according to his ongoing flux of feeling states. This is probably what fixes his immediate feeling state in such absolute control over his behavior.

The newborn infant begins life in a confined sector of the world with feelings based on his immediate internal state, as affected by largely novel stimuli arising from his array of visceral and body-wall sense receptors. When he gets hungry, wet, or is otherwise uncomfortable, he tenses up, wriggles his whole body, and may cry. Few-week-old baby who has been fed and relieved of major sources of discomfort indicates his delight and satisfaction with recognizable expressions of infantile pleasure. He comes with a feeling-assay system built into the chassis of his nervous system. Behavior accompanying his various feeling states is at first largely undirected. Infants the world over display similar movements and sounds and presumably share the same elemental feelings which are generative of later approach and avoidance behaviors. The feelings and behaviors at this early stage are expressions of an organism which, while still highly undifferentiated, is nevertheless fully integrated for behavior as a whole. Yet these earliest experiences and expressions are probably not yet appropriate for the designation of terms such as *mind* and *self*.

Movements generated by an infant's feeling states may be associated, according to their consequences, with more or less abrupt shifts in level of contentment or discomfort, which in turn will likely lead to memory storage as a result of the shift in feeling state that accompanied behaviors just experienced. Now print! orders are presumed to be generated by any such abrupt shifts in feeling state. The infant thereby learns to rehearse behaviors that led to agreeable consequences, and to act increasingly in ways that will yield consequences which can satisfy his feelings. In short, the infant very early learns actions that will enhance his feelings of satisfaction and minimize his feelings of dissatisfaction. His nervous system differentiates, selects, and prints those aspects of his internal neuronal experiences which constitute biological significances for him.

Feelings of satisfaction and positive reinforcement as a consequence of successfully coping with and overcoming frustrations and challenges quickly broaden the infant's acquaintance with different stimulus situations and his behavioral options in relation to them. This emerging insight is enhanced by his discovery that certain of his actions will arouse behaviors in the people around him that can redound to his own satisfaction. He has begun to enjoy a measure of social control, thus making it increasingly likely that he will be able to generate more such satisfying experiences. A baby soon "learns" that his soft babbling sounds return parental attention and that one "goo" leads to another. He has already begun to control social signaling both by his own bodily expression and also by using a primitive form of language—gesture vocalization. In short, his original, largely undifferentiated, and poorly directed expressions of feeling become increasingly differentiated and focused as (1) significances become learned, (2) behaviors become increasingly specific and appropriate, and (3) the learned significances become increasingly specific prognostications for generalization and selection of future behaviors. We conceive that mind emerges as an identifiable aspect of nervous system functions at this stage of development.

Throughout this process, the infant's guide for behavior is the increasing range and quality of feelings that he finds satisfying and dissatisfying. Satisfaction is the touchstone for the lodging of images in memory, which in turn provide him with powers for the initiation and control of his behavior. Behavior becomes increasingly directed as the consequences of additional experiences are built into memories and as the infant's capabilities continue to expand. Emergent awareness contributes to the joy of anticipation, the excitement of exploration, and the delight of novelty. Prognostications of the probable consequences of action are composed from weighted averages of past experiences concerned with objects, people, and situations. Perceptions become increasingly reliable sequences of cues prognosticating behavior. He begins increasingly to control his own sensory input in accordance with his past experiences, expectations, and purposes.

The infant begins to appreciate things *outside* himself, and *otherness*, and *externality* that is relatively independent of his own feelings and behaviors. He begins to develop impressions of the constancies apparent in certain objects, people, and situations as the consequences of his own actions among them are brought home to him. The infant becomes directly aware that many of his feelings attach to things outside himself, "out there," that are seen, heard, smelled, and felt, and that yield in himself changes of feelings indirectly, as compared with events arising from within his own body, both of which may lead to direct shifts of feeling. He senses the externality of his mother's breast and of other parts of his environment. He discovers his own hands and begins to organize the personal body imagery essential for controlling his arms and legs well enough to push or pull himself away from things that cause distress. He becomes increasingly aware of his body parts and of his own different reactions to different objects and individuals throughout his environment. He becomes increasingly aware of constancies relating to himself and his environment and his own behavior, on which his perception of his body image and self-image depend. We conceive that *self* is born at this stage.

An essential aspect of the emergence of both mind and self is consciousness. Consciousness is an evolutionary development that has survival value because it can serve as a determinant of behavior and choice, and ultimately because it involves imagination, inventiveness, and creativity. Interest, curiosity, and persistence are complemented by increasingly self-conscious individual efforts, ingenuity, and invention of behaviors to solve increasingly complex problems. Consciousness creates opportunities for escape from otherwise imperious reflexive reactions to the immediate situation. Consciousness allows an individual to take into account the past experiences stored in his memory and prognosticated into the future on the basis of increasingly refined expectancies and longer-ranging purposes. The present becomes oriented toward an anticipated future in accordance with a biologically meaningful past. Consciousness, when extended to social and cultural transmission, to reading and other forms of communication, becomes an increasingly powerful tool for transmission of prognostications for action from the remotest past and extremest distances.

Dualism has persisted as an unresolved problem largely because of the scarcity of adequate information to establish a scientific version of the neural bases for subjective experience. The dynamics of *being* and *becoming* emanate from a sequential, interdependent succession of experiences which accompany species-specific developmental processes in the composition of a functional unity of brain–mind–self. The combined form of brain–mind–self is not simply a complex of mechanisms reacting and interacting with the environment; it is a time-bound process of interdependent systems that cannot be understood except by examining the complex as a whole—from the inside out as well as from the outside in.

The holistic entirety constitutes a dynamic system of transactions by which multiple, interdependent systems in simultaneous action express species-specific and increasingly individual-specific internal experiences and internally controlled behaviors. The brain–mind–self unity emerges as a consequence of complementary qualities of the underlying physical and chemical processes. Integrative actions are continuously insuring that the system operates as a unified whole, linking mechanisms of appetite and satisfaction with underlying feeling states and overlying consciousness, perception, and behavior. It is only by conceptual artifice that the three—brain, mind, and self—are considered independently of one another. Recent convergent discoveries from the behavioral and neurological sciences indicate that brain, mind, and self can usefully be treated in theory and practice as an ensemble rather than as isolable and independent domains of insight. We believe that the changes in outlook now taking place will radically affect research, training, and professional service in the health and behavioral sciences.

References

Allen, W.F. 1932. Formatio reticularis and the reticulo-spinal tracts. *J. Washington Acad. Sci.,* 22: 490–5.

Livingston, W. K., Haugen, F.P., and Brookhart, J.M. 1954. Functional organization of the central nervous system. *Neurology:* 485–96.

Snell, B. 1960. *The discovering of the mind: the Greek origins of european thought.* New York: Harper Torchbooks.

Epilogue

Hadley Cantril (1906–1969): The transactional point of view

F.P. Kilpatrick

With the death of Hadley Cantril on May 28, 1969, at the age of 62, psychology lost a scholar who embraced pioneering as a way of life, not because he wanted to be known as a pioneer, but because his quest for increased understanding of human behavior would not let him do otherwise. His extraordinary talent for recognizing new and fertile territory at the frontier, plowing it and demonstrating its productivity, and then moving on, resulted in major contributions in the psychology of propaganda; public opinion research; applications of psychology and psychological research to national policy, international understanding, and communication; developmental psychology; the psychology of social movements; measurement and scaling; humanistic psychology; the psychology of perception; and, basic to all of them, the analysis of human behavior from the transactional point of view. According to Cantril, *transaction* is to be differentiated from *interaction*. While the latter posits two entities, the individual and his environment, transaction implies that the two are interdependent: The individual is a creative agent in his perception of the external world, and the environment is a creative agent in shaping an individual's perceptions.

The influence of Cantril's ideas was felt not only in psychology but in education, law, philosophy, politics, and psychiatry as well. Those who knew well the man and his writings recognized that each of his interests was the manifestation of a single driving purpose, and that each was pursued in the manner and to the extent that it contributed to that purpose. He was engaged in the constant task of building and refining a point of view and a system which would give ever better understanding of human behavior, not just in the laboratory, but in the full range and subtlety of everyday life, that is, in what he called "ongoing, full-bodied, experience." Within this framework, he constantly pursued the task of abstracting and describing

Reprinted by permission from *Journal of Individual Psychology* 25 (Nov. 1969): 219–25.

variables, *not as causes* of specific aspects of behavior, but as elements or factors in a complex, dynamic matrix *except for which* human beings would not behave as they do, and he accepted fully and imaginatively the task of devising means for assessing or measuring these variables in ways which would compromise neither their subtlety nor the complexity of their interdependence.

This, then, was his enduring theme and challenge, and the focus of his great intellectual drive and curiosity. But it was only the major theme. He, like all men, was a part of what he called the "full-bodied orchestration of living," which for him blended into the whole many factors including a deep love and enjoyment of his family, a love of country and a desire to serve it, an almost compulsive need to help further the legitimate aspirations of others, a sensitivity to the loneliness and frequent harshness which results from asking new and difficult questions of one's contemporaries, and a belief in freedom as a necessary condition for individual and social emergence and effectiveness. It is in this context that his contributions can best be understood and accounted for.

Contributions as a critic. Critical paragraphs were contained in viri   y all of his writings. His targets were many, but his favorites were simplistic explanations, reifications of variables, dualisms, taxonomies, statistical over-refinements, and faddish multiplications of methods-for-methods-sake studies. He feared, he often said, that we would become lost in "proliferating sideways instead of pushing forward."

Public opinion research. In 1935, when Cantril read about the surveys being launched and reported in the newspapers by George Gallup, Elmo Roper, and Archibald Crossley, he "felt that here was a new instrument the social scientist, particualrly the social psychologist, had better look into. The survey technique seemed to hold potentialities for the study of genuine problems, for learning how people look at things, and for understanding better than we did why people of various backgrounds, interests, loyalties, and information levels hold the opinions they do" (1967a: 22). He became the first or one of the first, to bring the teaching of public opinion research into the college classroom. In 1940 he established the Office of Public Opinion Research at Princeton and in 1944 published the still widely used volume *Gauging Public Opinion* (1944). The chapter headings have a very modern ring to them and show a strong concern (with which he was not always credited) for methodological rigor.

Policy research. Cantril was concerned with "relevance" long before it became the catchword of a youth movement. Throughout his career, he endeavored to bring the insights and tools of social science, particularly opinion research and the transactional point of view, to bear on the problems of the nation and the world. His adventures before and during World

War II in policy research for Franklin D. Roosevelt, in the use of opinion survey techniques in political and military intelligence and in the postwar international struggle for the minds of men, make up a fascinating drama of successes and disappointments which contain important lessons in this age of increasing pressures on the social sciences for "relevance" (1967a).

In 1955, he left Princeton University to establish, with Lloyd Free, the Institute for International Social Research under a grant which gave him the freedom and the means to choose and pursue his own intellectual course for the rest of his life. He felt deeply the obligation and the loneliness placed upon him by this freedom. The volume and quality of what he produced during the remaining fourteen years more than vindicate the faith placed in him. The eight books and more than two dozen articles he authored or coauthored during that period were devoted to what, for him, was the unitary task of advancing transactionalism, humanism, and individual, national, and international understanding (see especially 1958, 1960, 1961, 1965, 1967b).

Humanism and humanistic psychology. Because of his holistic approach and his conviction that "the outstanding characteristic of man is his capacity to participate in the creation of emergent value attributes which enrich the quality of his experience" (1950: 159), he never backed away from such value-laden abstractions as faith (1957), hope, happiness, surety, aspiration, and the like. Although the term "humanistic psychology" is not new, its current usage stems primarily from a 1955 article by Cantril entitled *Toward a Humanistic Psychology* in which he stated that we must take into account "in any psychology which pretends to be adequate those problems which are common problems to the humanist and the true scientist" (1955: 279; also included in this volume as Chapter 6). He saw the conceptual framework of transactional psychology as both the catalyst and the analytic tool for making progress toward a humanistic psychology.

The transactional point of view. Transactional psychology is a point of view, not a theory, and Cantril carefully distinguished between the two. A point of view is broader, while a theory is less inclusive and usually attempts to make precise predictions on the basis of specific assumptions. Within the evolutionary point of view there are various evolutionary theories. Within the transactional point of view are several more or less well developed transactional theories, two of which are briefly presented below. What Cantril meant by transactional psychology, that is, the analysis and description of human behavior from the transactional point of view, is implicit in much of what has been said so far. His own words offer the best summary:

The ultimate goal of psychology is the understanding of human living so that individuals can live more effectively. The psychologist's aim is that of formulating a set of constructs which will enable him conceptually to "understand," "explain," and "predict" the activities and experiences of the functional union we call a behaving person. . . .

The psychologist interested in understanding the process of living must start from naive experience in the phenomenal area. For only then will he be able to undertake investigations that will disclose the nature of the processes playing a role in behavior which the experiencing individual is taking [into] account. The words "experience" and "behavior" are used here as *interdependent* abstractions man has created, neither of which would be meaningful except for the other. . . .

If the psychologist is to be faithful to his subject matter, he must always bear in mind that living is an orchestration of ongoing processes and that any process he may choose to differentiate out of this aggregate of ongoing processees of living can be understood only if it is recognized as referring to a phase of man's orchestrated functioning. It is, for example, a commonplace of philosophical and psychological thinking that "cognitive" and "motor" processes are themselves distinctions that can be misleading unless there is full cognizance of the fact that there can be no "knowing" without "doing," just as there can be no "person" except for an "environment," nothing "subjective" except for what is "objective," nothing "personal" except for what is "social," nothing experienced as existing "out there in its own right" except for the organizations and significances to an individual of the happenings going on in the world around him which he associated with light waves, sound waves, and so forth, as instruments of explanation. . . . This does not in the least, of course, imply that we turn our backs on the results of rigid scientific experimentation. (1955: 271-81)

Transactional perceptual theory. In 1947, Cantril met and began to work closely with Adelbert Ames, Jr., a leading authority in physiological optics, whose experiments and demonstrations showed not only that man is an active participant in the construction of what he "sees," but also revealed many of the variables "except for which" the processes involved in the creation of one's perceptual world would not occur as they do. Shortly, others were attracted to this work, and transactional perceptual theory and research began to develop rapidly.

Stated briefly, the theory suggests that perception can best be conceived of and treated as process. It further proposes that there is never one and only one thing which "must be there" in order to account for a pattern of stimulation on the organism; that any pattern of stimulation, no matter how complex, is necessarily ambiguous with respect to its referent. The resolution of the ambiguity is a learned response. Thus perceiving is primarily a learned activity of the organism. "Stored feedback," generally originating in actions and their consequences as they are registered in relation to our motives or purposes, is instrumental in the construction of what we perceive. Thus, the perceptual organization of the moment cannot be an absolute revelation of "what is," but is instead a sort of "best bet" based on past experience. This "best bet" based on the consequences of past dealings with the environment is reflected in awareness as perceiving, and serves as a directive for further dealings with the environment. Consequently, we are motivated and behave in terms of the world as we perceive it, and the world as we perceive it is in large part a product of our past motivations and behavior and our present purposes.

Transactional neurological theory. Early in the development of transactional psychology and especially transactional perceptual theory, one of our major concerns was that many of the processes postulated had no known correlates in neurological processes; as a matter of fact, much of the neurological evidence suggested rather forcefully that we were on the wrong track. Some examples are: (1) the functional organization into definite tracts and nuclei that characterize the arrangement of the sensory and motor systems of classical neurology lacked "transactional" components; (2) evidence was lacking for postulated central modulation, based on experience, feeling, and purpose, of sensory systems at relay stations and at the periphery; (3) evidence was lacking for a pervasive positive–negative feeling-state system which would attach a valence "of a kind and in a degree" to behavior as experienced (in Cantril's words, "the value quality of experience").

Thus, it was with great excitement that Cantril witnessed over the last decade and a half the emergence of new neurological evidence based primarily on techniques for studying the activity of the conscious brain by the use of implanted microeletrodes: (1) The reticular formation, once thought to be mainly excelsior-like padding for the known sensory and motor systems, is being found to possess all the functional attributes of a central transactional core. (2) Evidence now indicates that the brain can "police" its own input; that the cortex can modulate activity in and through the reticular formation, and at all points clear out to the sensory receptors. (3) Two "affective" systems, which can be characterized as generally positive and generally negative, have been identified in the brain, and seem to form the mechanisms for the directional feeling-states associated with experience. Cantril took account in his writings of the significance for psychology of these developments (1963, 1967c), and in the last months before his death he wrote in a major article on the subject: "Contemporary neurological and psychological disciplines are converging toward simpler, more holistic views" (unpub: 6, included as chapter 15 in this volume).

Cantril often expressed his fascination with "becoming," with the "ongoing changes exhibited by all forms of life in their progress from birth, through growth and maturation, to old age and death" (1963: 3). Certainly his "becoming" was directional and emergent. It is appropriate that he was writing a chapter on "change" when the final interruption to his work occurred.

Hadley Cantril was born in Hyrum, Utah, in 1906 and received his B.S. from Dartmouth College in 1928 and his Ph.D. from Harvard in 1931 after graduate study at the Universities of Munich and Berlin. He was awarded honorary degrees from Dartmouth and Washington and Lee University. He began his career as an instructor at Dartmouth and two decades later was Stuart Professor of Psychology and chairman of the Department of Psychology at Princeton University. He was a founding member of the Society for the Psychological Study of Social Issues, past president of the Eastern Psychological Association, and received the American Association for Public Opinion Research award for distinguished achievement. In 1955, Dr. Cantril left Princeton University to become chairman of the board of the Institute for International Social Research, a position he occupied until his death in May of this year. He is survived by his wife, Mavis L. Cantril, two children, Albert H. Cantril and Mrs. Donald C. Jansky, and his sister, Mrs. Warren B. Walsh.

References

1950. *The "why" of man's experience.* New York: Macmillan.
1955. Toward a humanistic psychology. *ETC.: A Review of General Semantics* 12(4): 278–298.
1957. The nature of faith. *J. Indiv. Psychol.* 13(1): 24–37.
1958. *The politics of despair.* New York: Basic Books.
1960. *Soviet leaders and mastery over man.* New Brunswick, N.J.: Rutgers University Press.
1961. *Human nature and political systems.* New Brunswick, N.J.: Rutgers University Press.
With Livingston, W.K. 1963. The concept of transaction in psychology and neurology. *J. Indiv. Psychol.* 19: 3–16.
1965. *The pattern of human concerns.* New Brunswick, N.J.: Rutgers University Press.
1967a. *The human dimension: experiences in policy research.* New Brunswick, N.J.: Rutgers University Press.
With Free, L.A. 1967b. *The political beliefs of Americans.* New Brunswick, N.J.: Rutgers University Press.
1967c. Sentio, ergo sum: "motivation" reconsidered. *J. Psychol.* 65: 91–107.
With Livingston, W.K., Previously unpub., included as chapter 15 in this volume. Brain, mind, and self.

Publications of Hadley Cantril

Books

1932. *General and Specific Attitudes.* Psychological Monographs, vol. 42, no. 5, whole issue no. 192.

1935. *The Psychology of Radio.* With Gordon W. Allport. New York and London: Harper.

1940. *The Invasion from Mars: A Study in the Psychology of Panic.* Princeton, N.J.: Princeton University Press. Also published as *La Invasión desde Marte: Estudio de la psicologiá del pánico.* Madrid: Revista de Occidente, 1942. (Paperback in Torchbook Series, New York: Harper & Row, 1966 and reissued by Princeton University Press, 1982.)

1941. *The Psychology of Social Movements.* New York: John Wiley; London: Chapman & Hall. (Paperback in Science Editions; Wiley & Sons, 1963.)

1944. *Gauging Public Opinion.* Contributing ed., Princeton, N.J.: Princeton University Press; London: Oxford University Press. (Reissue)

1947. *The Psychology of Ego-Involvements.* With Muzafer Sherif. New York: John Wiley; London: Chapman & Hall. (Paperback in Science Editions; Wiley & Sons, 1966.)

1947. *Understanding Man's Social Behavior: Preliminary Notes.* Princeton, N.J.: Office of Public Opinion Research.

Ed. 1950. *Tensions that Cause Wars: Common Statement and Individual Papers by a Group of Social Scientists brought together by UNESCO.* Urbana: University of Illinois Press. (Translations: French, Japanese.)

1950. *The "Why" of Man's Experience.* New York: Macmillan. (Translations: Italian, Japanese.)

Ed. 1951. *Public Opinion 1935–1946.* Princeton, N.J.: Princeton University Press. (Reissued by Greenwood Press, 1978.)

1953. *How Nations See Each Other: A Study in Public Opinion.* With William Buchanan. Urbana: University of Illinois Press.

1958. *The Politics of Despair.* New York: Basic Books. (Paperback, New York: Collier Books, 1962.)

1960. *Reflections on the Human Venture.* With Charles H. Bumstead. New York: New York University Press.

1960. *Soviet Leaders and Mastery over Man.* New Brunswick, N.J.: Rutgers University Press. (Paperback, Rutgers University Press, 1960.) (Translations: Spanish, Japanese, Hindi, Portuguese, Bengali.)

Ed. 1960. *The Morning of Adelbert Ames, Jr.* New Brunswick, N.J.: Rutgers University Press.

1961. *Human Nature and Political Systems.* New Brunswick, N.J.: Rutgers University Press. (Translations: Portuguese, Korean, Japanese.) (Also published in Bombay, India: Popular Prakashan, 1966.)

1965. *The Pattern of Human Concerns.* New Brunswick, N.J.: Rutgers University Press.

1967. *The Human Dimension: Experiences in Policy Research.* New Brunswick, N.J.: Rutgers University Press.

1967. With Lloyd A, Free. *The Political Beliefs of Americans: A Study of Public Opinion.* New Brunswick, N.J.: Rutgers University Press. (Paperback in Clarion Books; New York: Simon and Schuster, 1968.)

Articles and reports

With William A. Hunt. 1932. "Emotional Effects Produced by the Injection of Adrenalin." *American Journal of Psychology* 44 (April): 300–7.

1933. "The Range and Nature of Rural Attitudes." In *Research in Social Psychology in Rural Life,* ed. J.D. Black, pp. 127–30. New York: Social Science Research Council.

1933. "Recent Trends in American Social Psychology." *Sociologus* 9: 125–200.

With Gordon W. Allport. 1933. "Recent Applications of the Study of Values." *Journal of Abnormal and Social Psychology* 28, no. 3 (Oct.–Dec.): 259–73.

With Gordon W. Allport. 1933. "Studies in the Psychology of Radio." In *Education on the Air,* ed. J.H. Maclatchy, pp. 317–20. Columbus: Ohio State University Press.

With H.A. Rand and Gordon W. Allport. 1933. "The Determination of Personal Interests by Psychological and Graphological Methods." *Character and Personality* 2, no. 2 (Dec.): 134–43.

1934. "Attitudes in the Making." *Understanding the Child* 4 (Jan.): 13–14.

1934. "The Roles of the Situation and Adrenalin in the Induction of Emotion." *American Journal of Psychology* 46 (Oct.): 568–79.

1934. The Social Psychology of Everyday Life." *Psychological Bulletin* 31, no. 5 (May): 297–330.

With Gordon W. Allport. 1934. "Judging Personality from Voice." *Journal of Social Psychology* 5: 37–55.

With H.A. Rand. 1934. "An Additional Study of the Determination of Personal Interests by Psychological and Graphological Methods." *Character and Personality* 3, no. 1 (Sept.): 72–8.

1935. "A Psychological Reason for the Lag of 'Non-Material' Culture Traits." *Social Forces* 13, no. 3 (March): 376–9.

1936. "Education and Propaganda." *Proceedings of the Middle States Association of History and Social Science* 34: pp. 43–7.

1936. "Research in Public Opinion." *Public Opinion Quarterly* 1: 105–9.

1937. "A Comparative Study of Radio and Face-to-Face Stimulus Situations." *Journal of Social Psychology* 8: 443–58.

1937. "The Effect of Modern Technology and Organization upon Social Behavior." *Social Forces* 15, no. 4 (May): 493–5.

1937. "Experimental Studies of Prestige Suggestion." *Psychological Bulletin* 34: 528ff.

1937. "Prediction of Social Events." *Public Opinion Quarterly* 1: 83–7.

1937. "Propaganda and Radio." In: *Seventh Yearbook, National Council for the Social Studies,* ed. Elmer Ellis, pp. 87–100.

With Kenneth Fink. 1937. "The Collegiate Stereotype as Frame of Reference." *Journal of Abnormal and Social Psychology* 32, nos. 3–4 (Oct.–Dec.): 352–6.

With Daniel Katz. 1937. "Public Opinion Polls." *Sociometry* 1, nos. 1–2 (July–Oct.): 155–79.

1938. "The Prediction of Social Events." *Journal of Abnormal and Social Psychology* 33, no. 3 (July): 364–89.

1938. "Propaganda Analysis." *English Journal* 27: 217–21.

With Muzafer Sherif. 1938. "The Kingdom of Father Divine." *Journal of Abnormal and Social Psychology* 33, no. 2 (April): 147–67.

1939. "Attitudes toward Picketing." *Journal of Social Psychology* 10: 153–5.

1939. "Freedom and Adequacy of Information Furnished by Channels of Communication," *Contemporary Social Problems,* General Education Board, 1939.

1939. "The Role of the Radio Commentator." *Public Opinion Quarterly* 3 (Oct.): 654–62.

With Hazel Gaudet. 1939. "Familiarity as a Factor in Determining the Selection and Enjoyment of Radio Programs," *Journal of Applied Psychology,* vol. 23, no. 1, February 1939, pp. 85–94.

With Daniel Katz. 1939. "Objectivity in the Social Sciences." In *Industrial Conflict: A Psychological Interpretation,* ed. G. Hartmann and T. Newcomb, pp. 9–12. New York: Cordon.

1940. "America Faces the War: A Study in Public Opinion." *Public Opinion Quarterly* 4: 387–407.

1940. "Experiments in the Wording of Questions." *Public Opinion Quarterly* 4 (June): 330–2.

1940. Introduction to "The Public Opinion Polls: Dr. Jekyll or Mr. Hyde?" *Public Opinion Quarterly* 4 (June): 212–17.

With Daniel Katz. 1940. "An Analysis of Attitudes toward Fascism and Communism." *Journal of Abnormal and Social Psychology* 35, no. 3 (July): 356–66.

With Donald Rugg. 1940. "Looking Forward to Peace." *Public Opinion Quarterly* 4 (March): 119–21.

With Donald Rugg. 1940. "War Attitudes of Families with Potential Soldiers." *Public Opinion Quarterly* 4 (June): 327–30.

With Donald Rugg and Frederick Williams. 1940. "America Faces the War: Shifts in Opinion." *Public Opinion Quarterly* 4: 651–6.

1942. "Public Opinion in Flux." *The Annals of the American Academy of Political and Social Science* 220, (March): 136–52.

With Donald Rugg. 1942. "The Wording of Questions in Public Opinion Polls." *Journal of Abnormal and Social Psychology* 37, no. 4 (Oct.): 469–95.

1943. "Causes and Control of Riot and Panic." *Public Opinion Quarterly* 7 (Winter): 669–79.

1943. "Educational and Economic Composition of Religious Groups: An Analysis of Poll Data." *American Journal of Sociology* 48, no. 5 (March): 574–9.

1943. "Identification with Social and Economic Class." *Journal of Abnormal and Social Psychology* 38, no. 1 (Jan.): 74–80.

1943. "The World in 1952: Some Predictions." Clinical Supplement to the *Journal of Abnormal and Social Psychology* 38, no. 2 (April): 6–47.

With John Harding. 1943. "The 1942 Elections: A Case Study in Political Psychology." *Public Opinion Quarterly* 7: 222–41.

With Gerard B. Lambert. 1943. "Informing the Public: A Test Case." *Public Opinion Quarterly* 7 (Fall): 457–65.

1944. "The Issues–As Seen by the American People." *Public Opinion Quarterly* 8 (Fall): 331–47.

1944. "The People and the Government: Should Congress Lead or Follow Public Opinion." *Historical Service Board Pamphlet.*

With Gerard B. Lambert. 1944. "Increasing Public Understanding of Inflation." *Journal of Abnormal and Social Psychology* 39, no. 1 (Jan.): 112–18.

With J.M. Wallace, Jr., and F.W. Williams. 1944. "Identification of Occupational Groups with Economic and Social Class." *Journal of Abnormal and Social Psychology* 39, no. 4 (Oct.): 482–5.

1945. "Do Different Polls Get the Same Results?" *Public Opinion Quarterly* 9 (Spring): 61–9.

With Frederick Williams. 1945. "The Use of Interviewer Rapport as a Method of Detecting Differences between 'Public' and 'Private' Opinion." *Journal of Social Psychology* 22: 171–5.

With Muzafer Sherif. 1945–6. "The Psychology of 'Attitudes'." *Psychological Review.* Part I: vol. 52, no. 6 (Nov. 1945): 295–319. Part II: vol. 53, no. 1 (Jan. 1946): 1–24.

1946. "The Intensity of an Attitude." *Journal of Abnormal and Social Psychology* 41, no. 2 (April): 129–35.

With Richard Centers. 1946. "Income Satisfaction and Income Aspiration." *Journal of Abnormal and Social Psychology* 41, no. 1 (Jan.): 64–9.

1947. "The Place of Personality in Social Psychology." *Journal of Psychology* 24: 19–56.

1948. "The Human Sciences and World Peace–A Report on the UNESCO Project: 'Tensions Affecting International Understanding'." *Public Opinion Quarterly* 12, no. 2 (Summer): 236–42.

1948. "The Nature of Social Perception." *Transactions of the New York Academy of Sciences,* series II, vol. 10, no. 4 (Feb.): 142–53.

1948. "Polls and the 1948 U.S. Presidential Election: Some Problems It Poses." *International Journal of Opinion and Attitude Research* 2, no. 3 (Fall): 309–20.

1948. "Trends of Opinion during World War II: Some Guides Interpretation." *Public Opinion Quarterly* 12, no. 1 (Spring): 30–44.

With Norman Frederiksen. 1948. "Social Functions of the Individual." In *Foundations of Psychology,* ed. Edwin Garriques Boring et al. Chap. 2, pp. 8–47. New York: John Wiley; London: Chapman & Hall.

1949. "Psychology for Public Relations Practice." *Public Relations Journal* 5: 26–8.

1949. "Psychology Working for Peace." *American Psychologist* 4, no. 3 (March): 69–73.

1949. "Reply to Myers on Pollsters" (comment). *American Psychologist* 4, no. 1: 23.

1949. "Toward a Scientific Morality." *Journal of Psychology* 27: 363–76.

With Adelbert Ames, Jr., Albert H. Hastorf, and William H. Ittelson. 1949. "Psychology and Scientific Research." *Science* 110. Part I: "The Nature of Scientific Inquiry," no. 2862, (Nov. 4): 461–4. Part II: "Scientific Inquiry and Scientific Method," no. 2863 (Nov. 11): 491–7. Part III: "Transactional View in Psychological Research," no. 2864 (Nov. 18): 517–22. (Reprinted in F.P. Kilpatrick, *Explorations in Transactional Psychology* pp. 6–35. New York: New York University Press, 1961.)

With Albert H. Hastorf. 1949. "Some Psychological Errors in Polling: A Few Guides for Opinion Interpretation." *Journal of Educational Psychology* 40: 57–60.

1950. "An Inquiry Concerning the Characteristics of Man." *Journal of Abnormal and Social Psychology* 45, no. 3 (July): 490–503.

1950. "Psychology." *Scientific American* 183, no. 3 (Sept.): 79–84.

1951. *What Should Our Message be?* Distributed by The Inwood Institute; reprinted in *Congressional Record,* May 2.

1951. Foreword to *The Art of Asking Questions* by Stanley Payne. Princeton: Princeton University Press. (Reissued by Princeton University Press, 1980.)

1952. *The Cantril Report on Plausible Appeals in Psychological Warfare.* Princeton: Institute for Associated Research. (Multilith report.)

1952. *Recent Experiments in Perception and Their Implications in the Mind-Body Problem.* Paper delivered at Conference on Methods in Philosophy and the Sciences, New School for Social Research, Jan. 13.

With William Buchanan. 1952. "The Shadow of the Bear." *United Nations World,* 6, no. 7 (special issue, July): 42–4.

1953. Preface to *The Design of Human Behavior* by L.O. Kattsoff. St. Louis: Educational Publishers.

1953. "Public Opinion–Its Formation and Change." *Princeton Alumni Weekly,* Nov. 6, pp. 10–13.

1953. "Sex without Love." Review of Alfred C. Kinsey, et al., *Sexual Behavior in the Human Female. The Nation,* Oct. 10.

With William H. Ittelson. 1954. *Perception: A Transactional Approach.* (Doubleday Papers in Psychology.) Garden City, N.Y.: Doubleday.

1954. Foreword to *Human Beings and Psychological Systems* by Horace M. Kallen. Remarks at dedication of The Perception Demonstration Center, Princeton University, March 6.

1954. "The Qualities of Being Human." *American Quarterly* 6, no. 1 (Spring): 3–18.

With Albert H. Hastorf. 1954. "They Saw a Game: A Case Study." *Journal of Abnormal and Social Psychology* 49, no. 1 (Jan.): 129–34.

1955. "Concerning the Nature of Inquiry." In *Sociologica* (Frankfurter Beiträge zur Soziologie), ed. Max Horkheimer, pp. 293–304. Frankfurt am Main, Europäische Verlagsanstalt.

1955. "Ethical Relativity from the Transactional Point of View." *Journal of Philosophy* 52, no. 23, (Nov.): 677–87.

1955. "Toward a Humanistic Psychology." *ETC.: A Review of General Semantics* 12, no. 4: 278–98.

With David Rodnick. 1956. *On Understanding the French Left.* Princeton: Institute for International Social Research. (Multilith report.)

1957. "The Nature of Faith." *Journal of Individual Psychology* 13, no. 1: 24–37. (Reprinted in *Pastoral Psychology,* Oct. 1962, pp. 38–47.

1957. "The Nature of Our Reality Worlds." *Indian Journal of Psychology* 32, parts I–II, pp. 51–63.

1957. "Perception and Interpersonal Relations." *American Journal of Psychiatry,* 114, no. 2: 119–26.

With Hans Toch. 1957. "A Preliminary Inquiry into the Learning of Values." *Journal of Educational Psychology* 48, no. 3: 145–56. (Reprinted in F.P. Kilpatrick, *Explorations in Transactional Psychology* pp. 321–31. New York: New York University Press, 1961.

1958. "Effective Democratic Leadership: A Psychological Interpretation." *Journal of Individual Psychology* 14: 128–38.

1958. "Moral Ideas: Toward a Humanistic Psychology." In *Proceedings of the Second International Congress of Classical Studies.* Vol. II: *The Classical Pattern of Modern Western Civilization.* pp. 183–204. Copenhagen: Ejnar Munksgaard.

1958. *Some Observations of a Psychologist after Visiting the Soviet Union.* Princeton: Institute for International Social Research. (Multilith report.)

1958. *Some Observations of a Psychologist in India: An Informal Discussion.* Princeton: Institute for International Social Research. (Multilith report.)

1958. *What People in Kerala are Concerned About: Report on a Small Sample Survey of India's Communist State.* Princeton: Institute for International Social Research. (Multilith report.)

With Henry A. Murray and Mark A. May. 1959. "Some Glimpses of Soviet Psychology." *American Psychologist* 14, no. 6: 303–7.

1960. "Concerning the Nature of Perception." *Proceedings, American Philosophical Society* 104, no. 5: 467–73.

With F.P. Kilpatrick. 1960. "Self-Anchoring Scaling, a Measure of Individuals' Unique Reality Worlds." *Journal of Individual Psychology* 16, no. 2: 158–73. (Reprinted by The Brookings Institution, 1960, reprint no. 47.)

1961. "The Nature of Faith." In *Reconstruction in Religion,* ed. Alfred E. Kuenzli, chap. 2, pp. 23–44. Boston: Beacon Press, 1961. (A revision of previous article on faith.)

With F.P. Kilpatrick. 1961. "The Constancies in Social Perception." In F.P. Kilpatrick, ed. *Explorations in Transactional Psychology,* chap. 21, pp. 354–66. New York: New York University Press, 1961.

1962. "A Transactional Inquiry Concerning Mind." In *Theories of the Mind,* ed. Jordan Scher, pp. 330–53. New York: Free Press.

With Lloyd A. Free. 1962. "Hopes and Fears for Self and Country: the Self-Anchoring Striving Scale in Cross-Cultural Research." *American Behavioral Scientist* 6 no. 2, supplement, (Oct.).

1963. "A Study of Aspirations." *Scientific American,* 208, no. 2 (Feb): 41–6.

1963. "The Individual's Demand on Society." In *Conflict and Creativity,* Seymour M. Farber and R.H.L. Wilson, eds., pp. 185–99. New York: McGraw-Hill, 1963.

With William K. Livingston. 1963. "The Concept of Transaction in Psychology and Neurology." *Journal of Individual Psychology* 19 (May): 3–16.

1964. "The Human Design." *Journal of Individual Psychology* 20 (Nov.): 129–36.

1965. "Evaluating the Probable Reactions to the Landing in North Africa in 1942: A Case Study." *Public Opinion Quarterly* 29, no. 3 (Fall): 400–10.

1967. "A Fresh Look at the Human Design." In *The Challenges of Humanistic Psychology,* ed J.F.T. Bugental, chap. 2, pp. 12–18. New York: McGraw-Hill.

1967. "Sentio, Ergo Sum: 'Motivation' Reconsidered," *Journal of Psychology* 65: 91–107.

1968. "Some requirements for a political psychology." In *Perspectives in the Study of Politics*, ed. Malcolm B. Parsons, pp. 124–46. Chicago: Rand McNally.

1968. *The Pattern of Human Concerns in Czechoslovakia in February 1968*. Princeton: Institute for International Social Research.

With William K. Livingston. "Brain, Mind, and Self." Previously unpub; included as chapter 15 in this volume.

Newspaper articles

1936. "The Bombardment of Ballots." *New York Times Magazine*, June 14.

1936. "Straw Votes." *New York Times*, Oct. 25.

1941. "How Good Is Our Morale?" *New York Times Magazine*, Nov. 16.

1942. "The Mood of the Nation." *New York Times Magazine*, Sept. 27.

1942. "Propaganda for Victory." *New Republic*, Feb. 23, pp. 261–3.

1944. "What We Don't Know Is Likely to Hurt Us." *New York Times Magazine*, May 14. Reprinted in *Redbook Magazine*, August 1944.

1944. "The Issue Behind the Issues." *New York Times Magazine*, Oct. 22.

1944. "Political 'Dopesters' Expect a Close Race." *New York Times*, Nov. 5.

1944. "Why We Vote the Way We Do." *New York Times Magazine*, Sep. 24.

1947. "Don't Blame It on Human Nature." *New York Times*, July 6.

Index of Subjects

Index of Names